THE ILLEGITIMACY OF JESUS

THE ILLEGITIMACY OF JESUS

A Feminist Theological Interpretation of the Infancy Narratives

Jane Schaberg

1817

Harper & Row, Publishers, San Francisco

Cambridge, Hagerstown, New York, Philadelphia, Washington
London, Mexico City, São Paulo, Singapore, Sydney

Library of Congress Cataloging-in-Publication Data

Schaberg, Jane.
  The illegitimacy of Jesus.

  Includes bibliographical references.
  1. Jesus Christ—Genealogy—Biblical teaching.
2. Bible.   N.T.   Matthew I, 1–25—Theology.
3. Bible.   N.T.   Luke I, 5–11, 30—Theology.
4. Virgin birth—Controversial literature.   I. Title.
BT314.S33   1987   232.9′21   86-50250
ISBN 0-06-254688-0

87 88 89 90 91 RRD 10 9 8 7 6 5 4 3 2 1

Contents

Preface

This book is a birthday present for my mother, Helen Walsh Schaberg, on her eighty-first birthday, a token of appreciation for her constant encouragement, her sense of humor, and her mental and spiritual flexibility. It is also in loving memory of my father, Kenneth Dewar Schaberg, in appreciation of his questioning.

My thanks to many others for the enriching gift of their criticism and their interest in this work: my sisters, Helen Kauffman and Kathy Violette; my brother-in-law, Christopher J. Kauffman; my colleagues at the University of Detroit, especially Justin Kelly, George Pickering, T. K. Venkateswaran, Barbara Butler, Edwin DeWindt, Sarah Gravelle; friends and scholars Patricia Geoghegan, William Reader, James Buckley, Adele Fiske, Cora Brady, Kathy Wider, Jean Lambert, Sharon Ringe, Elaine Schapker, James A. Sanders, Schuyler Brown, Carolyn Osiek, Delores Kincaide, Marietta Jaeger, Kit Concannon, Grace Lee, Marcella Martinez, Susan Bascom, Leianna Rabenau Spurgeon, Clayelle Dalferes, Carol Hofer. Justus George Lawler has been a tremendously supportive editor and friend. My thanks also to two children, Darius and Carolyn Johnson, for sharing their lives with me.

When this book was about two-thirds written, it was discovered that I had breast cancer. I am grateful to my brother, Kevin Schaberg, my surgeon, Gary Talpos, and my oncologist, Robert O'Bryan, for getting me back to work and "going for a 'cure.'" Their awareness and admission of what is not known about cancer and its treatment parallel my awareness and admission of what is not known about the New Testament. We work in ignorance and in hope of discovery.

The Illegitimacy of Jesus has been written for my scholarly peers and also for a more general audience; for the first, anticipated gratitude for their criticism; for the second, in the belief that biblical studies should never be the restricted province of the experts, and that this Book, like all classics, belongs to all of us. What is presented here is a new interpretation of the New Testament Infancy Narratives—new claiming to be old. The hope is that it will send the general reader back to the biblical texts and to the work of other scholars, with lively interest in the basic issue raised.

The unforeseen delay in publication allowed me to benefit from some initial criticism based on the advertisement. Four negative criticisms are worth mentioning and responding to. First, some object to the title, regarding it as unnecessarily inflammatory, indelicate, crassly sensational, or even blasphemous. The title, however, tells what the book is about in a way that no other title could. The gospels themselves are sensational and scandalous. Familiarity with them and certain bland interpretations obscure that aspect, even with regard to the crucifixion of Jesus and the claims of the resurrection narratives. This reading of the Infancy Narratives draws them into the shadow of the larger gospel scandal and deepens that shadow.

Second, one scholar active in Jewish-Christian dialogue remarked that he supposed that this book will be one "in which the Jews will be the villains of the piece." His reaction is probably due to the correct assumption that there will be discussion of Talmudic and medieval Toledoth traditions of Jesus' illegitimacy (see chapter 4), and perhaps due to the opinion, which I regard as incorrect, that traditions of this kind are best forgotten in the interests of "brotherhood." These traditions contain valuable information for the New Testament student; they are polemic but not just polemic. Jewish-Christian dialogue occurs in its deepest sense when there is awareness and discussion of past differences and shared insight. This dialogue has a strong future as well as a strong recent past in the work and collaboration of Jewish and Christian women.[1] Christian feminist biblical scholars are seeking our Jewish feminist roots, and this book is offered as an aid in that search.

Third, some interested in what they call the pastoral and priestly dimensions of New Testament scholarship comment that the average churchgoer—layperson or cleric—has no access to the specifics of this kind of research and will not understand this book, that it will generate more heat than light, and issue in slogans, name calling, squabbling among Christians, to no one's benefit and not "to the honor of the Lord." The gap between the desk and the pew, the classroom and the pulpit, is admittedly enormous. But that gap can be bridged with education, and there is an obligation to bridge it. I hope this book will lend itself to open discussion. Minear speaks of those who are "overcredulous because of complacent orthodoxy," who read the Infancy Narratives "too hastily in terms of their own prior solutions of dogmatic problems," those whose credulity is "complete and aggressive."[2] The minds of those with this attitude are the most difficult to change or persuade; they may often be the most vocal churchgoers, but they are not the majority or the average. The exegete is responsible as well, moreover, to other communities.

Fourth, some have said the book sounds "too imaginative." Whether this is so or not can be judged only after the arguments for what is "imagined" have been assessed, and it is seen whether or not they are plausible or convincing. Without what Schüssler Fiorenza calls "historical imagination,"[3] aspects of the worlds and imaginative powers of the biblical writers are closed to the critic. The effort to understand and to empathize across the centuries can fail, of course, when projection of later attitudes and realities blurs those of the distant past. The attempt is made here to imagine without that kind of projection. Now that this book is finished, one of my own criticisms of it is that it is not imaginative *enough:* for example, in chapter 2, what could have happened *to* a woman in the situation described in Matthew 1 is imagined and studied; what such a woman might *do* should also have been imagined.

In the spirit of the insight that engaged scholarship, committed to the struggle for human equality, can result in new and valid perceptions, I dedicate this book to the millions of women who have borne illegitimate children, and to those often "fatherless" children, a few of whom are friends of mine. Their shared concerns have sent my thought spinning in new directions.

1. Introduction

"... legends cannot flourish at the source of all legends ..."[1]

A. OVERVIEW

This book is written primarily as a contribution to scholarly interpretation of the New Testament Infancy Narratives. On every page a debt is owed to other scholars who have written on these texts.[2] But the use made here of their scholarship in many instances contributes to turns of argument and to conclusions that go against the scholarly consensus (as well as against what might be called the ecclesiastical consensus). My claim is that the texts dealing with the origin of Jesus, Matt 1:1–25 and Luke 1:20–56 and 3:23–38 originally were about an illegitimate conception and not about a miraculous virginal conception.

It was the intention—or better, *an* intention—of Matthew and Luke to pass down the tradition they inherited: that Jesus the messiah had been illegitimately conceived during the period when his mother Mary was betrothed to Joseph. At the pregospel stage, this illegitimate conception had already been understood theologically as due in some unexplained way to the power of the Holy Spirit. Both evangelists worked further with this potentially damaging and potentially liberating material, each developing his own brilliant and cautious presentation. Chapters 2 and 3 of this book are exegeses of the parts of Matthew's and Luke's narratives through which the tradition was transmitted. The evangelists' caution and their androcentric perspectives—as well as the history of interpretation of the narratives, and our own presuppositions about them—make this aspect of their meaning difficult to perceive. To borrow Emily Dickinson's words, they told the Truth, but they told it "slant." In their telling, they presupposed the illegitimacy tradition, of which Christians soon became unaware.

In chapter 4, the pre-gospel tradition is reconstructed as far as possible. Attempts are then made to further analyze the redaction by each evangelist and to briefly trace the early interpretations of their narratives and of the illegitimacy tradition. On the one hand, in Christian reports of claims and charges made by Jews concerning Jesus' origin and in the Jewish writings themselves, the tradition was preserved and polemicized. On the other hand, as far as we can tell, Jewish Christians and Gentile Christians erased the illegitimacy tradition in three different ways: some claimed that Joseph was the biological father of Jesus; some that Jesus the Christ was a supernatural being with no human parents; some that Jesus was virginally conceived, without male sperm or intercourse. By the end of the second century of the Common Era (C.E.), this last belief, in the virginal conception, had become the dominant Christian understanding of Jesus' origin, the dominant Christian reading and meaning of the New Testament narratives. The tradition of his illegitimate conception was lost to Christians, but it was passed on and developed in Jewish circles. In the Epilogue, we will return to the Infancy Narratives in the light of the foregoing analysis, commenting on the question of the status of the Roman Catholic doctrine of virginal conception and on contemporary understandings of Mary or the Virgin as an empowering figure.

B. THE ORIGIN OF THIS BOOK: A PERSONAL REFLECTION

A few words are appropriate here about how this book came to be. Awareness of the process is significant methodologically and raises the important issue of presuppositions. The study began with an "objective," rather innocuous question concerning the Immanuel prophecy, Isa 7:14. In the Hebrew Bible this passage reads, "Behold, a young woman shall conceive and bear a son, and shall call his name Immanuel" (RSV); in the Septuagint (LXX) Greek translation, "Behold, a virgin shall conceive in the womb, and shall bring forth a son, and you shall call his name Emmanuel." Many commentators hold that the LXX translator probably understood the Hebrew text to mean that one who is (now) a virgin will conceive (in the normal way women conceive).

Matthew, however, who used this verse as a fulfillment citation in 1:23, is thought to have understood it differently. That is, Matthew read it as Isaiah's prediction of a miraculous conception by a biological virgin without intercourse with a male. But how do we know that Matthew did not understand the verse as the LXX translator did? Is there evidence in the first chapter of Matthew that forces us to the conclusion that he did not? To turn the question around, does the notion that the Matthean Infancy Narrative is about a virginal conception depend primarily on the idea that Matthew read and used Isa 7:14 in a new way?

Experimentation and dialogue expanded the original question into a series of technical exegetical questions, into exploration of the legal aspects of the situation presented in Matthew's first chapter and of Old Testament[3] and intertestamental traditions drawn on by Matthew. Approach from this last angle made the notion of a virginal conception seem more and more odd, and even an inaccurate interpretation of the New Testament Infancy Narratives. There is no text in that earlier literature in which the action of God or the Spirit of God is said to replace or cancel natural human sexual activity in such a way as to render the human role superfluous. In spite of ecclesiastical and scholarly insistences to the contrary, the notion of virginal conception seems to say something negative about human sexuality, something opposed to the positive aspects of major Israelite and Jewish tradition (even given the sexism and androcentrism of that tradition). While it is certainly not inherently impossible that an early Christian tradition uniquely stood against the positive Jewish orientation, it seemed more and more unlikely in this case. The Infancy Narratives are widely acknowledged to be some of the most markedly Jewish material in the New Testament.

It became clear that if the texts were not about a virginal conception, they were about an illegitimate conception. This appears to be the only alternative, if we take seriously the claim of both evangelists that Joseph was not the biological father of Jesus, and if we attempt to account for the story Matthew tells, of Joseph's dilemma.[4] It became necesary for me to explore in an on-going way my own attitudes and presuppositions with respect to both alternatives and the choice between them, in order to help ensure as far as possible that the choice was made on the basis of exegetical issues, and not unduly influenced by prior under-standings.

In section D of this chapter, I will discuss contemporary fem-inist attitudes and presuppositions regarding belief in a virginal conception and the image of Mary. Ancient and modern atti-tudes toward women and children who do not fit "legitimately" into patriarchal family structures also play a significant role in exegesis of the Infancy Narratives. Women who willingly or un-willingly conceive outside of marriage, women raped or seduced and impregnated, illegitimate children who are often "fatherless" in the sense that their biological father plays no part in their lives: this vast population began to stand behind the texts for me and to widen my horizons.

We cannot make progress in New Testament study if we as-sume that the novel or uncomfortable answer (in this case, the alternative of illegitimate conception, uncomfortable to some) "is always the true one just because it is uncomfortable, and that any objections can be swept aside as the vain struggles of the traditionalist."[5] Or, to put it another way, we cannot assume that the reading is always true which causes a "collision of history and doctrine"[6] (in this case calling into question what had seemed to some to be "the sure religious instinct behind the development of Mariology"[7]). Neither can we assume that untraditional read-ings are untrue. The interpretation of the narratives that was taking shape—illegitimate conception, not virginal conception— is not fully represented elsewhere[8] in the two thousand years of serious Christian interpretation. But for these two thousand years only half of the Christian population has been represented in the commentaries and analyses. Cynthia Ozick labels as "a plain whopping lie" the statement of Adin Steinsaltz that the Talmud "is the collective endeavor of the entire Jewish people."

The truth is that the Talmud is the collective endeavor not of the entire Jewish people, but only of its male half. . . . What we have had is a Jewish half-genius. That is not enough for the people who choose to hear the Voice of the Lord of History. We have been listening with only half an ear, speaking with only half a tongue, and never understanding that we have made ourselves partly deaf and partly dumb.[9]

The same, of course, is true of the Christian tradition; it has been produced by only the male half. Realization of this partial deafness and dumbness allows us to imagine that some Jewish and Christian feminist interpretation today may be—though we will never know—the voice of some silenced ones of the past.[10] That silent tradition has its own strange weight, which should embolden us to experiment responsibly. It can give a sense of community and courage to the individual critic.[11] (Further, one aspect of this experimentation turned out to be listening hard to the silences within the texts, as will be seen below.)

Only a cooperative effort by a team of scholars could produce the kind of study this topic requires, refining the exegetical analysis at every stage, and extending the investigation into the areas of Gnostic studies, the history of ideas, sociology and psychology. This book is less than I had in mind, but it is a beginning.

C. A FEMINIST THEOLOGICAL INTERPRETATION

This is a feminist work because it draws its motivation, ambition, whatever courage it exhibits, and important aspects of its methodology from feminist criticism. Theories of feminist biblical interpretation have been treated at length in several recent publications.[12] Here those elements of special significance to this study will be briefly discussed. In part, they became clear only by reflection on the exegesis in process and finished.

The approach used is grounded in feminism as Hilda Smith defines it: "the view of women as a distinct sociological group for which there are established patterns of behavior, special legal and legislative restrictions, and customarily defined roles,"[13] which are based on neither rational criteria nor physiological dictates. Feminists, she notes, will more quickly than nonfeminists pose the question "why?" about any difficulty that befalls an individual woman. The feminist answer will include this understanding of women as a sociological group whose rights have been restricted systematically by the powerful within a given society. In the next chapter, it will be obvious that Matthew 1 is read as being about a difficulty that befalls Mary of Nazareth. The question "why?" is asked, and answers are pursued based on the understanding of women as an oppressed but powerful group.

The feminist sense of women's rights and of their unjust denial flows from growing experience of the oppression and power of women and from a vision of an egalitarian society. Just how biblical that vision is, and in what writings or levels of the biblical tradition it may be found, are matters of current debate.

Feminist interpretation adds to other considerations this focus on the position and role of women in the society in which the texts and traditions under examination were produced. The biblical society, like ours, was patriarchal, and dominated by a dualistic mind set. "Feminist criticism is the name that should be applied to all criticism alert to the critical ramifications of sexual oppression, just as in politics 'women's issues' is the name now applied to many fundamental questions of personal freedom and social justice."[14] As part of a worldwide social change movement this criticism is "a political act whose aim is not simply to interpret the world but to change it by changing the consciousness of those who read and their relation to what they read."[15] Feminists, male and female, are embarking on a revisionist reading of the entire literary inheritance, entering old texts from a new critical direction. This rereading offers us all "a potential enhancing of our capacity to read the world, our literary texts, and even one another, anew."[16]

An important aspect of feminist interpretation is its frank interest in the interplay between text and contemporary situation as both are illuminated by the women's movement. This interplay can sensitize the interpreter's empathy, imagination, and analysis. But the goal is not to manipulate the texts into anachronistic usefulness and relevance, nor "to construct history *as it ought to have been* to authenticate women's aspirations and sense of self."[17]

Neither is the goal to achieve a purely objective reading and a scientific presentation of historical "facts" for a value-neutral, detached interpretation. Contemporary hermeneutics recognizes that attaining such a goal is impossible and undesirable. We have become increasingly aware of the importance of the interpreter's own bias in shaping her or his interpretation: what we see is substantially influenced by what we are prepared to see, by our commitments, experiences, the way we live, the communities within which we live and to which we are accountable. Thus the importance of (a) self-consciousness and acknowledgment of our perspective; (b) a self-critical stance concerning it; and (c) an openness to new discoveries. The most common objection to a feminist reading is that it is subjective and results from the vested interests of the perspective; it tends to distort what the text is really saying. But all interpretation is subjective, and acceptable and unacceptable readings must be adjudicated by scholarly criteria.[18]

The basic goal here is to present an accurate grasp of the intention of Matthew and of Luke, and of the history and tradition they interpret, concerning the conception of Jesus. This goal is pursued in the conviction that understanding that intention, whatever it may be, or coming as close as possible to it using historical-critical methodologies, is an indispensable stage in the search for a usable past. Tremendous difficulties are involved in any effort to discover an author's intent, especially across twenty centuries, and many insist that such an effort is absurd. Authors have many intentions when they write, and all are not equally conscious or equally important to them. Some intentions may fall short of being achieved. A written work assumes a life of its own and takes on meanings and functions beyond the author's intention, acquiring new meanings for different readers in different times. Great works divulge covert or latent intentions in different settings and under new stresses; they have a potential for metamorphosis. Every strong reading is a misreading, in that it can be shown by later interpreters to be partial and wanting and in need of correction.[19] It is virtually an epistemological impossibility for biblical scholars to achieve scientific *certainty* about what the text meant. And yet the narrow and concentrated effort to determine what the writers "thought that they thought" and intended to communicate is an essential part of the task of biblical scholars who hear "the call to historical honesty."[20] Further, the effort has met with real and significant success.

Feminist biblical criticism accepts the general tenet of historical-critical scholarship, that biblical texts are historical formulations within the context of religious communities of different times and places, articulated in historically limited and culturally conditioned human language. To this, feminist criticism adds the sharpening awareness that such contexts are patriarchal and androcentric, and that the Bible should be approached with a hermeneutics of suspicion. The biblical texts themselves are androcentric, and a dangerous misogynist bias in them is to be expected,[21] just as it is to be expected in the history of interpretation. In contrast, until recently even liberal Christian theologians tended to insist that biblical passages that confirm women's status as the second sex must have been misinterpreted.[22]

When biblical sexism is squarely faced, it proves to have an important educative role. Biblical sexual politics must be explored, and the literary strategies that are used by the biblical narrative to promote patriarchal ideology must be analyzed.[23] We are required to accept the ambiguous nature of the whole Bible with its internal contradictions, to critically assess and evaluate, to discriminate between oppressive and liberating biblical traditions and aspects of traditions, to make decisions about what constitutes the true word of God. The interpreter is freed by this suspicion and identification of biblical sexism for the surprising possibility of new discoveries and new appreciation, for the possibility of participating in the biblical heritage in new ways.

Feminist hermeneutics, then, is profoundly paradoxical. It sees the Bible as both ally and adversary in the struggle for human rights, equality, and dignity. The biblical God, both helper and enemy, friend and tormentor, cannot simply be identified with God. Feminist interpreters who appreciate this paradox approach the Bible not only with suspicion but with the hope that it will be possible to read it (or part of it) in such a way that it becomes (almost in spite of itself) a historical source and theological symbol for women's power, independence, and freedom. For these interpreters a shift of perception may occur that results in a new appropriation of certain positive dimensions of the text.

Some feminist critics are ambitious to claim the center of biblical religion for women. This must be distinguished from the claim of others to be "centrist," by which they mean that they are neither liberal nor conservative, that they disclaim radical statements and express the moderate, middle-of-the-road consensus of the "mainline" church.[24] But that "center" is the center of only half of Christianity, of a half-church that has marginalized and subjugated women, excluded them from contributing in any meaningful way to its consensus, denied them equal access to its power. When Schüssler Fiorenza writes of feminists "claiming the center," the word "center" takes on new meaning. She does not aspire to existence at the center of the male-dominated half, nor of a female-dominated half, but to existence at the center of a whole church.[25] In that church, for which this book was written, empowered women will speak for themselves, name their own experience, and contribute equally with men to the formation of the tradition, which will reflect the specific realities of their lives as well as those of men. Claiming the center has to do with claiming the past, the biblical heritage, and the future. It has to do with telling the truth about women and men, which should bring all of us closer to telling the truth about God.

Read as being about an illegitimate conception, the Infancy Narratives turn out to contain a mixture of liberating and oppressing elements. They are no escape from biblical sexism. Further, these texts stand as a source of the belief in a virginal conception, a belief that some feminists regard as a negative influence, but one that others have been able to turn to positive use. It will be helpful at this point to explore feminist attitudes toward this belief and toward the figure of Mary. The first aim must be to examine the New Testament materials and the tradition not without bias or presuppositions of any kind, but with an admission and exploration of bias and presuppositions.[26]

D. THE VIRGIN MARY

Let us examine what the idea of a virginal conception is meant to convey, and what religious values it enshrines. In what way is it a tribute to Jesus, and what experience of Jesus does it express? It was not thought to account for his sinlessness, since nowhere in the Infancy Narratives is it explained this way; nor is it necessary to account for his divine Sonship, since Mark, Paul, John, and other New Testament writers who do not have any notion of a virginal conception call Jesus the Son of God. Many contemporary scholars think of this fatherless conception as a new creation, "a direct act of the Creator himself such as never happened before in the case of any other human being. . . . God, in his free, underivative action, causes Jesus to be born, who, entirely under the control of his Spirit, will accomplish the saving presence of God."[27] It is not clear how this notion of new creation is compatible with the belief that Jesus was human (not seemingly human) and had a human mother. She seems to be reduced, in this line of thinking, to an emptiness, a space, a nurturing container, ultimately excluded from consideration in the formation of this child.[28] The point, according to some critics, is to show that God takes the initiative in this conception. "In human society, it is man who represents individual initiative, while woman represents the continuity of the species. The Messiah was not the child of this or that father, but of the race. He was not a son of any individual, but He was 'the Son of Man.' "[29] For others the virginal conception was necessary in some sense, "in order that one could be present once and for all at the triumph of spirit over flesh, and that eternity could definitively take precedence over time."[30] But even allowing for ignorance concerning the specific biological roles of male and female, and rigidity concerning their social roles, there is little evidence in the New Testament Infancy Narratives that these ideas capture the evangelists' thought.

The psychological meaning of the belief that Jesus had no male parent, that Mary was a virgin mother, has yet to be extensively explored. One wonders if it is a projection of male fantasy and wishes: for a tame and "pure" woman who is asexual or does not exercise her sexuality; for a woman especially untroubling to the celibate male psyche; for a mother who has no partner; for the annihilation of the human father; for the replacement of the human male by the male god. Is it an expression of male awe and reverence,[31] or a compensation for male shame and anguish over the violation of women,[32] an element, hitherto unexplained, of what Engelsman calls "the patriarchal guilt feeling"[33]—or what?[34] Keith Thomas writes that all men "(and, for that matter, all women)" unconsciously desire a tender, loving, and virginal mother.[35] But do they? Do all women desire a virginal mother, except insofar as "virginal" means free, independent, unsubordinated, unexploited?[36]

I do not know what to make of these words of Karl Barth:

"Mary's virginity in the birth of the Lord is the negation—not of man before God, but of his possibility, of his aptitude, of his capacity for God." Man participates here "only in the form of the unwilling, nonaccomplishing, noncreative, nonsovereign man, only in the form of the man who can only receive, who can only be ready, who can merely allow something to happen to and with him." Therefore precisely the man had to "be eliminated here."[37] Man's elimination seems to somehow humble him and give him the attitude and the aptitude of a stereotypical woman. I do not know what to make either of "the negative value" given to the virginity of Mary: that through which the flesh has been redeemed has not been touched or possessed.

Discomfort with and bewilderment concerning the belief in the virginal conception may be derived in part from the fact that women had little or nothing to do with the construction and development of the belief. But there may be some positive value in it as well for women. Chodorow mentions Deutsch's reports that in women's fantasies and dreams, sexuality and eroticism are often opposed to motherhood and reproduction; women's "parthenogenic fantasies" appear.[38] Mary Daly insists that a woman's creation of her Self is parthenogenic, not requiring a "father."[39]

There is no denying the strong appeal to some of the image of Mary and of "the feminine dimension of the divine" in her cult; as a Roman Catholic I experience that appeal. But it is difficult to associate it with the notion of virginal conception. Elizabeth Cady Stanton asks, "If a Heavenly Father was necessary, why not a Heavenly Mother? If an earthly Mother was admirable, why not an earthly Father?"[40] "Anon." expresses the thought that lurks as a suspicion of many: "I think that the doctrine of the Virgin Birth as something higher, sweeter, nobler than ordinary motherhood, is a slur on all the natural motherhood of the world."[41]

In modern times, popular cults of Mary have had a tremendous attraction for the downtrodden and exploited.[42] There is power in the Catholic experience of the love of God in the figure of a woman, in the tradition that demonstrates that female language and symbols encompassing the myth and symbols of the Goddess have a transparency towards God.[43] Some feminists have been able to claim for themselves the image of Mary in positive ways, seeing her as one who embodies and personifies the oppressed who are being liberated.[44]

Even so, the idealized Virgin Mother of God is a tool of the institutional sexism so strongly entrenched in Roman Catholicism. Schüssler Fiorenza has rightly noted that the Mary myth has not been used to promote the liberation of women. It almost never functioned as a symbol or justification of women's equality or leadership in church or society. Rather, traditional Mariology demonstrates "that the myth of a woman preached to women by men" has served and can serve to deter women from becoming fully independent and whole human persons,[45] to confine ambitions. In countries where the cult of Mary is strong, women have not become significantly involved in public and political life; in churches that have the strongest official attachment to Mary, women are most strongly denied full participation.[46] This seems to be part of a broader picture: mother goddesses are dominant figures in cultures that ideally polarize male/female roles and idealize woman in compensation for her actual social position. The data from Hindu and Buddhist countries as well as from many Roman Catholic countries indicates that mother goddess worship stands in inverse relationship with high secular female status.[47]

Mary is presented as "the great exception," unlike all others in that she alone conceived virginally. In this the Christian Virgin Mother is a great contrast to the virgin goddesses of other religions, who were "virgins" with lovers. Their virginity was not a biological statement but a powerful symbol of their autonomy and independence from male control. But Mary is honored for the nonuse of her sexuality. Far from being autonomous, she is glorified for her passive subordination to the role assigned to her, for her receptivity. She is without real strength or power in herself, and she only points to Christ and his Father. The image of Mary kneeling before her son, says Simone de Beauvoir, is "the supreme masculine victory."[48]

The Virgin Mary is also a great contrast to real human women. Mary establishes the child as the destiny of woman, but does not experience the sexual intercourse necessary for all other women to fulfill this destiny. Defined as wholly unique, she is set up as a model of womanhood that is unattainable.[49] As the male projection of idealized femininity, a patriarchal construction, she is the good woman, stripped of all dangerous elements; she receives worship, not equality. Man exalts Mary for virtues he would like woman to exhibit, and projects onto her all that he does not resolve to be.

Evil, on the other hand, is projected onto the rest of women. The shadow side of the glorification of the passive and dependent Virgin Mary is the denigration of women. Carl Jung comments that the consequence of increasing Mariolatry in the later Middle Ages was the witch hunt.[50] The Mary myth reduces woman to something less than a whole human being. This symbolic reduction then becomes a rationale for the unequal treatment of women and for women's self-devaluation. As Mary Gordon asks, "What hope is there for the rest of us, who eat, breathe, menstruate, make love, bear children?" She holds it is necessary to reject the traditional image of Mary created by some men "in order to hold onto the fragile hope of intellectual achievement, independence of identity, and sexual fulfillment."[51] At her deadliest, Mary is the mother who—unlike Demeter—conforms to patriarchal expectations, and pushes or pulls her daughters into that conformity.

The charge of contemporary feminists, then, is not that the image of the Virgin Mary is unimportant or irrelevant,[52] but that it contributes to and is integral to the oppression of women. As "the most fully realized and generally venerated image of woman regenerated and consecrated to the good,"[53] Mary represents a central theme in the history of Western attitudes to women. While one scholar can speak of "*the* Roman Catholic attitude toward Mary" (emphasis mine) which may be a key to the specific nature of Catholicism,[54] what we really have had is the *male* attitude toward her, as John McKenzie recognizes.[55] According to *that* attitude, the belief in the virginal conception is "a traditional formulation of faith that has served Christianity well." It has "given *a woman* a central role in Christianity, and today we should appreciate more than ever before what a service that was."[56]

Feminist exploration of the New Testament texts on which the image of the Virgin Mary draws is therefore relevant and pressing. This is true whether the belief in the virginal conception is present in the texts or (as I think) is not present. We contribute to the changing, the revisioning of myth, which eventually may make cultural change possible. Such biblical interpretation becomes a political and spiritual task with potentially radical—if presently incalculable—institutional implications.[57] The "symbols of the mother that people use are neither idle nor haphazard elements, but active forces that work for people, bring desired ends, unify people, lead to change, and disclose in a variety of ways inescapable aspects of our human condition, as well as our attempts to comprehend and transcend it."[58] The Virgin Mary at this point in Christian history is the symbol of the mother of men. How will women represent her as the mother of women?

E. READING AS A WOMAN

Further comments are in order about the type of feminist criticism *The Illegitimacy of Jesus* is. Feminist biblical criticism approaches texts directly in at least four different ways, which are not mutually exclusive. (1) One approach exposes the androcentrism and the sexism (gross and subtle) in the text and its interpretation. (2) Another approach attempts to counter biblical sexism by reinterpreting texts that have been distorted, revisioning previous androcentric exegesis, or by highlighting countercultural texts positive to women, ones that challenge patriarchal structures, attitudes, images, and presuppositions. (3) Some criticism is a retelling, sympathetic to the woman victim, of a "text of terror." Sometimes the critic interprets against the narrator, plot, other characters and the biblical tradition; at other times forgotten or neglected nuances in the text are discovered. (4) In some cases there is a shift from the text to a reconstruction of biblical history, in an attempt to show that the actual situations of the Israelite and Christian religions allowed a greater or different role for women than the canonical writings suggest. (5) In addition to these four direct approaches to the text, a fifth approach focuses not on individual texts but on the Bible in general, in the hope of finding a theological perspective, such as the prophetic insistence that God sides with and liberates the oppressed—some central witness that offers a critique of patriarchy.[59]

This book does not fit neatly into any one of these categories but overlaps all of them. In this revisionist reading of the Infancy Narratives, they are discovered to be in part illustrations of the prophetic liberating principle and applications of this principle to the endangered woman and child. A story of terror (and perhaps a woman's theological tradition) lies behind and within the story of the appearance of the Messiah. The tradition also comes to us filtered through patriarchal aspects of the evangelists' mentality.

But primarily this exegesis is an exercise in "reading as a woman."[60] It is true that all five approaches mentioned above are different ways of reading as a woman, in that feminist hermeneutics always attempts to ground its analysis in the experience of women's oppression and power. What is different here is the explicit interest in how the sex of a woman reader/interpreter influences the reading of male texts. Every woman who reads does not read as a woman, just as every woman who speaks does not speak as a woman. Women, in fact, have been trained to read as men, to identify against themselves with a masculine perspective and experience, which is presented as the human and universal one.[61] Women are lead to participate in an experience from which they are explicitly excluded, asked to identify with a male selfhood that defines itself in opposition to them. The most insidious form of women's oppression is alienation from their own experience and interests; and the most basic step toward liberation is coming to consciousness of this alienation. The first act of a feminist critic is "to become a resisting rather than an assenting reader, and by this refusal to assent, to begin the process of exorcizing the male mind that has been implanted in us."[62] Annette Kolodny writes that "reading is a *learned* activity which, like many other learned interpretive strategies in our society, is inevitably sex-coded and gender-inflected."[63] Feminist criticism, according to Elaine Showalter, is concerned with "the way in which the hypothesis of a female reader changes our apprehension of a given text, awakening us to the significance of its sexual codes."[64]

Reading as a woman is reading sensitive to women's history of suffering, survival, and courage; it is reading from the usually ignored and devalued vantage point of women's experience. Reading as a woman is based on the conviction that experience as a woman is a source of authority for response as a reader, on the assertion that there is continuity between women's experience of social and familial structures and their experience as readers.[65] Women learn to bring their own experience, questions, and concerns to texts, to trust their responses even when they raise questions that challenge prevailing critical assumptions. Conclusions derived from these questions are then tested against the text itself, its contexts, and the explorations of other critics. Reading as a woman reverses the usual situation in which it is assumed that the perspective of a male critic is sexually neutral, while a feminist reading is regarded as a case of special pleading and an attempt to force the text into a predetermined mold. By confronting male readings with the elements of the text they neglect, and by identifying specific defenses and distortions, feminist criticism tries to get at the broad and undistorted vision. The aim is not to produce a woman's reading that would parallel a man's reading, but rather to produce a comprehensive perspective, a compelling reading, a human reading. "The conclusions reached in feminist criticism of this sort are not specific to women in the sense that one can sympathize, comprehend, and agree only if one has had certain experiences which are women's. On the contrary, these readings demonstrate the limitations of male critical interpretations in terms that male critics would purport to accept, and they seek, like all ambitious acts of criticism, to attain a generally convincing understanding—an understanding that is feminist because it is a critique of male chauvinism."[66] More importantly, it is feminist because it is an expression of women's insight and power.

Such an understanding of the interpreter's task is compatible with the understanding of gender dimorphism as socially, politically, and theologically constructed and not "natural." It need not perpetuate the patriarchal myth of innate and absolute female and male psychological differences and characteristics, nor deny that great literature and maybe even great literary criticism (like a great person) in some ways transcend gender differences. Cynthia Ozick holds that such literature universalizes, does not divide; it is "hungrier" than the separating self-consciousness.[67] But belonging to or identifying with a group whose rights have been systematically restricted and which has been socialized differently causes perceptual differences that can be empirically verified. Jean Baker Miller speaks of perceptions that men, because of their dominant position, could not perceive.[68] Carol Gilligan produces evidence that women, because of their history, training, and conditioning, speak to moral issues "in a different voice."[69] Since the 1960s some feminist critics have been developing theories of sexual difference in reading, literary interpretation, and writing as well, arguing that women readers and critics bring different perceptions and expectations to their literary experience. One can say that the greater the work, the more it demands feminist criticism, in order for its greatness as well as its flaws to be seen. It draws us out of our segregated worlds. What is needed, and what feminist critics are demanding, is "a new universal literary history and criticism that combines the literary experiences of both women and men, a complete revolution in the understanding of our literary heritage."[70]

Analysis of this kind is helpful in explaining the process of the following exegesis of the Infancy Narratives, and in understanding why the conclusions reached differ from those of other interpreters. In the next chapter it will become apparent that I am a "resisting reader" of the first chapter of Matthew. Against the desires of the author, I do not initially identify with Joseph and his troubles, but with Mary, a figure who is spoken about but never appears. Initially, I also resist the efforts of both evangelists to direct the attention of their readers away from the tradition of the illegitimacy of Jesus (knowledge of which they both presume on the part of at least some readers), and toward the distinctive theological and christological points each makes on the basis of that tradition. Neither evangelist intends to deny the tradition of Jesus' illegitimacy. If each were asked about it, he would reply, "Yes, I do intend to hand down this tradition. Yes, but . . . " Both want to focus the attention of their readers on this "but," on the distinctive meanings they find in and beyond the "scandal"; this is their major intention. The resisting reader attends here to their minor intention, highlights it, and makes it explicit, whereas the evangelists do not. The resisting reader talks about it, where they are silent; recognizes evasiveness, obliqueness, suppression, and the tendency to mystify as literary strategies sometimes used to promote patriarchy, and sometimes used to communicate realities that are considered socially unacceptable.[71]

This brings us to a consideration of the reading of silence. Feminist critics are beginning to study the silence in the text concerning women (male silence about women; women's own silence[72]), and to understand that aspects of the reality of women have been erased. This silence is not allowed to prove the absence of women or their nonexistence at the center of foundational events of the Israelite and Christian communities. Schüssler Fiorenza insists that we must "find ways to break the silence of the text," searching for clues and allusions that indicate the reality about which the text is silent.[73] This is true also of the silence in the Infancy Narratives. A biological father of Jesus is never mentioned or named; he is absent from the stories. But silence about him, his absence, should not be read to mean his nonexistence. Women, perhaps more than men, would not be inclined to draw from the absence of a male figure in such a story the conclusion of that figure's nonexistence. This is so because women are accustomed to the absences of men: real, imagined, physical, mental, psychological, emotional; absences caused by irresponsibility, violence, inattention, different values, desire for distance and separation; absences caused by women remaining behind, out of fear or constraint; absences caused by the relegation of the sexes to two different spheres, by social pressures, poverty, and by a thousand other things. Even more is male absence felt when the story is one of a dangerous pregnancy, outside the structures of patriarchal marriage—a situation as ancient as it is common. As a woman, I read Matthew 1 as a chilling evocation of realities women encounter daily even today.[74]

A feminist Christian would have less difficulty than a nonfeminist Christian in thinking that Jesus was illegitimate, and that the evangelists handed down such a tradition. She or he would have less difficulty making sense of this tradition theologically. A feminist Christian would be less inclined to think that this necessarily denigrated Mary or Jesus, and more inclined to be open to an experience of the sacred in such a situation.

Reading as a woman confronts male critics with elements that they have neglected or overlooked. The exegesis in the next two chapters will stress several such elements. One of the most striking is the mention and exploration of the possibility that rape as well as seduction or adultery would be a normal way of accounting for Mary's pregnancy. Even those few critics who do turn to Deut 22:23–27 to elucidate Matthew 1 almost never raise the possibility of rape. As we will see, most common is the discussion of the two alternatives of adultery or virginal conception. But "All women live with male violence. . . . A feminist biblical interpretation must have this consciousness at its center" in tension with the consciousness of women's power.[75]

We turn in the next two chapters to the attempt to read Matthew's and Luke's Infancy Narratives as a woman reads.

2. Matthew's Account of Jesus' Origin

Reading the New Testament Infancy Narratives in terms of an illegitimate conception (rather than a virginal conception) offers a consistent explanation of many small details. Some of these are puzzling, and all of them have been given other explanations. Some explanations attribute carelessness or ignorance to the author, while others involve excising or staging portions of the text to make sense of it at different levels of composition. None of the explanations offered here, taken alone, is convincing enough to challenge the traditional interpretation of the Infancy Narratives. But the cumulative effect of these explanations does pose that challenge. As this is not a full commentary on the Infancy Narratives, not all aspects of the texts will be treated, but only those directly pertaining to our subject, the origin of Jesus. I assume that the reader will turn first to the narratives themselves, so familiar to many, and attempt by careful attention to break through the haze of that familiarity.

A. THE FOUR WOMEN

Matthew begins his Gospel with the genealogy of Jesus Christ (1:1–17). An unusual feature of this genealogy is the mention of four women:[1] Tamar the mother of Perez and Zerah; Rahab the mother of Boaz; Ruth the mother of Obed; and the wife of Uriah, mother of Solomon. Several explanations have been given for their inclusion, which is probably the work of Matthew himself.[2] (a) They are named because they are sinners, preparing for the presentation of Jesus as the one who will "save his people from their sins" (Matt 1:21). Perhaps, some critics argue further, as four sinners in the Davidic line they are a *contrast* to the sinless Mary, already defamed by "Jewish calumny."[3] However, the Old

Testament and later Jewish traditions do not present the four as sinners. And if by including the women Matthew is refuting or mitigating attacks on the legitimacy of Jesus, pointing to blemishes in David's pedigree, his refutation seems to be of such a nature as would only encourage "calumny." The reminder that there was illegitimacy in the royal line was no defense of the "purity" or "legality" of Jesus' birth.[4] Some think Matthew's narrative itself probably stimulated attacks concerning Jesus' origin. (Let me anticipate my own view, by saying that I think that scandal both preceded and was stimulated by Matthew's account.)

(b) The four women are included because they were regarded as foreigners, preparing for Matthew's presentation of Jesus as Lord of all nations (28:19)[5] and showing that his own ancestry was mixed. In the Old Testament, Rahab and probably Tamar were Canaanites, Ruth a Moabitess, and Bathsheba probably a Hittite like her husband. However, according to this theory the four women would not be linked to the fifth woman, Mary, since they have nothing in common with her. Moreover, in postbiblical Judaism Rahab and Tamar were considered Jewish proselytes.

(c) A third explanation is that the women were each involved in extraordinary or irregular sexual unions, which were scandalous to outsiders. This is thought to prepare for the account of the irregular union that produced Jesus. In addition, each of the women, like Mary, showed initiative or played an important role in the plan of God, and thus they were vehicles of divine intervention. In spite of the fact that Matthew's Mary is a completely passive character, acted upon and spoken about in chapter 1, and in spite of the fact that the stories of the four women show a significant *lack* of intervention on the part of God (intervention understood in any direct or miraculous sense), I agree with the direction of this last explanation. I do not agree with the way it is usually spelled out, with Matthew's reasoning understood, for example, as follows: he has chosen women who foreshadowed the role of Mary. Her pregnancy was a scandal, since she had not lived with her husband; yet the child Jesus was actually begotten through the Holy Spirit and not by any man, so that God had intervened to bring to fulfillment the messianic heritage. "And this intervention through a woman was even more dramatic than the Old Testament instances; there God had overcome the moral or biological irregularity of the human parents, while here He overcomes the total absence of the father's begetting."[6] The way in which the authors of *Mary in the New Testament* characterize this theory ("The Four OT Women, Marked by Irregular Marital Unions, Were Vehicles of God's Messianic Plan"[7]) avoids the stress on intervention, simply arguing that through these unions God carried out the divine promises and plan. But this obscures the fact that Tamar's union with Judah was not a marriage; and Matthew's phrase, "the wife of Uriah," seems to indicate that he is thinking of Bathsheba's adultery with David, not their later marriage.

Our discussion will profit from a careful look at the Old Testament stories of the four women, stories that can be classified with those Phyllis Trible calls "texts of terror, unpreached stories of the faith."[8] We will consider as well aspects of later tradition possibly available to Matthew.

TAMAR

As the account stands in Genesis 38, Tamar was taken by Judah as a wife for his son Er, who was "wicked in the sight of Yahweh; and Yahweh slew him" (v. 7). Er's brother Onan refused to perform the duty of levirate marriage and produce a male descendant for his brother; instead he practiced coitus interruptus, for which he in turn was slain by Yahweh. Tamar's father-in-law Judah then refused her his third son Shelah "till Shelah my son grows up," because he feared for his son's life, suspecting Tamar was in some way responsible for the other two deaths (cf. Tobit 3:7–9; 8:9–10). Tamar was sent back to live as a widow in her father's house. Judah wrongfully considered this solution as final for himself, but presented it to Tamar as an interim solution.[9]

Eventually Tamar understood that Judah wanted to get rid of her permanently, and she acted for the first time on her own. Disguising herself as a prostitute, she tricked Judah into having intercourse with her, and she became pregnant. When the pregnancy was discovered, Tamar was accused of being "with child by harlotry."[10] Her father-in-law pronounced the terrible and extraordinary sentence of death by burning.[11] The accusation against Tamar is on the basis of her prostitution as a betrothed woman, that is, betrothed to Judah's third son.[12] Those who accused her to Judah assumed that he would honor his obligation, and Judah took the role of judge, thus recognizing her as part of his family. Tamar's own act, however, proceded from the assumption that Judah had released her permanently (and unjustly) from the family.

The death sentence was overturned by a disclosure. When Tamar revealed the identity of the one who impregnated her, Judah admitted, "She is more righteous than I, inasmuch as I did not give her to my son Shelah" (v 26). Though Tamar's action bordered on a crime, she was not guilty, and the line of Judah continued through her. Childs comments, "Judah demonstrated an unfaithfulness which threatened to destroy the promise of posterity, which was only restored by the faithfulness of a Canaanite wife."[13] However, just whose wife Tamar was, if anyone's, is unclear. Judah "did not lie with her again" (v 26),[14] and it is not said that she was given to Shelah. (According to *Jub.* 41:21 she was *not* given to Shelah since she had had intercourse with Judah.)

This strange ending to the story leaves the reader with the impression of a legitimated illegitimacy. In the biblical genealogies Tamar's children from Judah are considered Judah's legitimate sons. But 1 Chr 2:4 mentions that Tamar was Judah's daughter-in-law, and in later rabbinic sources her place in David's ancestry seems to have been used to castigate his genealogical purity.[15] Nevertheless, this later tradition highlights Tamar's righteousness.[16] In Philo's convoluted allegorizing, she becomes a sign of victory,[17] and of chastity "inviolate, undefiled and truly virginal."[18] Her conception is seen as a reception of "divine impregnation."[19]

No intervention by Yahweh on Tamar's behalf has marked the story in Genesis 38. Because of her own action, "an attractive symmetry has been achieved. Judah who had lost two sons, Er and Onan, now begets twins—a sign certainly that Judah has been forgiven."[20] For Tamar the twins replace, as it were, the two lost husbands, in that they secure for her a place in the patriarchal social structure, in the role at least of mother if not of wife. Judah's acknowledgment of her as the mother of his children-to-be regularizes her position in that society. Tamar herself has acted to secure her rights and demonstrate her righteousness. Suspected of bringing death and disgrace, she has in the end brought life: for Judah the honor of an honest reaction and responsibility accepted, and the continuation of his name and of the covenant promise. Tamar is willing to risk her life in order to bear a son who would continue her husband's name, Er. She takes initiative selflessly and in an indirect way on behalf of her dead husband, showing more loyalty to the name of Judah than Judah himself, and she is rewarded for these actions. The dominating role of human beings and human things becomes clear from the fact that the actual narrative in vv 12–30 does not mention Yahweh's acting and speaking. Actually, males and male values dominate, through the female who reintegrates herself into the structure.

Intervention of a sort does appear in the accounts of this narrative in the Targums, Aramaic translations of the Old Testament.[21] In the Targum Pseudo-Jonathan, after Judah declares that Tamar is innocent and pregnant by him, a divine voice from heaven declares, "It is from me that this thing comes." Renée Bloch neatly captures the idea of dual causality in her translation: "C'est de moi [Judah] qu'elle est enceinte. . . . C'est de moi [God] que vient cette chose."[22] After the voice has spoken, the tribunal sets both of them free. In the Fragmentary Targum, Judah admits responsibility for the pregnancy, insisting Tamar is not pregnant with a child of fornication and that this happened because he did not give Shelah to her; then a heavenly voice is heard: "Both of you are acquitted at the tribunal. This thing has come from God." In Targum Neofiti I, the voice announces, "They are both just; from before the Lord this thing has come about."[23] I call this intervention of a sort, because it only serves to underline that the action of God (if we can speak of that here) has been hidden in or even identified with the action of the human drama. As in the Joseph story, into which the story of Judah and Tamar has been inserted as an interlude or "structural parasite"[24] or, better, "oblique commentary,"[25] in Genesis 38 the theological component has been kept discreetly in the background.[26]

RAHAB

The inclusion of Rahab (Matt 1:5: *Rachab*) in Matthew's genealogy cannot be fully explained from the traditions now available to us. The statement that Boaz was her child by Salmon and that she was an ancestress of David (cf. Ruth 4:21; 1 Chr 2:11) has no support in the Old Testament or elsewhere, and it is strange since the biblical Rahab (*rāḥāb;* LXX; *raab*) lived at the time of the conquest, nearly two hundred years before Boaz. This Rahab is not mentioned in the apocrypha, pseudepigrapha, or Philo. The name spelled *Rachab* does not appear elsewhere in the New Testament, nor in the LXX or second-century Fathers. Origen, commenting on Matt 1:5, speaks of *Rachab* as "an insignificant woman, mentioned nowhere else in Scripture, who has dropped *ex machina*—so to speak—into the sphere of the gospel."[27] In spite of the difference in Greek spelling and the dating difficulty, most scholars conclude that it is virtually certain that Matthew means the Rahab of the conquest.[28]

Her story is told in Joshua 2, 6. Two men sent by Joshua to spy out the city of Jericho "came into the house of a harlot whose name was Rahab, and lodged there" (2:1). The reader is not told why they came to her or why she received them; presumably her reputation attracted them and she welcomed them first on the basis of her occupation. The narrator makes no comment of scorn or condemnation on Rahab's harlotry. Apparently she was accepted as an outcast who survived in an institutionalized status outside the family unit, beyond the normal social structure and its boundaries and rules. Nor does the narrator comment on the presence of the Israelite spies in her house. The Old Testament discourages unions with prostitutes (Prov 2:16–22; 29:3; 31:3) and warns fathers against their daughters becoming prostitutes (Lev 19:29; cf. Deut 23:17), but it also recognizes that prostitutes were patronized.[29] Their sexual activity, not under the control of a husband or a father, was probably tolerated if not encouraged, when it did not disrupt the paternity system.[30]

In a surprising move, Rahab defied the king of Jericho by hiding the spies and sending their pursuers off on a false trail. She told the spies, "I know that Yahweh has given you the land . . . for Yahweh your God is he who is God in heaven above

and on the earth beneath" (vv 9, 11).[31] The basis of her knowledge and faith was not direct experience of Yahweh, but the
fear of the Canaanites at hearing of the exploits of Yahweh on
behalf of the warriors. In payment for her kindness, Rahab extracted a promise that she and her father's house would be left
alive when the city was conquered; the daughter was to secure
the safety of the entire family. Rahab let the spies down by a
rope through a window in her apartment in the city wall. She
was told to bind a scarlet cord in that window when the spies
returned with the army. When the city and all within it were
destroyed, Joshua honored the promise: "Rahab the harlot, and
her father's household and all who belonged to her, Joshua
saved alive; and she dwelt in Israel to this day, because she hid
the messengers whom Joshua sent to spy out Jericho" (6:25).
Rahab was, then, a survivor in the world of men at war, unfaith-
ful to her own people but faithful to her own household and to
Israel and its God. Yahweh did not intervene to save the spies
or to save Rahab and her family from utter destruction; instead,
her ingenuity and second-hand, partial faith accomplished this.

Rabbinic tradition mainly magnified her profligacy, in order
to emphasize her repentance and conversion.[32] She is said to
have married Joshua and become the ancestress of prophets, and
to have been gifted with prophecy. Heb 11:31 and Jas 2:25
underline her hospitality to the spies. We can do no more than
speculate, on the basis of these traditions and on the basis of the
stories of the other women in Matthew's genealogy, that Matthew
may have seen in her profession of harlotry the paradoxical opportunity of safety and success for Israel, and for her and her
family.

RUTH

Trible describes the story of Ruth in this way:

With consummate artistry, the book of Ruth presents the aged Naomi
and the youthful Ruth as they struggle for survival in a patriarchal
environment. These women bear their own burdens. They know hardship, danger, insecurity and death. No God promises them blessing; no
man rushes to their rescue. They themselves risk bold decisions and
shocking acts to work out their own salvation in the midst of the alien,
the hostile, and the unknown.[33]

Their "salvation," like that of *all* female biblical characters, is their eventual integration into the patriarchal social structure, outside of which there was believed to be no salvation.[34] "The overriding concern of the author of Ruth is the history of the royal line of Judah."[35]

The death of Naomi's husband and sons left her and her Moabite daughters-in-law Orpah and Ruth as three childless widows, sociological misfits, with no security, worth, protection, or identity in a male-dominated culture. Ruth unexpectedly elected to link her destiny with Naomi's and return with her to the latter's homeland, Judah. In Bethlehem where they settled, Naomi had a kinsman, Boaz, "a man of substance" (2:1). By chance, according to the patriarchal design of the author, Ruth gleaned in Boaz's field, met him, and acquired his favor. When Naomi learned of the kindness of this relative, she contrived to "seek a home" (3:1) for Ruth. She told her, "Now is not Boaz our kinsman, with whose maidens you were? See, he is winnowing barley tonight at the threshing floor. Wash therefore and anoint yourself, and put on your best clothes and go down to the threshing floor; but do not make yourself known to the man until he has finished eating and drinking. But when he lies down, observe the place where he lies; then go and uncover the lower part of his body;[36] and he will tell you what to do."

Ruth obeyed, but instead of waiting for Boaz to take charge and tell her what to do, she told Boaz, "Spread your wing over your maidservant, for you are a redeemer" (3:9), a request that he marry her, thus fulfilling his obligation as a kinsman. Boaz's reaction was to bless and praise her and to assure her that he would do as she asked, providing that a nearer kinsman would not play that role for her. He asked her to lie down until morning, and Ruth's departure before dawn kept the encounter secret.[37] When the nearer kinsman was confronted by Boaz, the right of redemption—to buy Naomi's property and to marry Ruth—was turned over to him. The elders and all the people were called to witness that Boaz had bought all that belonged to Naomi's husband and sons, including Ruth the widow of Naomi's son, "to restore the name of the dead in his inheritance" (4:10). The elders replied with a prayer that Yahweh "make the woman who is coming into your house like Rachel and Leah, who together built up the house of Israel" (4:11), reminding the reader of the role of two women together in this story. They prayed also, "May your house be like the house of Perez, whom Tamar bore to Judah, because of the children that Yahweh will give you by this young woman" (4:12), reminding the reader of parallels between the stories of Tamar and Ruth: trickery,[38] the levirate obligation,[39] and the taint of scandal.

"So Boaz took Ruth and she became his wife; and he went in to her and Yahweh gave her conception and she bore a son" (4:13). Trible remarks: "The gift of life resides neither in male nor in female, but in God."[40] God does not intrude in this narrative, by speech or miracle. God's activity "is very much that of the one in the shadows, the one whose manifestation is not by intervention but by a lightly exercised providential control."[41] In contrast, *Ruth R.* 7.14 interjects a "miraculous" element into the story and links it to other Old Testament stories with the statement that Boaz was eighty years old and Ruth forty, so that it ambiguity was against all expectations that they would have a child. The biblical narrative ends with a genealogy (4:18–21), and it is worth noting that four of the men listed are associated with the four women in Matthew's genealogy: Perez, Salmon, Boaz, and David.

Ruth alone among the four women of Matthew's genealogy is free from a taint of immorality in the rabbinic tradition, which stresses the problem of her Moabite ancestry. (Deut 22:3, which reads "No Ammorite or Moabite shall enter the assembly of Yahweh, even to the tenth generation," could be applied to David through Ruth.) But a glance at some of the material from the rabbinic literature, targums, and translations shows that there is intense concern that the threshing floor scene receive careful exegesis by various methods in various periods, lest the reader conclude from the sexual allusions in 3:4, 7–9, 12–13 that Ruth and Boaz had intercourse there.[42] We can conclude that such strenuous efforts to remove any hint of indelicacy implicitly acknowledge that a different reading was possible and persistent, even popular.

In any case, it is clear that like Tamar Ruth risked an accusation of harlotry, and like Tamar she was praised for taking the risk. The actions of Naomi and Ruth ultimately summoned

Boaz to his duty, and resulted in the reintegration of both women into the social structure through Ruth's marriage and the legitimate birth of a child, Obed.

THE WIFE OF URIAH

In many ways the story of Bathsheba is the most horrifying of the four Old Testament stories. She is not mentioned by name in Matthew's genealogy, probably because identification of her as the wife of Uriah stresses her adultery and not her subsequent marriage to David, or because even as married to David she was still in some way the wife of Uriah. In her appearance in 2 Samuel 11, she is so colorless, passive, and pathetic a figure that she is nearly anonymous there also. From his palace roof, David the king saw her bathing.[43] The reader is told nothing about her except that she "was very beautiful" (v 2). David inquired about her and was informed to whom she belonged: she was a daughter of Eliam and wife of Uriah. The verbs used in the next verse are plain and blunt: "David sent messengers, and took her; and she came to him, and he lay with her." The happening "has all the appearance of a casual affair, a king's whim."[44] In an aside the narrator remarks that she was purifying herself from her menstruation; this implies that the child she would soon conceive could not possibly be that of her husband Uriah. The blunt talk continues: she returned home, she conceived, and she sent word to David, "I am pregnant" (vv 4–5). Nothing is said about her reaction to any of this. No one speaks to her, including David. There is no hint of any resistance or protest on her part (who could resist the king?), or of fear that the adultery be discovered.[45]

David plotted to bring Uriah home from battle and make him sleep with his wife, so that the pregnancy would appear to be due to him. When his plan failed,[46] David plotted and executed the murder of Uriah, in order to keep the adultery secret. And "when the wife of Uriah heard that Uriah her husband was dead, she made lamentation for her husband" (v 26); three times in this one verse her marital relationship is stressed. Whether the lamentation was a formality or grief, the author does not say. Again the blunt talk: "when the mourning was over, David sent and brought her to his house, and she became his wife, and bore him a son" (v 27).[47]

Does the writer of the Succession Narrative have no interest at all in Bathsheba: in her motives, her ruin, her compromises? That the terseness in the text is not due to this writer's lack of sympathy and imagination in dealing with women in general is shown by his more nuanced and sensitive portrait of Tamar, raped by her half brother Amnon (2 Samuel 13). But here the author communicates outrage at David's treatment of Bathsheba by treating the crimes in the same rough, brutal fashion in which they were committed. "The figure of Bathsheba haunts the whole narrative with extraordinary ambiguity. . . . One is forced to guess, without being able to conclude, what meaning these events had for her, whether she was victim, or accomplice, or somehow both at once."[48] The author may intend to portray not her shallowness but her entrapment, a total entrapment, in a situation where her feelings, rights, plans, perhaps love all counted for nothing. She had no recourse. The narrator is interested in David's blame: "The thing that David had done displeased Yahweh" (v 27).

In the incident that follows, Bathsheba played no part. David was confronted by the prophet Nathan with the parable about the poor man's little ewe lamb. Bathsheba as wife of Uriah is symbolized by a pet, a pet like a daughter, a pet contrasted with a flock or herd, a pet needlessly slaughtered. David, unaware of the symbolism, judged that the rich man who took (*lqḥ*) the lamb (12:4) deserved death, but he designated a monetary penalty for the crime. The conclusion of David's speech shows that the issue was not simply theft (or adultery). The issue was lack of pity (12:6), the lack of compassion and sympathy, even physical mercy that would spare a potential victim from some form of violence. The oracle condemning David frames a single reference to the adultery with two references to the act of murder in 12:9, but in 12:10 the focus is on the adultery. The verb *lqḥ* appears in vv 9, 10 as in 11:4, for David's act (cf. 12:4). David, it is implied, also showed no pity—for Uriah or for Bathsheba. "And for David to show no pity . . . is for David to despise God" (12:9, 10).[49]

In punishment, David was told that evil would be raised up

against him out of his own house; his wives would be taken before his eyes and given to his neighbor.[50] Further crimes against women were to compensate for the crime against Uriah. Although Uriah died, and "the man who has done this deserves to die" (12:5), David did not die. Instead, the child born to him died. Then "David comforted his wife, Bathsheba, and went in to her, and lay with her" (v 24). She bore a son, whom David named Solomon, and whom Yahweh loved.[51]

Bathsheba appears again, in 1 Kings 1, when David was near death. She plays here the role of the pawn of Nathan, who counseled her to remind David of a promise that Solomon would be king, not Adonijah his eldest. The reader has no way of knowing whether David made such a pledge or whether this is a hoax foisted on the old king. Bathsheba did as she was told, and David promised. Whether or not she was merely the mouthpiece for Nathan and his colleagues, or acting to save the life of Solomon and her own life, as Nathan insisted, David bent to her will as she once bent to his.

In Bathsheba's last biblical appearance, 1 Kings 2:13–25, she is again a messenger, this time from Adonijah to Solomon. She delivered the alleged request of Adonijah that he be given Abishag the Shunammite, David's concubine, royal property that should be passed on to Solomon. The last words spoken to her are Solomon's sarcastic refusal to a woman he regarded as unable to function intelligently and independently in the world of high politics.

Her story, then, is the story of a woman taken in adultery, pitied rather than scorned or blamed by the storyteller. She is presented without options, without recourse, without a personal history of significance. She does not act but is acted upon, and then she barely reacts. Her wordless submission renders her a thing passed from man to man.[52] She personifies tragic passivity, unlike Tamar, Rahab, and Ruth who stood up against the fates offered them by society, took matters into their own hands, and bettered their positions within the patriarchal framework. Bathsheba who survives as a queen never emerges as a person.

Like the stories of the other three women in Matthew's genealogy, Bathsheba's story is one that stresses not the God who intervenes, disrupting human events, but the God who creates the context for human freedom.[53] Human acts are destiny-producing deeds[54] in which there is a tight connection between sin and suffering, and in which God is somehow seen as involved and at work. Yahweh is mentioned by the narrator explicitly in 11:27 ("the thing that David did displeased Yahweh"); 12:1 ("Yahweh sent Nathan to speak to David"); 12:15 ("Yahweh struck the child") and 12:24–25 ("Yahweh loved" Solomon, whose name was called Jedidiah "because of Yahweh"). The net effect of these "interventions" is that confidence is expressed that the whole story pertains to God and that God prevails in what happens, though God does not will whatever comes to pass. These theological asides have an important and "oddly abrupt effect" in this story, which is without miracle. They involve the reader in judgment passed by God on human beings, and the last aside (12:24) states the "act of choice," the "divine turning" toward the newborn child, "without making any attempt whatsoever at explanation or substantiation."[55]

Later tradition passes over Bathsheba to focus on the sin of David,[56] or makes her responsible for the crime of murder.[57] It is difficult to understand her later inclusion in the twenty-two women of valor listed in *Midrash Ha-Gadol* 1, 334–39.[58] It was enough, perhaps, that she was the mother of Solomon and instrumental in his acquisition of the throne.

CONCLUSION

What conclusions can be drawn from these stories and traditions to explain Matthew's choice of these four women for mention in the genealogy of Jesus? What do they have in common, which may prepare the reader for the story of Mary that follows? As Niditch has seen, the sociological situations of all four women are comparable.[59] (I recognize that we cannot be sure if or how some aspects of the following profile apply to Rahab, since the full story of her that Matthew knows is unknown to us.)

(1) All four find themselves outside patriarchal family structures: Tamar and Ruth are childless young widows, Rahab a prostitute, Bathsheba an adulteress and then a widow pregnant with her lover's child.

(2) All four are wronged or thwarted by the male world. Without claiming a full feminist consciousness for the authors of these

narratives, we can claim an awareness, however dim, that society was patriarchal, that this caused suffering for women in certain circumstances, and that certain women and men sometimes rectified or manipulated those circumstances in extraordinary ways to lessen the suffering. Alter speaks of "extra-institutional awareness of women's standing."[60]

(3) In their sexual activity—or in Ruth's case perhaps only suspicion of sexual activity—all four risk damage to the social order and their own condemnations. Accusation of improper sexual conduct is actually made in the case of Tamar, implicit in the case of Rahab, avoided in Ruth's case by the secrecy of Boaz, and leveled in Bathsheba's case against her partner.

(4) The situations of all four are righted by the actions of men who acknowledge guilt and/or accept responsibility for them, drawing them under patriarchal protection, giving them an identity and a future within the patriarchal structure, legitimating them and their children-to-be. In the final analysis, they are exalted for their acceptance of the patriarchal status quo,[61] because it is believed that within that status quo the covenant promises to Abraham and David are being kept, and the generations move toward the establishment of the nation of Israel and the monarchy.

Mention of these four women is designed to lead Matthew's reader to expect another, final story of a woman who becomes a social misfit in some way; is wronged or thwarted; who is party to a sexual act that places her in great danger; and whose story has an outcome that repairs the social fabric and ensures the birth of a child who is legitimate or legitimated. That child, Matthew tells us (1:1), is "the son of David, the son of Abraham."

Further, what do the four stories have in common theologically, and what is the reader led to expect theologically? The stories, as we have seen, show a significant lack of intervention on the part of God. There has been no miraculous, direct intervention to right the wrongs, or remove the shame, or illuminate the consciousness, or shatter the structures. The references to divine activity are strikingly sparing. God does not intrude by speech or miracle, but overrules without interfering with natural causation. In Matthew's genealogy, the promises to Abraham and to David undergird the movement down the generations. Fathering after fathering, and pregnancy after pregnancy, the movement is toward the one believed to be the Messiah. Four special pregnancies are chosen for emphasis; chosen rather than the difficult pregnancies of barren women like Sarah are the distasteful ones of fruitful women. Matthew leads his reader to expect a story that will continue this discrete theologizing. It will be a story marked by *lack* of miraculous, divine intervention, a story rather of divine accommodation to human freedom in the complexity of near-tragedy. What the reader gets is more than what is expected, but Matthew has done a brilliant job with the traditions at hand. The story that follows is even more difficult to present theologically. Matthew has seen it as a story without precedent but not without preparation.

If we look at the four stories through the eyes of the later writers and compilers of the Mishnah's tractate Nashim, they represent what Neusner calls the dangerous moment in which woman is seen as threatening, not related (or not properly related) to man. It is the critical moment of her transfer from one man to another, from one setting and status to another. This is the moment in which woman is not sanctified, her position not secured either in heaven or on earth, when the anomaly of woman is at its most anomalous.[62] The work of sanctification becomes necessary precisely here, at the point of danger and disorder. According to the Mishnah, man is capable of effecting sanctification through his will and works, since what corresponds to God's word on earth is the will of man. All the wild potentialities of female sexuality, with their threat to the order of the stable, sacred society must be brought under control. This must be done to preserve the normal modes of creation, how things really are—or how a small group of men wanted things to be—so that maleness, that is, normality, may encompass all. From this viewpoint, what has occurred in the stories of the four women, and what will follow in the fifth story, is sanctification. But in the fifth, sanctification fiercely challenges notions of "how things really are."

B. V 16: THE SHATTERED PATTERN

In v 16, Matthew reaches the final names of his genealogy with the statement that "Jacob begot (*egennēsen*) Joseph the husband of Mary; of her was begotten (*ex hēs egennēthē*) Jesus, called the Christ." We have reached the thirty-ninth occurrence of the verb *gennan*, "to beget." But the pattern, A begot B, B begot C, which has been used throughout the genealogy, is here broken in dramatic fashion. What is not said is clearly important. It is not said that Joseph, the husband of Mary, begot Jesus. And it is not said who begot Jesus.[63] V 16 cries out for clarification.

By shattering the pattern, Matthew is apparently trying to prevent the conclusion that Joseph was the biological father of Jesus. But precisely that conclusion was drawn by some. In *The Dialogue of Timothy and Aquila,* an anonymous work revised in the fifth century from a work that may be as early as 200 C.E., the text of Matthew is quoted as above in a discussion between a Jew and a Christian. The Jew apparently drew the conclusion from v 16 that Joseph was the father of Jesus. It is not, after all, incomprehensible that one would suppose that the husband of a woman of whom a child was begotten was the father of that child (cf. Luke 3:23).

The reading of Matt 1:16 given above is supported by the overwhelming weight of manuscript evidence. In the opinion of most contemporary critics, other readings of this verse are stages of copyists' corrections of the original.[64] One variant is especially interesting. In the Old Syriac (Sinaiticus) version, published in 1894, there is an attempt to restore the "A begot B" pattern. It reads, "Jacob begot Joseph; and Joseph, to whom the virgin Mary was betrothed, begot Jesus, called the Christ." What is meant by this restoration of the genealogical pattern, in a work that also contains Matt 1:18 and 20? Did the translator see no incompatibility between the description of Mary as betrothed virgin, pregnancy, and begetting through the Holy Spirit (vv 18, 20), on the one hand, and the biological fatherhood of Jesus by Joseph, on the other hand?

Some argue that the author of this version thought of a virginal conception. The pattern of the genealogy has not been restored completely. Mention of Mary as virgin and as betrothed has been added, replacing the statement that Joseph was the husband of Mary. This tinkering with the original text may have been designed primarily to safeguard belief in a virginal conception and in Mary's perpetual virginity. In this case, Joseph's fatherhood may be understood in terms of legal paternity.[65] Or the use of an active verb in this variant may be an unthinking, purely mechanical, and careless imitation of the preceding pattern.[66]

The insistence that the Old Syriac translator did not mean to name Joseph as Jesus' biological father is not totally convincing. It seems possible that the translator could have drawn from the original a conclusion similar to that of the Jew in *The Dialogue of Timothy and Aquila* (and, as we will see, to that of some Jewish Christians and Gnostics)—that Joseph was Jesus' father—and then changed the text to better reflect that conclusion. The presupposition behind that conclusion would then be the one that we will explore in the following pages: that divine and human begetting are not necessarily mutually exclusive.

If we read Matt 1:16 open to the same presupposition, but giving more weight to Matthew's intentional breaking of the genealogical pattern, the suspicion presents itself that Matthew is speaking of an illegitimate pregnancy. Silence about a human father—the lack of mention of his name—need not mean he did not exist. And the verb *egennēthē* in 1:16 need not be understood, as it often is, as a theological passive, meaning that in the place of a human father, God begot Jesus.[67] This interpretation occurs only to one who reads v 16 through the lens of the traditional interpretation of vv 18–25.

C. V 17: FOURTEEN GENERATIONS

One further curious element in Matthew's genealogy requires comment. In v 17, he insists that "all the generations from Abraham to David were fourteen generations, and from David to the deportation to Babylon fourteen generations, and from the deportation to Babylon to the Christ fourteen generations."[68] But the actual number of generations in the three sections does not seem to support his claim. In the first section, from Abraham to David (vv 2–6), fourteen men are named, but there are only thirteen generations or begettings. Probably Matthew intends the begetting of Abraham himself to be counted, which brings the number to fourteen. The second section, from David to the Babylonian exile, does list fourteen generations. But the third, from the exile to the Christ, has only thirteen. Unlike the first section, the first man named here, Jechoniah, cannot be counted because his generation has already been counted as the last of the previous section. Joseph, who is said to beget no son, is the twelfth generation, and Jesus appears to be the thirteenth.

It is possible that the number thirteen in the third section is simply due to the inaccuracy of Matthew's work, or the inexactness of his sources, or faulty transmission of the text,[69] but this is unlikely[70] in such a carefully composed passage that emphasizes the enumeration. Many different proposals have been offered for finding a fourteenth generation in this section, and it will be helpful to look at a few of these.

(1) One suggestion is that Matthew counts Jesus as the thirteenth and Christ as the fourteenth, since Jesus becomes the Christ only in his risen state and/or at his parousia. He is Christ before that, only proleptically.[71] But this cannot be Matthew's understanding, since he writes his Infancy Narrative to show that Jesus was the Christ from his conception; also, in this Gospel Jesus is acknowledged as the Christ during his lifetime (2:4; 16:16).

(2) It has been argued that Jesus should be counted twice, as representative of the thirteen and fourteen generations. According to this proposal, Matthew knew of a numerical interpretation of history in fourteen epochs: the second to last is the apocalyptic tribulations and the last is the Messianic age. In Matthew's Gospel, the life and death of Jesus is "the event in which the darkest moment in history occurs," but Jesus is also "the event in which restoration is effected."[72] However, this ingenious theory causes us to lose sight of the issue of begetting and sonship.

(3) Another suggestion is that Mary be counted, as the biological parent of Jesus. This would rank her in the masculine succession of generations, passing over her affinity with the four other women, and would involve an understanding of her role as unique.[73] It has been objected that counting her as the biological parent of Jesus would cancel out Joseph and still leave only thirteen begettings, "since one can scarcely count Jesus' not being begotten by Joseph as the thirteenth, and his being begotten of Mary as the fourteenth."[74] If, on the other hand, Joseph's role is counted as legal, and Mary's as physical, the one

chronological generation carries two other kinds of generations within it. But through Mary what is really being counted is the miraculous, divine generation of Jesus,[75] which leads us to the next proposal.

(4) God should be counted as the one who begets Jesus. "The 'miscalculation' is deliberate, and points reverently to the mysterious conception from the Spirit. The anonymous progenitor is the Lord God."[76] The verb in v 16 is read as a theological passive. But this is the reading I am challenging as unnecessary and as foreign to the intention of the Evangelist.

(5) Some suggest a solution based on the inaccuracies regarding the names of kings in the genealogy. Perhaps among the historical omissions in the genealogy available to him, Matthew recognized the omission (v 11) of Jehoiakim, son of Josiah and father of Jehoiachin (Jechoniah), an omission that may have been caused by the similarity of the names Jehoiakim and Jehoiachin, and by the use in the LXX of *Iōakim* for both. Matthew, it is reasoned, counted the implicit generation by mentioning Jechoniah again at the beginning of the third section. He did not change the name in v 11, nor did he insert "Jehoiakim begot Jechoniah," perhaps because he regarded the genealogical list he was using as sacred, and because the insertion of Jehoiakim in the second section would bring the number of generations to fifteen. Jehoiachin (Jechoniah) would have to remain in this section because he was begotten before the exile.[77] But this explanation for the double mention of Jechoniah is less convincing than that which understands it as coordinated with the double mention of David in v 6. Both men are transitional figures who demarcate different periods in Israel's history,[78] and the double mention of them emphasizes the transitions. Matthew intends that neither be counted twice.[79]

My own theory is that a name, the thirteenth, is conspicuously and consciously omitted from the genealogy. Joseph *is* counted by Matthew as a father of Jesus, though he is not thought or said to beget him. Anticipated by the broken pattern of v 16, the narrative in vv 18–25 will clarify that Joseph accepts the child as his own, by completing his marriage to the pregnant Mary. It is this legal fatherhood that makes sense of beginning this Gospel with a Davidic genealogy, Joseph's genealogy up to v 16a.

But Joseph is not Jesus' biological father, as Matthew tries to make plain by his avoidance of the expected formulaic statement, "Joseph begot Jesus." In place of the thirteenth name, of the biological father of Jesus, and of the active verb "begot," there is the passive, "was begotten." This should not be read as a theological passive. The verb is mysterious, "fraught with background," immediately raising the question, "begotten by whom?" To the loud "suggestive silence" and suspense[80] created by the ending of the genealogy, the narrative responds in the following verses, but not to our complete satisfaction. The biological father is never explicitly mentioned by Matthew. He is never named, either because Matthew and his sources did not know the name, or because it was suppressed. He is erased, but not completely; absent but not completely. Jesus' genealogy, then, does involve two kinds of human fatherhood: legal (Joseph's) and physical (the biological father). Matthew will insist in the narrative that the begetting is also "of the Holy Spirit"; in virtue of this Jesus can be called God's Son (2:15). As we will see, such divine begetting does not negate human begetting.

Certainly this is a very strange thing: the creation and use of a genealogy whose functions are (a) to admit or at least raise the possibility of illegitimacy; and (b) to insist, via someone other than the biological father, on legitimacy of a social/legal type (here, via Joseph, on Jesus' Abrahamic and Davidic descent). But, whether read with or without the following narrative, the Matthean genealogy of Jesus can be interpreted to have these functions.

Moreover, we do know of another Jewish genealogy from antiquity which has been interpreted to include an illegitimacy. In *m. Yebam.* 4:13, Rabbi Simeon ben Azzai, who lived at the end of the first and beginning of the second century C.E., is said to have responded to the question, "Who is accounted a bastard (*mamzēr*)?" He said, "I found a family register (*mglt yḥsyn*) in Jerusalem, and in it was written, 'Such a one (*plwny*) is a bastard (*mamzēr*) through [a transgression of the law of] thy neighbor's wife.' "[81] Danby cites Lev 18:20 as the law of thy neighbor's wife ("And you shall not lie carnally with your neighbor's wife, and defile yourself with her"). But it is possible that the law referred to is Deut 22:23–27, on the rape or seduction of a betrothed virgin; v 24 refers to the violation of a neighbor's wife, as a betrothed girl or woman was legally considered a wife. The Mishnah text goes on to say that this confirms the words of Rabbi Joshua,[82] who argued that a *mamzēr* is the offspring of any union "for which the partakers are liable to death at the hands of the court."

The genealogy probably dates from the period before 70 C.E., and some critics, including Klausner, Herford, and Johnson, have seen in this passage from the Mishnah an indirect reference to Jesus.[83] Klausner does not give the charge of illegitimacy any credence, nor does he connect the genealogy mentioned with any Christian document.[84] Herford ties the charge of illegitimacy to Jesus' death: Simeon ben Azzai brings the evidence of the scroll he has discovered, "to show that in the case of a notorious person the penalty of a judicial death had followed upon unlawful birth" from a union prohibited under penalty of death, according to Rabbi Joshua. For Herford, the alleged discovery of the scroll may be historical; the Jews were not prohibited from entering Jerusalem until 135 C.E., and Rabbi Simeon ben Azzai was dead before that time. What the scroll was, he says, cannot now be determined. But it is "just possible" that it was the Gospel of Matthew (which begins with the words, "the book of the genealogy of Jesus Christ"), or an Aramaic forerunner of it, or a scroll containing one of the genealogies given in Matthew and Luke.[85] Johnson raises the possibility that Simeon ben Azzai was referring "with polemical irony" to Matthew 1 as an example of a birth which (according to Rabbi Joshua) is illegitimate, "Jewish calumnies" having been suggested by Matthew's account.[86]

We will return in chapter 4 to a discussion of this passage and others like it that refer to *peloni* (a certain person, known but unnamed; here translated "such a one"); this term is sometimes regarded as a veiled reference to Jesus. The points to be made here are the following. (1) If there is a reference to Jesus in *m. Yebam.* 4:13, then this text may be a reaction to Matthew 1 or to gospel sources. This would indicate that some contemporaries of the evangelists understood Jesus' genealogy as a statement of his illegitimacy, that is, understood his mother to have been married or betrothed to one man and impregnated by another. Whether or not this was a "polemical" understanding is presently beside the point. As we have seen, Joseph is clearly referred to in Matt 1:16 as the husband of Mary, but he is not said to have begotten Jesus. This information, plus the mention of the four women and the missing fourteenth generation in Matthew's third division of the genealogy, are all peculiarities of the Matthean genealogy, which can be read to imply illegitimacy. However, we cannot be certain that the reference in *m. Yebam.* 4:13 is to Jesus. (2) If this Mishnaic text is not a reference to Jesus (and we cannot be certain either that it is not), we have evidence of at least one other genealogy that included an illegitimate birth or was worded in such a way that it was open to the interpretation that it included an illegitimacy.

D. VV 18–25: THE STORY OF THE CONCEPTION AND NAMING OF JESUS

The narrative in these verses is considered by Stendahl "the enlarged footnote to the crucial point in the genealogy."[87] The narrative serves to explain the details of v 16, to describe the break in the expected pattern and the engrafting of Jesus onto the Davidic line. With the genealogy, the narrative answers the question *Quis?* (Who?). The child is son of David, son of Abraham (1:1), Jesus, Savior of his people (1:21), Emmanuel (1:23). Brown expands Stendahl's treatment, arguing that 1:1–17 concerns the *Quis?* of Jesus' identity, and 1:18–25 the *Quomodo?* (How?). The narrative is said to present a virginal conception: Jesus "is son of David not through physical begetting, but through an acceptance by the Davidic Joseph of a child conceived through the Holy Spirit." This miraculous conception further clarifies the *Quis?*: Jesus is the Son of God, Emmanuel. Read this way, 1:18–25 points backwards to the genealogy but contains a progression of thought beyond the genealogy.[88]

I agree that the narrative deals with *Quis?* and *Quomodo?*, but I understand the answers given to these questions differently. The narrative elucidates not only v 16, but also v 17 of the genealogy. The narrative tells us that someone other than Joseph was the biological father of Jesus, and that Joseph was his legal father (explaining why the Gospel opens with Joseph's genealogy), thus showing that there are indeed fourteen generations in the period from the exile to the Messiah. The fact that chapter 1 is centered around personal names deepens the silence concerning the name of the thirteenth man. A significant aspect, therefore, of Jesus' identity remains unclarified. Matthew's answer to the question *Quomodo?* is indirect and discreet.

In addition, it is important to note that Jesus is not called the son of God in chapter 1. That aspect of his identity does not appear until the fulfillment citation in 2:15: "Out of Egypt I have called my son" (Hos 1:11), in which Matthew expresses his belief that the relationship of Israel to God is now summed up in Jesus. This is confirmed by the divine pronouncement at the baptism (Matt 3:17): "This is my beloved Son with whom I am well pleased." (In contrast, Luke 1:35b declares that directly on the basis of the Holy Spirit coming upon Mary, the child will be called Son of God.) For some, the theme of divine sonship (though not the title) is already present in Matt 1:18–25, because the phrase in 1:20, "begotten through the Holy Spirit," is thought to be a counterexplanation to human parentage. A different explanation of the phrase in 1:20 is offered below, one in which divine parentage is compatible with human paternity.

1. THE LEGAL SITUATION MATTHEW DEPICTS

An understanding as accurate as possible of the legal situation in Matthew's story of Mary and Joseph is crucial to the interpretation of that story. Matthew presumes that understanding on the part of his readers.

Mary the mother of Jesus

(18b) had been betrothed to Joseph; but before they began to live together, it was found that she was with child—through the Holy Spirit. (19) Her husband Joseph was an upright man, but unwilling to expose her to public disgrace; and so he resolved to divorce her quietly. (20) Now, as he was considering this, behold an angel of the Lord appeared to him in a dream, saying, "Joseph, son of David, do not be afraid to take Mary your wife into your home, for the child begotten in her is through the Holy Spirit. (21) She will give birth to a son; and you will call his name Jesus, for he will save his people from their sins." (22) All this took place to fulfill what the Lord had spoken by the prophet who said, (23) "Behold, the virgin will be with child and will give birth to a son, and they will call his name Emmanuel (which means 'God with us')." (24) So Joseph got up from sleep and did as the angel of the lord had commanded him. He took his wife home, (25) but he had no sexual relations with her before she gave birth to a son. And he called his name Jesus (Brown translation).

In this period in Palestine, the marriage of a young girl took place in two stages. First came the engagement or betrothal (*'ērû-sîn*), which was a formal exchange in the presence of witnesses of the agreement to marry and the paying of the *môhar*, the bride price. The usual age for a girl's betrothal was between twelve and twelve and a half, that is, at puberty or a little before. The betrothal constituted a legally ratified marriage, since it began her transfer from her father's power to her husband's, giving the latter legal rights over her, and giving her the status of a married woman for many purposes. She could be called his wife (see Matt 1:20, 24) or become his widow.[89] The betrothal could be broken only by his divorce of her, and any violation of his marital "rights" by her during this period (when she continued to live in her father's house for about a year [*M. Ketub.* 5:2]) was considered adultery. The second stage was the marriage proper (*nîśśû'în*), the transfer of the girl to her husband's home, where he assumed her support. Only at this point did she definitely pass to her husband's power.[90]

It was normally assumed that the girl was a virgin at the time of her betrothal, and, at least in Galilee, also at the time of her completed marriage. According to the Mishnah, in Judea the husband was allowed to be alone with his wife in the period between betrothal and marriage, so interim sexual relations were permitted.[91] But this was not the custom in Galilee. Therefore in Galilee the husband could bring a charge of adultery against his wife in court soon after the marriage if he suspected that she had not been a virgin at the time of their marriage,[92] and certainly also if she was found pregnant in the interim between betrothal and marriage. Under the more lenient custom in Judea, could he bring charge? According to *m. Ketub.* 1:5 (cf. *t. Ketub.* 1:4), "If a man in Judea ate in the house of his father-in-law [and had an opportunity to be alone with his betrothed wife] and had no witnesses [to prove he did not have sexual relations with her], he may not lodge a virginity suit against her, since he had [already] remained alone with her."

It is risky, however, to apply the difference between Judean and Galilean marriage customs to the situation of Mary and Joseph. In the first place, some scholars think that the difference arose because of the danger that occupying Roman troops might rape or seduce a betrothed virgin; the difference, then, may stem from a post–70 c.e. period.[93] Second, in Matthew's story Mary and Joseph lived in Bethlehem of Judea and had their home there (2:11);[94] if the customs were already different, we would expect that the Judean practice would have applied to them. "Yet the tone of scandal implicit in the Matthean narrative would better fit the Galilean practice."[95]

The pregnancy of Mary was discovered[96] in the period between her betrothal and completed marriage, before she and Joseph "came together" (*prin ē sunelthein*), probably meaning before Mary was brought to Joseph's home.[97] Joseph's reaction in Matt 1:19 makes it plain that in Matthew's mind he was not the biological father. Whether or not Joseph was legally allowed to have sexual relations with Mary during this period, according to Matthew he had not. He knew that the child could not be his. "A just man" (*dikaios*)—that is, Torah-observant—Joseph was "unwilling to expose her to public disgrace," and so "resolved to divorce her quietly." Was he just *and therefore* unwilling to expose Mary to disgrace, or just *but* unwilling to expose her? Was his justice exemplified in his decision, or was his decision a touch of mercy that modified his justice?

Our interpretation of Matt 1:19 and of the dilemma it proposes depends on what we think it implies about Joseph's belief or suspicion concerning the cause and circumstance of the pregnancy, and on what law or laws dealt with such a case. The logic of the story indicates that Joseph understood the situation to obligate or at least allow him, legally and morally, to divorce Mary rather than complete the marriage with the home-taking. But his judgment was overruled by the angelic command, "Do not be afraid to take Mary your wife" (that is, to take her home),[98] with its causal explanation concerning the Holy Spirit (v 20).[99] The logic and structure of the story are violated if we assume with some critics that before the encounter with the angel Joseph knew that the pregnancy was "through the Holy Spirit" (*ek pneumatos hagiou;* v 18)[100] This theory requires the reader to guess blindly at the source of Joseph's information, and to presume that "religious awe" would lead him to decide on divorce. It also makes redundant, anticlimatic, and nonrevelatory[101] the angel's words to him at the end of v 20: "what is begotten in her is through the Holy Spirit" (*to gar en autȩ gennēthen ek pneumatos estin hagiou*).[102] It is better to understand the first mention of the Spirit in v 18 as an explanation Matthew addresses to the reader, which is "not part of the narrative flow."[103] Matthew wants the reader at this point to know more than Joseph does.[104] But given the strangeness of the phrase, "pregnant of (or through) the (a) Holy Spirit," and (as we will see) the lack of clear preparation within the framework of Jewish traditions for understanding what it might mean, the information given the reader does not really cancel or hinder participation in Joseph's suspicions or dilemma. At the least, the phrase in v 18 alerts the reader to the presence of something wonderful, startling, divinely empowered. We will suspend further discussion of the two references to the Holy Spirit until we have considered the laws that deal with the seduction or rape of a betrothed virgin.

Adultery or rape are two normal alternatives Joseph had for explaining the pregnancy with which he was confronted. And two alternative actions were considered by him: to expose Mary to public shame or to divorce her secretly—the action he chose.

The case of discovery of a betrothed virgin's sexual intercourse with someone other than her husband during the period of betrothal is handled only in Deut 22:23–27, which deals with seduction (considered infidelity) and rape. (The term *seduction* is used in discussions of Deut 22:23–24, with the implication that a betrothed virgin, normally very young, would have been partly victimized by her partner, although the act would still qualify as adultery.[105] Notice that the law seems to imply incorrectly that rape is a violent form of seduction, and that both situations covered in this law could amount to what we would call rape.) No Old Testament text envisages a situation in which it is discovered during the betrothal period that the betrothed girl was not "seduced" but willingly sought out intercourse with someone other than her fiancé. Some critics, however, think that the particular law that would have concerned Joseph in Matthew 1 is Deut 22:20–21.[106] But this law is part of a larger section, 22:13–21, which deals with the case of an accusation made by the husband *after* the home-taking and consummation (contrast Matt 1:18, 20), the accusation that he has not found in her "the tokens of virginity."[107] Deut 22:22 concerns the adultery that takes place after the marriage has been completed. There is, of course, a relationship between 22:20–21 and vv 23–24, in that in both cases the young woman would be considered to have "played the harlot in her father's house." Her transfer to the power of her husband would not have been completed at the time of her adultery.[108]

Dubarle raises the possibility that Matthew's Joseph supposed that Mary had become pregnant *before* her betrothal to him, and that the relevant laws concern the seduction or rape of a virgin not betrothed: Exod 22:15–16; Deut 22:28–29.[109] Joseph, he argues, might have thought that Mary had been previously betrothed (or potentially betrothed) to another by means of a rape or a seduction accompanied by a promise of marriage or a secret betrothal that "respect for parental authority" prevented from being declared.[110] This might have led Joseph to think Mary should be reserved for her first partner, and to wish to step aside by divorcing her so that she could marry the father of her child.[111] But Dubarle recognizes that no law forbade Joseph to complete the marriage, if or when it was impossible to observe the law of Exod 22:15; Deut 22:23–29.[112]

It will be helpful to look carefully at Deut 22:23–27 and to determine what we can of its interpretation in the first century C.E. The text (in RSV translation) reads:

If there is a betrothed virgin [MT: *năʿărā bĕtûlâ mĕʾōrāsâ lĕʾîš;* LXX: *pais parthenos memnēsteumenē andri*], and a man meets her in the city, and lies with her, then you shall bring them both out to the gate of that city, and you shall stone them to death with stones, the young woman because she did not cry for help though she was in the city, and the man because he violated [*ʿinnāh;* LXX: *etapeinōsen*] his neighbor's wife; so you shall purge the evil from the midst of you. But if in the open country a man meets a young woman who is betrothed, and the man seizes her and lies with her, then only the man who lay with her shall die. But to the young woman you shall do nothing; in the young woman there is no offense punishable by death, for this case is like that of a man attacking and murdering his neighbor; because he came upon her in the open country, and though the betrothed young woman cried for help, there was no one to rescue her ['ên môšia' lāh; or, another translation: "there was no saviour for her"[113]).

In the following pages, we will examine aspects of later interpretation and application of this law. This examination is necessarily complicated. First of all, the situation envisaged is itself complicated, humanly and legally, and the law apparently was not applied mechanically. Second, our evidence for its application in the first century c.e. is slight. Mishnaic and Talmudic opinions can only be relied upon as early when they corroborate earlier evidence. Where earlier evidence is lacking, the rabbinic material can only be mentioned with hesitancy as indicating application that may or may not have been in effect earlier. Third, in using legal texts, it is important to recognize that they are not direct reflections of social reality, but of the opinions, attitudes, and ideals of the lawmakers. In the process of this examination, we will learn something of the dangerous threats under which women lived, and, unfortunately, of how little change there has been.

We will take in turn these questions:

1. How was it to be determined legally whether the act was seduction or rape?
2. If it was determined to have been rape, what was the likely fate of the raped woman?
3. If it was determined to have been seduction, what was the fate of the seduced woman?
4. What would have happened if the case was not legally determined?
5. In a case involving pregnancy, what was the fate or status of the child?
6. What light does the legal background throw on the Matthean narrative?

(1.)

Deut 22:23–27 defines seduction as an act committed in the city, rape as an act committed in the open country. We know of early attempts to help further distinguish between the two acts on the basis of that text.[114] (a) In the Qumran Temple Scroll, the expression in Deut 22:25, "in the country," is said to mean "in a place far-away and hidden from the city" (11QTemple 66:4–5). (b) Philo (*Spec. Leg.* 3.77–78) stresses that there has to be "careful inquiry from the judge who must not make everything turn upon the scene of the act. For she may have been forced against her will in the heart of the city, and she may have surrendered voluntarily to unlawful embraces outside the city." What has to be determined is whether she cried out and resisted, or cooperated willingly, and further whether she even *could* cry out and resist, or was bound and gagged, overcome by superior physical strength, and whether the man had accomplices. If she was overpowered and silenced, says Philo, she is (even though in a city) in solitude, "being solitary so far as helpers are concerned." For seduction, there must be "mutual agreement" between the "fellow-criminals" (3.73). (c) Josephus (*Ant.* 4.8.23 ##251–52) characterizes seduction of a betrothed woman (*korē*) as persuasion, obtaining her consent whether for pleasure or for money. Rape occurs, on the other hand, if the man met her alone "somewhere" (*pou*) and forced her "when none was at hand to aid."

(2.)

What happened to the betrothed virgin determined to have been raped? According to Deut 22:26, to such a young woman "you shall do nothing." Philo (*Spec. Leg.* 3.76) insisted that "pity and fellow-feeling attend her."[115] Nothing is said about divorce. However, Tosato draws attention to *Targum Pseudo-Jonathan* Deut 22:26, which adds to the Old Testament passage the stipulation that the raped woman *must* be divorced: "But the husband shall divorce her with a bill of divorce."[116] Cf. *b. Ketub.* 51b: "Samuel's father ruled: The wife of an Israelite who had been outraged [raped] is forbidden to her husband, since it may be apprehended that the act begun under compulsion may have terminated with her consent."[117] This stipulation contrasts with that of Lev 21:7, 13–14 (according to which [only] a priest cannot marry a prostitute or a raped or divorced woman or a widow) and that of Ezek 44:23 (a priest in the new temple can marry only a virgin of Israel, or a widow of a priest). It contrasts also with that of *m. Ketub.* 4:8, which concerns a woman who has been taken captive and therefore is presumed to have been raped. The ordinary Israelite can redeem her and take her back as his wife. But if her husband is a priest, he can only redeem her and bring her back to her own city, to her father's house; she has become unfit to remain a priest's wife.[118]

The value of the *Targum Pseudo-Jonathan* for elucidating legal customs of the first century C.E. is debated. Some scholars accept as an axiom that what is anti-Mishnaic in a targum is pre-Mishnaic. This is contested by others, who argue that there was no objection to the presence of antihalachic teaching in private, non-official targums.[119] Tosato claims that the *Targum Pseudo-Jonathan* here "reflects the ancient pre-mishnaic halakah of more rigorous Palestinian religious circles," circles in which "norms of particular sanctity, applicable originally only to the priestly caste, were extended to all Israelites."[120] He attempts to support this claim concerning the antiquity of the targum's law by reference to three Jewish texts of the pre-Christian era: (a) *Jub.* 33:7–9 (cf. *T. Reuben* 3:11–15; (b) *Jub.* 41:20; (c) 1QapGen 20:15.[121] Only the third of these texts, however, may show that in some circles in the first century C.E. a raped woman was forbidden to her husband, without other conditions complicating the situation.

In these three texts examined for first-century C.E. corroboration of the law in *Targum Pseudo-Jonathan,* we have one rape (of Bilhah, Jacob's slave-wife or concubine, by Jacob's son Reuben), one sexual act between consenting adults, one of whom did not know precisely to what he was consenting (Tamar and Judah), and one possible threat of rape (of Sarah, by Pharaoh). The first two passages concern relations forbidden as incestuous.[122] Only the third focuses on rape as the very action by which the wife may be "precluded for ever from her husband."[123] This example comes from the Qumran community, but it is not necessarily of Qumran origin. We may wonder, however, whether Abram in this story was regarded as representing all future Israelite laymen.

My conclusion from this evidence is that it is possible that some Jewish laymen in the first century C.E. might have regarded themselves *required* to divorce a raped wife, but the evidence is very slim. It is more likely that some laymen regarded themselves *allowed* to divorce her.[124] The criteria for divorce were broad and vague. They range from Deut 24:1 ("when a man takes a wife and marries her, if then she finds no favor in his eyes because he has found some indecency ['*erwat dābār;* literally: nakedness of a thing] in her, and he writes her a bill of divorce and puts it in her hand and sends her out of his house, and she departs out of his house . . ."), to the interpretations by the schools of Shammai and Hillel (see *m. Giṭ.* 9:10: Shammai understands "indecency" as unchastity or sexual crime, Hillel as just about anything, including spoiling a dish for him),[125] to Josephus (who interprets Deut 24:1–4 in this way: "He who desires to be divorced from the wife who is living with him[126] for whatsoever cause—must certify in writing that he will have no further intercourse with her" (*Ant.* 4.8.23 #253; cf. Philo [*Spec. Leg.* 3.5 # 30], "for any cause whatever").[127] A divorce could be a quiet, private matter, since only contested cases came before the courts.[128] It is also possible that some men would simply complete the marriage process and retain the raped betrothed women as their wives or simply maintain a completed marriage.[129]

To summarize, then: after it had been determined by a formal hearing that a virgin betrothed to a layman had been raped, not seduced, one of two things would happen to her: divorce or the completion of the marriage. We cannot be certain that the law in the first century C.E. insisted on the first course of action, that is, that the stricter halakah was in existence and commonly followed. I think it is probable that both options were open to her husband, and his choice depended on his religious, sexual, and human sensitivities.

(3.)

What would have been the fate of the woman judged to have been seduced? As we have seen, she was regarded as an adulterous wife. According to Deut 22:24, she was to be stoned to death with her partner: the woman because she did not cry out when she (supposedly) could have gotten help, and the man because he violated his neighbor's wife. "So you shall purge the evil from the midst of you" (cf. v 22). Three questions must be raised here. (a) Was the death penalty threatened but not carried out in the first century C.E. under a less severe legal system? (b) Under this system, if it existed, was divorce of the adulteress required or only permitted? (c) Or could the adulteress be pardoned and retained as a wife?[130] Related matters—whether or not a legal determination had to be made, and the fate of a *suspected* adulteress—will be treated in the next section. Let us briefly examine some pertinent texts of patriarchal law.[131]

The whole issue is complicated by the difficulty of proving a wife's adultery. When adultery was suspected but could not be proved with witnesses, the legal means for making a judgment were very primitive. Philo recognizes that

> adulteries detected on the spot or established by clear evidence are condemned by law. But when they are a matter of suspicion, the law did not think good to have them tried by men, but brought them before the tribunal of nature. For men can arbitrate on open matters, but God on the hidden also, since He alone can see clearly into the soul.

Philo is referring here to the trial by bitter waters, described in Num 5:11–31: the suspected wife was made to drink filthy water and utter a self-curse; if she sickened,[132] she was regarded as guilty. According to *m. Soṭah* 1:5, this trial could be eliminated and divorce effected privately before two witnesses. This mishnaic passage has been cited as evidence of a less strict judicial procedure,[133] and so it is, since the guilty woman was not executed.[134] But it does not really help us determine the possible fate in the first century C.E. of a betrothed virgin who was seduced. First of all, according to *m. Soṭah* 4:1, the betrothed woman was to be excluded from the trial by bitter waters. When there was a lack of evidence in regard to her seduction (and this must have happened often), there may have been no established procedure for bringing the case "before the tribunal of nature," and we have no text stating that she could simply be divorced. Second, we cannot be sure these mishnaic regulations were in effect in the first century C.E.

From the Old Testament period there are examples of death stated as the legal penalty for an adulteress (Deut 22:22, 23–24; Lev 20:10), and even the story of the pregnant Tamar who (as a betrothed woman) was almost executed. In Proverbs there is also frequent mention of death in a metaphorical, figurative fashion, as the outcome of adultery.[135] But there is no text that narrates or mentions the actual execution of an adulteress for her crime. The inflexible laws taken by themselves are not an adequate indication of how adultery was dealt with. In Ezekiel 16, forgiveness (vv 63, 53–55) comes only after the metaphorical death of the nation (16:38–40; cf. 23:10, 45, 47), but this cannot, of course, be used as evidence that executions were performed.[136]

In fact, a wide variety of other punishments are mentioned for adultery, including the stripping of an adulteress and perhaps the public exposure of her genitals (see Hos 2:3, 10; Jer 13:26; Ezek 16:37, 39; 23:10, 26, 29).[137] In Hosea, divorce and punishment are followed by forgiveness.[138] Jer 3:8 reads, ". . . for all the adulteries of that faithless one, Israel, I had sent her away with a decree of divorce." With regard to the assumption that the Law *demanded* that a husband denounce or divorce an adulterous wife, neither Deut 20:20–21; 22:23–24 or any other Old Testament text provides solid proof that this obligation existed.

In the Deuterocanonical literature, two second-century B.C.E. texts are important for our study: the story of Susanna (Daniel 13 in the Vulgate), and Sir 23:22–26. The legend of Susanna contains the story of a Jewish wife falsely accused of adultery, convicted by the congregation, and sentenced to death. She was spared when Daniel showed that the witnesses had perjured themselves. But this story does not necessarily reflect contemporary Jewish custom. Ben Sira 23:22–26, a text to which we will be returning, appears to have in mind not the penalty of execution for an adulteress, but rather divorce or perhaps a beating. Execution for adultery in the Old Testament and intertestamental period, then, appears to have been extremely rare. Not a single case is reported.[139]

For the New Testament period, it is presently impossible to say for certain whether or not the Jews in Palestine had the authority under Rome to perform capital punishment,[140] and if they did, whether or not they used it to punish adultery. John 18:31 insists that the Jews did not have this power, and there is a later tradition[141] that around the year 30 C.E. the Romans took it away from the Sanhedrin. However, some think that the Jews may have retained it for nonpolitical offenses such as adultery. Philo lists adultery and the rape of a young person among the crimes for which death is the penalty.[142] In *m. Sanh.* 7:4–11:6 the sexual union of a betrothed woman with a man other than her husband is mentioned as threatened by the death penalty. Law such as this in the rabbinic literature seems to have become a theoretical teaching, not meant as a practical penal guide for the courts.[143] One instance of such an execution is reported in the Mishnah: Rabbi Eliezer ben Zadok tells of the burning of a priest's daughter who committed adultery (*m. Sanh.* 7:2; cf. *b. Sanh.* 52b, where he reports that he was a child riding on his father's shoulders when he witnessed this; here he tells also of one other instance that he witnessed as an adult).

The story of the woman caught in adultery in John 8:3–11 may be understood as an attempt to trap Jesus into repudiating either the Mosaic law (under which she was to be killed) or the Roman law (under which she would normally suffer a lesser punishment, and under which the Jews may have had no power of capital punishment).[144] Jesus neither forgives nor sentences,[145] and no execution takes place. This story cannot be used as proof that the death penalty for an adulteress was enforced in the first century C.E., but it does indicate that it was still discussed and threatened.

My conclusion is that there is enough evidence to support the claim that a less severe legal system probably did exist in first-century C.E. Israel and before. Under that system, divorce was most likely, if not strictly obligatory, for the convicted adulteress.[146] There is no evidence that in the New Testament period a man's forgiveness of his adulterous wife was forbidden.[147] But on the basis of the texts examined, it seems to me that forgiveness from a Law-observant man would follow the punishment and divorce, if not the death, of his convicted wife.

(4.)

What would happen if the husband of a betrothed virgin, who had been either seduced or raped, decided not to legally determine which was the case? Although it offends our sense of justice, it was probably true to life in many instances that the wife would be regarded by him as a suspected adulteress or even presumed guilty.[148] There is evidence that the complications of enforcing the law of Deut 22:23–24, concerning the seduction of a betrothed virgin, may have led a husband who wished to be free of his guilty wife to divorce her rather than denounce her. It is possible that in Matthew's time a man who was an observer of the Law might have *wished* to break his union with one whom he suspected of being an adulteress. This would not be because there was a law commanding him to do so, "but because of his repugnance to marry one who has, as it seems to him, grossly broken the Law." In this case, he might have divorced her without public accusation.[149] Tosato insists that while it was not obligatory to resolve the suspicion of adultery,[150] even a suspected adulteress legally had to be divorced. But the mishnaic texts he refers to concern suspicions made public and official, not private suspicions, and some do not apply to the betrothed virgin.[151] There is no evidence that a man was required not to keep his suspicions of adultery to himself, but to air them and divorce his wife.

On the basis of our study so far, we can attempt to reconstruct something of the husband's thought process here. If he were a layman, whether he followed the stricter or the less rigorous halakah, he would probably divorce his wife if seduction (adultery) were proven. If he followed the stricter halakah (forbidding both the seduced and the raped wife to layman as to priest), he would probably divorce her whatever the outcome of the hearing. (However, there is no conclusive evidence for the existence of this halakah in the first century C.E.)[152] So in either case, if he suspected seduction, he might well decide to forego accusing her and obtaining public "satisfaction," and might proceed with divorce on other grounds. This decision might be motivated by the desire to spare his wife (and himself) the public disgrace of a "defamatory process."[153]

What of the man in this situation who suspected rape, not seduction, or was uncertain whether it was rape or seduction? I suggest that he also might have decided on a quiet divorce, perhaps on trivial grounds, to spare the woman and himself the pain and humiliation of a public hearing, and/or to avoid the possibility that rape could not be proven. (Then as now that proof would not be easy to obtain.) But if he followed the less rigorous halakah and was not forbidden to marry a raped woman, and if he knew or believed it was a case of rape, he might decide to simply complete the marriage with the home-taking.

What would become of the wife who was divorced with or without being charged and convicted of adultery? Returned to her father's house, with or without disgrace, presumably she could marry again. But what if the betrothed woman was pregnant?

(5.)

This further complication, pregnancy, needs to be examined, since it is part of the situation of Mary and Joseph as Matthew describes it. What would be the fate or status of the child carried by the pregnant, betrothed woman in the scenarios that we have explored? First, of course, if the woman was executed (an outcome unlikely in the first century C.E.), either her fetus would die with her (cf. Tamar's story), or the execution would be delayed until after she had given birth (a practice followed in the early Roman Empire).

The divorce of a seductress who became pregnant by her lover is depicted in Sir 23:22–26, which contains some terrible words about the fate of her children.

So it is also with a woman who leaves her husband
And produces an heir by a stranger.
For first, she disobeyed the law of the Most High;
Second, she committed an offense against her husband;
And third, she committed adultery through fornication (*en porneia,*)
And produced children by a strange man.
She will be led away unto the assembly,
And punishment will fall on her children.
Her children will not spread out roots,
And her branches will not bear fruit.
She will leave her memory for a curse,
And her disgrace will not be blotted out.[154]

Not lust, but the desire for motherhood on the part of a childless woman is ironically regarded as her motivation.[155] The punishment that falls on her children may be the assembly's decision that they are illegitimate. The husband may have been thought of as publicly rejecting them as his own and as his heirs. They are piously wished premature deaths and sterile unions. Her cursed memory and her disgrace live on in them.

A similar attitude toward the children of adultery and a similar curse on them appears in Wisdom of Solomon 3:16–19; 4:3–6 (ca. 50 B.C.E.).

> But the children of adulterers will not come to maturity,
> and the offspring of an unlawful union will perish.
> Even if they live long they will be held of no account,
> and finally their old age will be without honor.
> If they die young, they will have no hope
> and no consolation in the day of decision.
> For the end of an unrighteous generation is grievous. . . .
> But the prolific brood of the ungodly will be of no use
> and none of their illegitimate seedlings will strike a deep
> root or take a firm hold.
> For even if they put forth boughs for a while,
> standing insecurely they will be shaken by the wind,
> and by the violence of the winds they will be uprooted.
> The branches will be broken off before they come to maturity,
> and their fruit will be useless,
> not ripe enough to eat, and good for nothing.
> For children born of unlawful unions
> are witnesses of evil against their parents when God
> examines them (RSV).

The punishments of these children are social and eschatological, their lives—the author hopes—a living death marked with failure and shame.

These texts show us some of the labels put on such children. But would they also be classified in the first century C.E. as *mamzērîm?* The term *mamzēr* is found in Deut 23:3: "No *mamzēr* will enter the assembly of Yahweh even to the tenth generation . . . " Its meaning is uncertain here: two verses before, there is reference to incest, followed by reference to a person with defective sex organs; the verse after 23:2 is about Ammonites and Moabites being forbidden to enter the assembly of Yahweh even to the tenth generation. The use of the term *mamzēr* in rabbinic literature is inconsistent: it is used to designate the offspring of Judahite mixed marriages, of incest, of forbidden unions, of unions punishable in the Torah by excision or death. Jeremias argues that the oldest rabbinic view is that a *mamzēr* is a child conceived in adultery.[156] He bases his opinion on *m. Yebam.* 4:13 (R. Simeon ben Azzai's claim to have found a family register in Jerusalem),[157] among other texts.[158] The *mamzērîm* were forbidden marriage with priestly families, Levites, legitimate Israelites, and even with illegitimate descendants of priests. At the end of the first century c.e. their rights to inherit from their natural fathers were in dispute. They could not hold public office, and if they took part in a court decision, the decision was invalidated. Their families' share in Israel's final redemption was vigorously argued. The word *mamzēr* was considered one of the worst insults to a man. *Mamzērîm* were among those called the "excrement of the community" (*pĕsûlê qāhāl*).[159]

But whatever the terms used to speak of the child of the seduced, divorced woman, it is clear that both the mother and child would suffer as social misfits. Perhaps the mother would not marry again. In the case of the raped and divorced woman, we would assume the penalties to be similar. At least no priest and no other man following the stricter halakah would be allowed to marry her. If after a hearing of the case, she was retained as wife by a husband following the less rigorous halakah, the child of the rape would somehow be part of this family unit; yet it is reasonable to suppose that the publicity surrounding the hearing of the case would negatively and seriously mark both mother and child. If divorce took place on trivial grounds without mention of seduction or rape, suspicion and rumor might attend her pregnancy. If the more lenient customs concerning betrothal were in effect in Judah at her time, the child might be believed to have been fathered by her exhusband. In any case, it is not difficult to imagine that she too might be regarded with her child as an outcast. But at least, in this scenario, open accusation and official, public stigma would be avoided.

The last possibility considered in the section above was the completion of the marriage between a betrothed, raped woman and a layman following the less rigorous halakah, without a hearing. In this instance especially, the child would benefit by what Tschernowitz calls the "humane provision" of Israel's regulations concerning adoption.

In ancient Israel, as in other nations of antiquity, no great distinction was made between blood relationship (cognation) and artificial kinship (agnation), created by any sort of attachment to a family, e.g., through

adoption and the like. The ruling principle was that one, whether kinsman or stranger, who was accepted under the rule of the head of the
family, was regarded as his son in all respects. . . . The right of inheritance always depended upon the father's identification of his son as
such. The evidence of the father was considered conclusive when he
testified that a given person was his son or first-born, as the case might
be, although the latter had not been known as such by common re-
pute.[160]

What Tschernowitz is mainly considering here is a man's acceptance of his own natural sons, begotten outside marriage. But
he stresses that sometimes even a stranger could become the heir
(for example, Eliezer would have inherited from Abraham had
not Isaac been born [Gen 15:3]). This practice in Israel could
lead to illegal actions on the part of the legitimate children, as
in the story of Jephthah's brothers who drove him out of his
father's house (Judges 11:2).[161] *M. B. Bat.* 8:6 states the principle
succinctly: "If a man said, 'This is my son,' he may be believed."
    Would this principle apply even in the case of a *mamzēr?* On
this point there was disagreement. *M. Yebam.* 2:5 speaks of "any
kind of son," a son from any source, and Danby comments,
"even a bastard."[162] However, it may be that the question of
whether or not a *mamzēr* could inherit, and therefore be regarded as a full son, was undecided in the era of the earliest
Tannaim.[163] Later, in *b. Yebam.* 22a, the *mamzēr* is explicitly included (opinion of Rab Judah). But Ben Sira's characterization
of the child of an adulteress as a (potential) heir (23:22) may
indicate that this opinion was common, if not universal, centuries
earlier.
    Of all the possible fates in store for the child of a woman in
the situation Matthew depicts, adoption into the family and protection of her husband was the kindest and most humane. But
because of the emotional obstacles and prejudices that would
have been involved in such a decision, we can conjecture that it
may have been the rarest and most unexpected.

(6.)

What light does this legal background throw on the Matthean
narrative?[164] We have explored many dimensions of the dilemma
facing a man like Joseph in the situation Matthew depicts. These

are options that the reader, informed in the area of contemporary Jewish law, would expect Joseph, "a just man," to consider carefully—even agonizingly—as he reached his decision. They are also options that Matthew wants his reader to consider. In this passage, Matthew's opening lesson on righteousness and the Torah, Matthew makes Joseph the engaging central character in the story. Attention is focused on him in this and in the subsequent narrative. The reader is given Joseph's genealogy; Joseph is mentioned by name seven times; he receives three messages in dream appearances of an angel of the Lord (and one message without an angelic appearance [2:22]). These messages concern the nature of the child to be born, and its fate and safety, which are dependent on Joseph's obedience. In contrast, Mary is spoken of by Matthew almost always in the passive. She is never addressed, makes no decision, and performs no action on her own.[165] It is difficult for the reader to identify with her character in this Gospel, without an effort to imagine the horror of her situation, an effort Matthew does not really encourage the reader to make.

"Her husband Joseph was an upright man, *and* unwilling to expose her to public disgrace; and so he resolved to divorce her quietly" (v 19). Matthew sees no contrast or tension between Joseph's Torah-observance and what we might term his lack of vindictiveness or his desire to avoid humiliation.[166] He was unwilling to "bring to public notice especially that which seeks concealment."[167] So he chose, among the several options open to him legally, a quiet divorce. This means that Joseph ruled out the hearing to determine whether Mary had been seduced or raped. It need not be argued, although it is one possibility, that this indicates that he suspected that she was an adulteress.[168] In ruling out the hearing, he was shielding her and himself (a) from the public shame and questioning involved in the hearing; (b) from the possibility of an accusation and conviction on the charge of seduction/adultery, with its punishment of either death or (more likely) a degrading divorce, perhaps with attendant indignities and certainly with a bleak future; (c) from the reasonable likelihood that rape could not be proved. The choice Joseph made—of a quiet, probably lenient, divorce[169]—would involve simply the delivery of the writ of divorce before two witnesses, and the return of the *Kĕtūbbâ*. He chose what amounted to a merciful alternative offered by the Law.

But the angelic message in vv 20–21 urged the home-taking. "Joseph, son of David, do not be afraid to take Mary your wife into your home, for the child begotten in her is through the Holy Spirit. She will give birth to a son; and you will call his name Jesus, for he will save his people from their sins." Tosato comments: "The angel, by removing the suspicion of adultery and of violence, makes Mary acceptable to her husband."[170]

Two issues are involved here, which I would like to separate for a moment: the role of the Holy Spirit in the pregnancy, which will be considered shortly, and the question of whether or not, apart from this role, home-taking would remove the suspicion of adultery and of violence. The examination we have done of how the legal situation would have been evaluated in the first century C.E. indicates that home-taking, the completion of the marriage, *would* remove the suspicion of seduction/adultery. A Torah-observant man would probably not complete the marriage with an adulteress. But home-taking *would not* remove the suspicion of rape. A Torah-observant man, following the halakah that allowed him to marry a raped woman, might proceed with the home-taking. "Do not fear to take Mary your wife into your home" can be seen as equivalent to: There is no legal impediment here.[171] Or perhaps: it is not necessary for you to follow the stricter halakah.

The words of the angel could also be read as a cancellation or suspension of any legislation forbidding the home-taking, even a cancellation of legislation forbidding Joseph to take home a seduced/adulterous woman. The angel's command would then be somewhat comparable to that in Hos 1:3: "And Yahweh said to me, 'Go again, love a woman who is beloved of a paramour and is an adulteress'" (contrast Deut 24:1–4). However, the words of Jesus about divorce in Matthew's Gospel may urge against such an interpretation of Matt 1:20–21. In 5:32, Jesus says, "But I say to you that everyone who divorces his wife, except on the ground of *porneia*, makes her an adulteress"; cf. 19:9: "Whoever divorces his wife, except for *porneia*, and marries another, commits adultery." If *porneia* means sinful sexual acts,[172] the command of Jesus (indicating that divorce is allowable on the basis of *porneia*) is consistent with Joseph's decision to divorce, if he is thought to assume Mary may be guilty of such acts. The angelic command could be read to mean she had not committed *porneia*, had not been seduced or committed adultery. The meaning of *porneia*, however, is disputed.[173] Whatever it means, Matthew's Infancy Narrative probably does not contradict what is said later in this Gospel about marriage and divorce. Matthew understands the situation in chapter 1 not to have been an instance of *porneia*.[174]

In any case, Matthew insists that the Torah is valid (5:18) and must be interpreted without relaxation (5:19), but on the basis of the hermeneutical principle of priority to the love command.[175] Matthew intends the angelic solution to the dilemma of Joseph to be a righteous and a legal one. It does not contradict, but properly interprets and applies the Law, removing Joseph's scruple.[176]

A Torah-observant man who completed the home-taking could also adopt the child of his wife into his family. Joseph, accepting the pregnant Mary into his home, accepted responsibility for the child she was carrying. In Matt 1:21, the angelic words, "You will call his name Jesus," are equivalent to a formula of adoption.[177] Joseph, by exercising the father's right to name the child, acknowledged Jesus and thus became his adoptive and legal father.[178] Since Joseph did not contest the existing marital status, the child born within it was regarded as his.

The name of this child, *Iēsous*, a Hellenized rendering of the Hebrew *Yēšûaʿ*, is given a popular etymological interpretation in v 21: "for we will save his people from their sins." That is, the name is connected with the root *yšʿ* (to save) and the noun *yĕšûʿâ* (salvation),[179] so that it means "Yahweh saves."[180] This popular etymology was well known,[181] and there was no need to spell it out for early Christians. It is spelled out here, however, possibly under pressure of the traditional form of angelic birth announcements, a form that will be discussed in the next chapter. It is striking that Matthew is the only evangelist who explains the name, since the idea of "saving" is not prominent in his Gospel; despite the Lucan emphasis on "salvation," Luke does not make use of such a meaning of Jesus' name in his Infancy Narrative.[182]

The explanation of the name in v 21 achieves an allusion (intended or not) to Deut 22:27 ("and though the betrothed young woman cried for help, there was no saviour for her"). In this child, God saves—not only the mother, but the people.[183] I am not arguing on this basis for a Semitic original of the Matthean narrative at v 21, but the allusion I propose to Deut 22:27 is to the Hebrew text, not to the Greek, and Matthew seems to know Hebrew.

Matthew's final remark concerning the marital situation of Mary and Joseph is in v 25. After Joseph took his wife home, "he had no sexual relations with her before she gave birth to a son." (Literally: "he did not know her until she gave birth to a son.") There appears to be in this remark no implication about what happened after the birth of Jesus. Matthew is stressing once again that Joseph could not be this child's biological father.[184]

2. BEGOTTEN THROUGH THE HOLY SPIRIT

As we have seen, Matthew claims in an aside to the reader in 1:18 that Mary was found to be pregnant "through the Holy Spirit." And in v 20 Joseph is told in an angelic revelation that "the child begotten in her is through the Holy Spirit." That Matthew is speaking of the Holy Spirit of God here is fairly certain. The wording in v 20 (*ek pneumatos estin hagiou*) puts emphasis on the adjective "holy," and could be translated, "of a spirit which is holy." This alone might lead one to understand that the revelation to Joseph is that what is conceived in Mary is of a *holy* spirit, not an evil or impure one (contrast Gen 38:24 LXX: Tamar is said to be pregnant *ek porneias* [through fornication or prostitution]; cf. Sir 23:23; Deut 23:2 LXX). But the phrase in v 18 (*ek pneumatos hagiou*) is a fairly normal way of referring to the Holy Spirit.[185] No developed idea of a personal Spirit is present here, or in the rest of Matthew's Gospel.[186] What did Matthew mean by these phrases?

They are usually interpreted solely with respect to their narrow context here in Matthew's first chapter, and with reference to Luke's annunciation scene. Virtually no modern critic thinks that Matt 1:18, 20 refers to anything but a virginal conception. Let us look for a moment at the way in which this is understood. Begetting through the Holy Spirit is thought to replace normal human begetting. Matthew takes pains to stress that divine sonship is not communicated through normal sexual relations between husband and wife, and he rules out any human sexual agent. Jesus is conceived without a human father, in a *nonsexual* virginal conception.[187] For most critics this does not mean that Mary is impregnated by a male deity or element, but that the child is begotten through the *creative* power of the Holy Spirit. Jesus' procreation, an eschatological event, is entirely the work of the Spirit who generates Jesus by a direct act of creation.[188] The Holy Spirit is not said to be the father of Jesus or to take the male role in begetting. There is no hint of intercourse between the human and the divine, and no indication at all of how the conception took place.[189] Jesus is begotten through divine intervention. "The nexus of cause and event which characterize human history are breached by a direct intervention *ab extra*."[190]

If the manner of begetting is implicitly creative rather than sexual, Matthew can be expected to have signaled this. Several scholars think that in Matt 1:18–20 there is a reminiscence of Gen 1:2: "As the Spirit of God hovered over formless matter when the miracle of creation took place, so there is a new creative act of God when Jesus is born."[191] The Spirit's role here is regarded as the nearest the New Testament comes to the idea of the Creator Spirit.[192] It is about a new act of creation, unprecedented as the creation of the universe itself; and the coming of Jesus Christ is discontinuous with Judaism in this sense.[193] The title *biblos geneseōs* in Matt 1:1 is said to show that Matthew is thinking of the book of Genesis, alluding to the creation story (Gen 2:4: "These are the generations [MT: *tôlĕdôt;* LXX *hē biblos geneseōs*] of the heavens and the earth"), and/or to the genealogy of Adam (Gen 5:1: "This is the book of the generations of Adam" [MT: *sēper tôlĕdôt 'ādām;* LXX: *hē biblos geneseōs anthropōn*).[194] The only analogy to the Matthean account of the begetting of Jesus, read as a virginal conception, is said to be the Old Testament and Jewish belief in a purely miraculous creation which God accomplishes.

But do we really find in Matthew 1 such a theology of a new creation and perhaps even a hint of the notion of Jesus as a new Adam? As we have seen, Matthew's phrase in 1:1 may be related not to Genesis, but to the rabbinic formula *sēper yûḥāsîn* (book of family [genealogical] records).[195] A new creation motif, if it is present at all in Matthew's Infancy Narrative, is minor in comparison to the motif of fulfillment of prophecy. There is no development at all in the rest of this Gospel of the creation motif. Jesus as a new Adam and author of a new race *is* found in the Pauline writings, but there the symbolism is linked with the obedience and resurrection of Jesus, not with his birth; there is no justification for using these Pauline ideas to interpret Matthew. Further, the idea of creation or new creation does not explain why the tradition of Jesus' conception took the form it did.[196] The Genesis creation story, then, does not appear to be a background that best elucidates the notion of begetting through the Holy Spirit.

Several elements of Matthew 1 are said to support and necessitate the interpretation of 1:18, 20 in terms of a virginal conception. There are seven of these elements: (1) the lack of mention of a human father of Jesus in 1:16, where the normal pattern of the genealogy has been broken; (2) the passives used in vv 16 and 20, understood as theological passives, meaning "Mary, from whom God begot Jesus," and "the child God begot in her is through the Holy Spirit"; (3) the marital situation described at the time of Mary's pregnancy (she and Joseph have not completed the final stage of their marriage, the home-taking, and have not had sexual relations); (4) the urging by the angel that Joseph complete the marriage, implying that there is no impediment; (5) the stress in v 25 that Joseph did not have sexual relations with Mary between the home-taking and the birth of the child; (6) the language of begetting appearing here in a context where it is capable of a more realistic, rather than figurative, sense; (7) the fulfillment citation of Isa 7:14 in Matt 1:23, which speaks of a virgin (*parthenos*) being pregnant.

Different critics treat different elements as the crucial factor in interpretation. [197] The claim is rarely found that the phrases about the Spirit in 1:18 or 1:20 by themselves indicate the notion of birth without a human father.[198] Rather, the opinion of Lagrange is common: "begotten through the Holy Spirit" "is not at all a current expression for designating a miraculous conception."[199]

In the section following this one, we will discuss element (7) in the above list, Matthew's citation of Isa 7:14, the meaning this text may have had for him, and the reason he may have used it in v 23. The interpretation I will offer removes it as a support for or factor necessitating interpretation of vv 18, 20 in terms of a virginal conception. I have already offered alternative interpretations of elements (1), (2), and (4). Elements (3) and (5) simply underline Matthew's insistence that *Joseph* is not the biological father of Jesus; cf. v 16.

As for (6), if the other aspects of the text do not require us to interpret the phrases about the Holy Spirit to mean that Jesus was conceived miraculously, without a human father, how then shall the phrases be interpreted? We will attempt to see them as part of the wider context of statements about divine begetting in the Jewish pre-Christian tradition and elsewhere in the New Testament. The methodological decision to give weight to this wider context is justified by the argument that the narrower context does not provide us with enough clues to surely determine the meaning of these phrases.

Seen as being about a virginal conception, Matthew's statements about begetting through the Holy Spirit[200] have been regarded as unique, exceptional. It is rapidly becoming a scholarly consensus that the idea of divine begetting as a virginal conception is found in the biblical and intertestamental periods only in the Infancy Narratives of Matthew and Luke. There are no real parallels to this belief in the Hebrew or Greek Bible, in Philo,[201] in the Old Testament apocrypha, or pseudepigrapha,[202] in the Pauline or Johannine writings, or anywhere else in the New Testament.[203] A tradition of the virginal conception of Jesus (in contrast to a tradition of his illegitimacy) was evidently not known to the other New Testament writers. Critics generally agree also that there are no stories of virginal conceptions—in pre-Christian or non-Christian literature (ancient Greek or Roman, Hellenistic, Assyrian, Babylonian, Zoroastrian, Mithraic, Arabic, Egyptian, or Indian) or in the beliefs of some "primitives" today—that are truly identical to the Christian notion of a virginal conception, or that could have given the first Jewish Christians such an idea. The non-Jewish "parallels" involve a type of *hieros gamos* "in which a divine male, in human or other form, impregnates a woman, either through normal sexual intercourse or through some substitute form of penetration."[204] The New Testament Infancy Narratives, then, are regarded as presenting a unique belief in divine begetting.

However, the lack of parallels may indicate that this aspect of the Infancy Narratives of Matthew and Luke has been misunderstood, in terms of the intention of the authors and the comprehension of their earliest readers. Of course, Matthew and Luke *could* have written of something unique, of a virginal conception without parallel.[205] But the combination of (a) the lack of parallels to that belief; and (b) what I judge to be the lack of factors in the immediate context requiring us to find it here leads me to suspect that Matt 1:18, 20 is not—or was not originally—about a virginal conception.

The relevant Jewish and Christian texts on the motif of divine begetting fall into two categories. (a) Some of them use the metaphor of divine begetting to stress that God's power is the ultimate source of human life and generation. God "acts" behind or in human parenting, that "danger-fraught, divinely supervised venture,"[206] *B. Qidd.* 30b states the principle succinctly: There are three partners in every birth: God, father, and mother.[207] In a sense, the initial act of creation is reenacted at the birth of every human being. (b) Other texts use the metaphor to stress that God sometimes communicates a spiritual/psychosocial dimension of life to humans, over and above ordinary human existence. This moves beyond the idea that the human being is physically related to God through creation and coming into existence, to the idea of a moral, spiritual relation in terms of status conferred by election and carrying special obligations.[208] In this sense, Israel is begotten by God,[209] and certain persons are empowered for exceptional destinies (for example, patriarchs,[210] kings,[211] prophets,[212] the messiah[213]). In this sense New Testament authors refer to the Christian begotten by the Spirit or by God.[214] The texts in this second classification have nothing to do with normal human conception/begetting. Note the strong contrast in John 1:12–13 between being begotten through the sexual act in all its stages, and being begotten of God.[215]

When Matt 1:18, 20 is read in the light of relevant Jewish and Christian texts on the motif of divine begetting, another option presents itself for interpreting Matthew's notion of begetting through the Holy Spirit. My suggestion is a simple one: since nothing in the context of Matthew 1 *requires* us to read Matt 1:18, 20 in terms of a virginal conception, these verses should be read against and as a part of the wider Jewish and Christian context. They are an instance of the theme Gese calls the interpenetration of divine and human fatherhood.[216] This means that the Matthean phrases should be read in a figurative or symbolic, not a literal, sense.[217] They are more like than unlike the other statements of divine begetting. In the post–New Testament period, the metaphor of the divine begetting of Jesus was rejected as metaphor.[218] Literalism produced the notion of a biological virginal conception, all but rupturing the connection with its Jewish and early Christian source in the metaphor.

The story of this conception is not "theologically mute."[219] It is about a creative act of God that does not replace human paternity. Sexual and divine begetting are integrated.[220] Jesus is begotten through the Holy Spirit in spite of—or better, because of—his human paternity. In the light of the wider context, Matt 1:18, 20 can be read to mean that the Holy Spirit empowers this birth as all births are divinely empowered, that this child's human existence is willed by God, and that God is the ultimate power of life in this as in all conceptions. My sense is that Matthew means more—but not less—than this. In the situation he describes, this dimension of meaning is extremely significant and should not be underestimated: this child's existence is not an unpremeditated accident, and it is not cursed. The pregnant Mary is not to be punished.

Is Matthew also speaking about the election of this child from the womb for a role in Israel's history? Clearly yes: Jesus will save his people from their sins (1:21), will be called Emmanuel (1:23). Matthew may also think of the Spirit's role in Jesus' conception as an explanation of his extraordinary career and his final transformation and empowerment.[221]

Matthew is thinking as well of the communication of a special kind of life or dimension of life from God to Jesus at his conception, of a special relation with God, when he speaks of Jesus as "begotten through the Holy Spirit." This begetting constitutes him Son of God in a special sense, as the one who sums up in his existence the whole history of Israel from Exodus onwards.

The citation of Hos 11:1 in Matt 2:15 is the first time Jesus is spoken of as God's son. Matthew understands Jesus as "begotten through the Holy Spirit" from the moment of his natural begetting, as one with God from his conception.[222]

An additional note: for Matthew the presence of this tradition of divine begetting, in the context of the legal situation we have explored (of Joseph's dilemma and Mary's entrapment) takes the form of a revelation. This revelation seems to be almost a lesson in God's own interpretation of Torah. Matthew initiates here one of the great themes of his Gospel: Torah is valid when interpreted validly. It bears witness to and is fulfilled in Jesus, and is to be interpreted with reference to him who Matthew will claim has the authority to prioritize and radicalize its commandments, invigorate them with new insight. Here in Matthew's Infancy Narrative, Jesus' conception poses a problem of interpretation of Torah. The problem is "solved" by the angelic revelation that the child is begotten through the Holy Spirit and, with his mother, should be accepted by Joseph. This solution is one within the area of the Torah's own most just and merciful legislation[223] and its contemporary interpretation.[224] The narrative moves beyond legalities when it implies that more profoundly than the unnamed biological father, more profoundly than Joseph the legal father, God parents the illegitimate Messiah.

E. MATTHEW'S USE OF ISA 7:14

Between the angel's words to Joseph and the statement of Joseph's obedience to those words, Matthew inserts the first fulfillment citation of his Gospel: "All this took place to fulfill what the Lord had spoken by the prophet: 'Behold, the virgin (*hē parthenos*) will conceive [*en gastri hexei*] and will give birth to a son, and they will call his name Emmanuel' (which means, 'God with us')" (vv 22–23).[225] The MT of Isa 7:14 reads, "Behold, the young girl [*hā'almâ*] will conceive [or: is pregnant: *hārāh*] and will give birth [*wĕyōledet*] to a son, and she will call his name Emmanuel."[226] The LXX: "Behold, the virgin [*hē parthenos*] will conceive [*en gastri lēpsetai*] and will give birth to a son, and you [singular] will call his name Emmanuel."

The Hebrew text concerns the sign given to King Ahaz of Judah during the Syro-Ephraimite war of 734 B.C.E. Because Judah refused to join the Syro-Ephraimite coalition against Syria, the two northern kingdoms threatened to remove Ahaz from the throne and replace him with "the son of Tabeel" (7:6). Isaiah was sent to reassure Ahaz that their plan would come to nothing. Although Ahaz would not do as he was told and ask for a sign from Yahweh, Isaiah gave him one in anger, a sign confirming the prophetic word of doom on the coalition, and expressing hope for the future. Word of the conception and birth of the child called Emmanuel, however, was followed by the threat of disaster and hardship for Judah.[227] Incapable of trust, Ahaz sent an enormous gift and a request for help to Tiglath Pileser III (2 Kings 16:7–8), surrendered his independence, and initiated calamity.

Various identifications have been suggested of the young woman[228] and her child. If she is Zion personified, Emmanuel may be understood collectively as the remnant. If she is the wife or concubine of Ahaz, the child would probably be his, perhaps Hezekiah, as later Jewish interpreters held (see Justin, *Dialogue* 67.1). If she is Isaiah's wife, the child would be another of his children with symbolic names (cf. 7:3; 8:3). If she is the totality of all the women pregnant at that time in the nation, the child represents the many to be born. Perhaps the child Emmanuel is to be identified with the child described in 9:6–7 and 11:1–9, an ideal king contrasted with Ahaz. It is unlikely the reference is to a goddess and/or a divine child.[229]

The presence of the definite article (*the* young woman) seems to indicate that a specific person known to both Isaiah and Ahaz is spoken of. In any case, it is important to note that the sign offered by Isaiah was the birth, probably imminent, of a child *naturally* conceived. He would illustrate God's presence and care for Judah; and he would participate in the coming hardships. This passage, as far as we know, was not understood messianically in Judaism.[230]

How did the Greek translator understand the passage? The LXX translates 'almâ by *parthenos*, instead of by the more common rendering *neanis*, which is used in later Greek translations. Neither *parthenos* nor *bětûlâ*, which it usually translates, are clinically exact terms necessarily meaning biological virgin. (In Gen 34:3 LXX, Dinah is twice called *parthenos* [translating *na'arā*] after Shechem has raped her.) However, some hold that the use of *parthenos* here may represent a deliberate preference for understanding the young woman of Isa 7:14 as a virgin.[231] But even if it does, no miraculous conception through the creative activity of God is supposed by the translator. He seems to have simply meant that one who is *now* a virgin will conceive by natural means. "Nothing in the context suggests that 'the virgin' remained a virgin."[232] The LXX here is not evidence that Alexandrian Judaism, influenced by Egyptian paganism, believed in the possibility of nonsexual divine begetting of a human being. Nor is there any evidence that the LXX translation gave rise to such a notion.[233]

It is now generally agreed that the story in Matt 1:18–25 was not created on the basis of Isa 7:14 LXX, but that Matthew himself added the citation to a preexisting narrative or body of infancy traditions, choosing the textual tradition best suited to his purposes and adapting it further.[234] The translation already contained the word *parthenos;*[235] and from Isa 8:10 Matthew drew the interpretation of the name Emmanuel, mentioned again in 8:8. Matthew appears to have been the first early Christian and the only New Testament writer to apply Isa 7:14 to Mary and Jesus.[236]

Of all the texts available to him, why did Matthew choose this one, as the first of his fulfillment citations, to support and elucidate his story of the origins of Jesus? The most common answer given has been that Matthew saw in this text about the pregnancy of a *parthenos* and about the child who would signal God's presence with Judah a text that could express his belief that over seven hundred years earlier Isaiah foretold the miraculous virginal conception of Jesus, in whom God was present in a new, final, and unique way. The linguistic and conceptual affinities between the citation and the narrative are said to have provided a catchword relationship that led to the association of v 21 with Isa 7:14.[237] Ignorant of or ignoring the meaning intended by the author of the Hebrew original and the Greek translator (and, as far as we can determine, the authors of later Jewish interpretive tradition), Matthew is said to have read the text to confirm his presuppositions about Scripture and his belief in a virginal conception, certain that it would have both didactic and apologetic dimensions in his own time. Understanding *parthenos* in its restricted (biological) sense,[238] he saw in the text scriptural support for both the Davidic[239] and divine aspects of Jesus' identity.[240] It is agreed, however, that Matthew's interest, like Isaiah's, is not centered on the manner of the child's conception, but on the meaning of his existence and on the name Emmanuel.[241] The Old Testament text, then, teaches the Christian community that Jesus' origin—begotten of a virgin through the creative action of the Holy Spirit, rather than through the sexual action of a man—was part of God's foreordained plan. If Matthew intends the child of Isa 7:14 to be understood as the child mentioned in Isa 9:6–7 and 11:1–9, he achieves an implicit allusion to the Spirit here (see Isa 11:2: "the Spirit of God will rest upon him").[242] Further, the citation of Isa 7:14 is thought to secondarily provide a refutation of the calumny that may have circulated among the adversaries of the Christian community: "If there were those in Matthew's ken who were calumniating that genesis [of Jesus] as illegitimacy, let them know that they were blaspheming against what the Lord Himself had spoken."[243]

But what evidence do we have that Matthew did not understand Isa 7:14 as the Greek translator did—understand it, that is, to refer to one who *was* a virgin, but who would conceive naturally? I have argued above that each of the aspects of Matthew 1 that supposedly supports or requires here the notion of a virginal conception is open to another interpretation. Let me now propose another way of looking at Matthew's choice of Isa 7:14.

It *is* likely true that the word *parthenos* in the LXX played a role in Matthew's choice of the citation. But Matthew was not thinking of a virgin conceiving miraculously. He was thinking rather of the law in Deut 22:23–27 concerning the rape or seduction of a betrothed virgin (*parthenos*), the law he presupposes in his presentation of the dilemma of Joseph. Although Matthew does not quote the law, and does not explicitly call Mary a virgin, this, I think, is the catchword association that triggered his use of Isa 7:14. This would mean that he *did* understand the text as the Greek translator did. The Isaian passage speaks mysteriously of the pregnancy of the virgin, but makes no mention of the man who would impregnate her. Delling remarks, "the promised son stands directly under God's protection; hence the father is not named."[244] The sign given by the prophet is given in an attempt to convince Ahaz to trust and to give up his own plans;[245] in a similar way, the placement of the fulfillment citation in Matt 1:23, immediately after the angel's address to Joseph, underscores the way the divine assurance leads Joseph to trust and overturns his decision to divorce Mary. It underscores as well the divine command that Joseph make the child his own by naming him. The text may serve, as has been claimed, to link Jesus like Emmanuel in some unspecified way to the Davidic line. The child himself, as in the Isaian text, is the first beneficiary of divine assistance and its gauge for all the people.[246]

My proposal, then, is this: that the problem before Matthew was to make theological sense of the tradition concerning an illegitimate pregnancy. If we pause and ask what texts and traditions were available to be used for this purpose, to illuminate the event and show that it was predicted, we find that none would have been a clear and unambiguous choice. No text in the Hebrew Bible that I can think of perfectly fits the situation. No text vindicates a wronged woman who has been seduced or raped, or legitimates the child born of such a union—much less prepares for the startling thought that this might be the origin of the expected Messiah.[247] The stories of rape—for example, of Dinah, of David's daughter Tamar, of the Levite's concubine—are stories of male revenge and bloodshed, and sometimes of further atrocities committed against women. They are not stories that really right the wrong. The stories Matthew alluded to in his genealogy (of Tamar, Rahab, Bathsheba, and Ruth) are the ones Niditch treats in her article, "The Wronged Woman Righted." Matthew saw them as preparation for the story of Mary (a story Matthew told, however, as the story of Joseph). But even they do not present a situation fully comparable to the one in Matthew 1. There were, in fact, no texts and traditions ready at hand for such a theological task as Matthew's. I submit that he had to create out of fragments, easily misunderstood. And one of these fragments was Isa 7:14 LXX.

The virgin betrothed and seduced or raped is, in the great Matthean paradox, the virgin who conceives and bears the child they will call Emmanuel. His origin is ignominious and tragic. But Matthew's point is that his existence is divinely willed and even predicted. That although—or even *because*[248]—he was born in that way, the claim of his messiahship was not thereby negated. It was, rather, in some strange way strengthened.

J. A. Sanders remarks that "early Christians searched scripture to understand why Christ suffered the fate of a common criminal, a *lēstēs*, why he was so ignominously treated, why he was crucified. They found help in the prophets, especially in Isaiah, to understand how God could turn tragedy into triumph."[249] What I am proposing is that they searched, with a great deal less success,[250] not to explain *why* he was ignominiously born (because no answer could be found for that in the tradition), but to show that *although* or, better, *because* he was born that way, he was the Messiah. Matthew found in the stories of the women in his genealogy some preparation for this belief. And he found, I think, in Isa 7:14 LXX a text to elucidate Deut 22:23–27. He inserted his fulfillment citation into a narrative possibly patterned in some ways on the infancy of Moses, presented it within the structure of stereotypical announcements of the births of patriarchs and heroes,[251] and joined it to the genealogy traced from Abraham.[252] In this way Matthew tried to ensure that the tradition of Jesus' illegitimacy would be read as the story of one who relived and lived within Israel's covenant history with God.

The wording in which the conception story survives is, as Vermes says, "when scrutinized closely, curious and equivocal."[253] That is due, I think, not to the desire to be enigmatic, nor to the theological stress and strain of presenting a novel notion of divine begetting without human paternity, while trying to avoid all suggestion of a *hieros gamos*. It is due rather to something I judge harder: the effort to be honest, delicate, and profound, in dealing with material that resisted—and still resists—in great part the theologians' arts and tools: the siding of God with the endangered woman and child.

CONCLUSION AND RESPONSE

Before we turn to the Infancy Narrative of Luke, several points regarding Matthew's should be reemphasized and commented on.

This new reading of several individual elements of the narrative results in a new understanding of Matthew 1 as a whole.[254] Matthew is handing down the tradition of the illegitimate conception of Jesus, of his divine begetting, and of Joseph's acceptance of the messianic child and his mother. Matthew's belief is that this child is truly God's transcendent Son, and that in him, God is with us (1:23). This God, I have argued, is shown by the story to be one who sides with the outcast, endangered woman and child. God "acts" in a radically new way, outside the patriarchal norm but within the natural event of a human conception.[255] God "acts" here not as a *deus ex machina* interrupting or bringing to an end the history of human betrayal and violence and subjugation, but as one who reaches into that history to name the messiah. The "siding with" is not divine intervention in any miraculous sense, though it is announced through angelic dream-revelation.

Matthew's presentation of this message, however, is androcentric. His story is primarily about and for males. Joseph, "a just man," is his central character in chapter 1. Assuming awareness of the legal options open to Joseph and their human consequences, Matthew encourages the reader to identify with Joseph's dilemma, with his confusion and perhaps his suspicions, and then with his decision to divorce quietly. The fact that the story is not told from Joseph's point of view prevents *total* identification; the reader, with information Joseph does not have but needs (1:18), watches his struggle from a superior vantage point. When Joseph's decision is overturned by the angelic revelation to him that the child so conceived is begotten through the Holy Spirit, Joseph's obedience in the act of completing the home-taking establishes him as a model of even greater righteousness.[256] He becomes the protector of the mother and child, incorporating them into the Davidic line and into "the male sphere, the ordinary scheme of things."[257]

What is reflected here, without comment, is the patriarchal social situation in which the power of such decision, with life-and-death consequences, resides in men, and men make themselves the authoritative interpreters of Scripture and its laws, as they have been its authoritative creators and transmitters.[258] The story so understood deals with a specific situation about which some of Matthew's male readers or hearers were themselves likely to have to make a decision; thus it could serve to illuminate their own decision making.[259] Matthew's community, probably a mixed community with a Jewish base and an increasing number of Gentiles, was deeply concerned over questions of the validity and interpretation of the Law. At some point in its history after the war of 70 C.E. this community may have been in intense dialogue and polemical argument with Jewish authorities at Jamnia.[260] If the question of Jesus' illegitimacy was part of these and other discussions (and I think this is quite likely),[261] Matthew has offered his understanding of its deep significance.[262]

Also reflective of patriarchal society and its values is the treatment, or rather lack of treatment, of the biological father. No reference is made to the rights, responsibility, and/or guilt of the seducer or rapist, who is unnamed. Whatever is evil in the situation goes unmentioned, unconfronted, unpunished, unforgiven, untransformed. Might this make God in some way responsible for evil, responsible in a way that makes the notion of God's siding with the oppressed an empty notion? Nothing is done about the causes or structures of oppression. Matthew's sense of propriety, and his awareness that the story of Jesus' conception could weaken his credibility for many, led him to create a presentation in which what Matthew seems to have regarded as the facts are obliquely reported and underplayed and even to a certain extent withheld from the reader. The "unnameable" is avoided. It is a presentation in which the author's intent in this matter is easily misunderstood, the task of the reader and the historian made difficult. There is so much "delicacy" here, so little blunt honesty, that it is necessary to search for rhetorical clues and allusions that indicate the reality about which the text is silent. It is necessary to imaginatively "read the silence" as indication of that about which Matthew does not speak directly. This silence and lack of naming weakens and obscures Matthew's theological message.

So too does Matthew's treatment of Mary. His interest in her as a person appears to be minimal. The reader is told nothing of her feelings, her fears, her attitude toward her pregnancy, her faith or lack of faith, and is not encouraged to identify or sympathize with her. Sidelined, she is not the agent of her own liberation from the situation that threatens her and her child; instead, they both are completely dependent on the protection of Joseph. There is no mention of communication between her and God or God's messenger. By linking her story, however, with those of the four women listed in the genealogy, Matthew implies that through Mary Jesus is linked to Israel's history, as through Joseph he is part of David's line. Salvation history cannot be viewed essentially as a male enterprise. Matthew does not exalt Mary as mother of the Messiah, and in fact he pays little attention to her in the rest of his Gospel. He communicates no empathy or admiration for her, but he does tone down Mark's negative picture of her relationship with Jesus.[263] Though Matthew's Mary is far from being a role model for women, it is significant that unlike other biblical women who were seduced or raped, she is not left devastated or desolate; she survives. Fuchs has identified in the Hebrew Bible's annunciation scenes a shift of focus from the father figure to a growing recognition of the mother, and with this, a growing emphasis on the social and legal institution of motherhood, that powerful patriarchal mechanism.[264] In its focus on Joseph, Matthew's narrative stands against this trajectory. Fuchs argues further that the message of the Old Testament scenes, delivered by male divine messengers, is driven home: "that woman has no control at all over her reproductive potential. Yahweh, who is often andromorphized in the biblical narrative, has control." This dramatizes the idea that women's reproductive potential should be and can be controlled only by men. In spite of its androcentrism, the Matthean narrative, in my opinion, does not deliver this message; the Holy Spirit, through whom Mary's child is begotten, is not a male figure.

Schüssler Fiorenza correctly holds that feminist theology cannot state without qualification that the God of the Bible is the God of women.[265] Is the God of Matthew's Infancy Narrative the God of women? Not without qualification. But the thesis that the siding of God with the endangered woman and child is an important aspect of Matthew's theological message here is supported by analysis of his redactional choices: in particular, his addition of the names of the four women to the genealogy, and of the fulfillment citation to the narrative, as well as by his decision to hand down, however subtly, the tradition of Jesus' illegitimate origin as a divine begetting. A clearer picture of these choices will be possible after we attempt in chapter 4 to reconstruct the tradition behind both Matthew and Luke.

Some confirmation of the thesis that this is Matthew's theology may come eventually from an examination of the rest of this Gospel in the light of the foregoing interpretation of his Infancy Narrative. This is not the place to undertake such an examination (nor can the study of Luke's Infancy Narrative be followed here by any extended analysis). In both Matthew and Luke, the Infancy Narratives "function as a sort of overture to the Gospels proper, striking the chords that will be heard again and again in the coming narratives."[266] But the muted chord of Jesus' illegitimacy and of his divine begetting is not heard again.[267] Let me suggest that it is played in at least two other keys: first, in the interest Matthew shows in the marginality of women, and in their strength. Female gender is paradoxically here a strength and a weakness; it seems to prevent women's identification as disciples and their membership in that inner circle, but it heightens their accomplishments. The important roles of women ("roles the disciples should have played") and Jesus' response to women supplicants strain the boundaries of the Gospel's patriarchal world view, but they still are contained within those boundaries.[268] This indicates, I think, that Matthew explored but not fully the transforming implications of the tradition of Jesus' origin.

Second, Matthew's understanding of God as Father is significant. The God believed to side with the outcast and marginal cannot be a projection or endorsement of patriarchal ideology. Matthew's Jesus commands, "Call no man father on earth, for you have one father who is in heaven" (23:9). In this community and in society in general no one has the right to claim this name or to exercise the power of the "father"[269]—a power that does not empower all. The Jesus movement, as Matthew understood and described it, tried to found a new family, a family of God.

If my reading of Matthew's Infancy Narrative is regarded as a possible reading, other ears may recognize its echoes in the rest of this Gospel.

3. Luke's Account

A. INTRODUCTION

1. DIFFERENCES AND SIMILARITIES BETWEEN THE MATTHEAN AND LUCAN ACCOUNTS

When we turn to Luke 1 to read of the conception of Jesus, we immediately encounter some striking differences from Matthew's account: in design, focus, tone, point of view,[1] and christology/theology. Some of the most obvious differences pertain to our investigation. Luke begins his Gospel not with a genealogy of Jesus (although he does indeed have a genealogy, placed later, after the baptism of Jesus), but with a formal prologue (1:1–4), stating his intention as an Evangelist, that his reader may be assured about the instruction received. His narrative begins with an angelic annunciation to the aged priest Zechariah telling him that his barren wife Elizabeth will bear him a son of greatness. Then, coordinated with this announcement in careful fashion, there is an angelic annunciation to Mary (not to Joseph) that she will conceive a son of superior greatness. This second annunciation is followed by a scene in which Mary visits Elizabeth, and then by parallel accounts of the birth, circumcision, naming, and maturing of John the Baptist and of Jesus. Matthew has no such parallelism in his narrative.

Allusions to the Jewish Scriptures are woven continuously into Luke's account, especially into the canticles spoken by Mary (1:46–55), Zechariah (1:68–79), and Simeon (2:29–32); these allusions contrast with the explicit fulfillment citations that Matthew has woven into his narrative. Whereas Matthew tells the story of Joseph's dilemma resolved by the angelic appearance to him in a dream, Luke focuses on Mary, to whom Gabriel comes and with whom she enters into waking dialogue. In Matthew's first scene, Mary is spoken of but does not appear, and the reader learns nothing of her attitude; in Luke's annunciation, she is the central character, a hearer and doer of God's word.

The role of the Holy Spirit in her pregnancy is articulated quite differently in Luke, as is the prediction of the nature and mission of her child. Mary and Joseph are natives of Nazareth in Galilee in Luke (1:26; 2:4, 39), but apparently of Bethlehem in Judea in Matthew (2:1, 11). Dark danger attends the story of Jesus' conception in Matthew, but celebration appears to be the dominant motif in Luke.

The details and events that attend and follow the conception and birth of Jesus in the rest of Luke's Infancy Narrative do not appear in Matthew's Gospel: these include Mary's trip to Judah to her kinswoman Elizabeth; the greeting by Elizabeth, and Mary's Magnificat; the journey of Mary and Joseph to Bethlehem to enroll in a census; mention of swaddling clothes, a manger, no room in the inn; an angelic annunciation to shepherds and their visit to the child; the circumcision and presentation of Jesus, and the purification in Jerusalem; recognition of the greatness of the child by Simeon and Anna in the Temple; the loss and finding of the twelve-year-old Jesus. And the following Matthean stories do not appear in Luke: the visit of the magi; the flight of Mary and Joseph and the child into Egypt; Herod's slaughter of children in Bethlehem; the return of Mary, Joseph, and the child to Israel; the shift of residence to Nazareth. The standard commentaries discuss the impossibility of harmonizing these accounts of the two Infancy Narratives. (In the narratives of the annunciation of the conception of Jesus, however, there are no inherent contradictions.)

A careful reading shows that Luke agrees with Matthew on many points. They both report that the parents of Jesus were Mary and Joseph, and that the pregnancy occurred when Mary was betrothed to Joseph (Matt 1:16, 18; Luke 1:27), who was of Davidic descent (Matt 1:16, 20; Luke 1:27). They agree also that Joseph was not the biological father of Jesus (Matt 1:18–19, 25; Luke 3:23). In both gospels, an angel announces the role of the Holy Spirit in this pregnancy (Matt 1:18, 20; Luke 1:35), gives the child the name Jesus (Matt 1:21; Luke 1:31), and predicts his role in the history of Israel (Matt 1:21; Luke 1:32–33). Matthew and Luke both consider Mary a virgin (Matt 1:23, by implication; Luke 1:27). They insist that the birth of Jesus took place after his parents had come to live together (Matt 1:24–25;

Luke 2:5–6), and in Bethlehem during the reign of Herod the Great (Matt 2:1; Luke 2:4–6; 1:5). Both evangelists speak of Jesus as accepted from the very beginning by the just and pious of Israel, the Torah-observant (Matt 1:19, of Joseph; Luke 1:41–45; 2:25–32, 36–38 of Elizabeth, Simeon, Anna; 2:29 of Mary and Joseph). They stress continuity between the event of Jesus' conception/birth and Israel's past, and continuity between the child's origin and his future. In addition, the themes of universality (Matt 2:1ff; Luke 1:32; 2:31–32) and of messianic epiphany appear in both Infancy Narratives.[2]

It is commonly claimed that both Matthew and Luke agree also that Jesus was virginally conceived. But some critics recognize a difference here as well. Taylor thinks that Matthew's narrative only presupposes or implies the existence of a virginal conception tradition as already known to the readers of his Gospel, and that the earlier explicit tradition was possibly similar to what appears in Luke's narrative.[3] Matt 1:18–25, Taylor insists, is misunderstood if explained as a virginal conception tradition; but not Luke 1:31–35. In this way, Matthew's first chapter has been read in the light of Luke's, whose presentation of this belief is thought to be clearer.[4] But in contemporary scholarship, as we will see below, the tendency is rather to find the virginal conception clearly asserted in Matthew and perhaps less clearly in Luke.[5]

My argument, however, is that the presentation of a virginal conception is intended by neither evangelist. Luke, like Matthew, hands down and theologizes the tradition of the illegitimate conception of Jesus, alluding to the law in Deut 22:23–27 to refer to the circumstances of that conception. But Luke's treatment of the tradition is startlingly different from Matthew's. We will return to the question of similarities and differences in the next chapter.

2. A LITERARY LINK?

On the basis of the similarities and differences between the two Infancy Narratives, scholars have proposed various theories about the literary connection or lack of connection between them. A few hold that Matthew is dependent in some way on Luke. According to R. Gundry, for example, Matthew is dependent in part on "an expanded version of Q" (a hypothetical document or body of traditions, material not found in Mark but available and common to Matthew and Luke),[6] which included among other things the Lucan Infancy Narrative. This would mean that the Matthean story is the result of Matthew's transformation of the annunciation to Mary before her pregnancy into an annunciation to Joseph after the pregnancy. Gundry assumes also that Luke may have used the final edition of Matthew as an overlay on his primary sources.[7] A number of others hold that the primary direction of the influence is from Matthew to Luke. Goulder and Sanderson, for example, argue that Luke is expanding Matthew, and J. Drury that Luke 1–2 is a midrashic composition by Luke, on the basis of Matthew 1–2 and the LXX.[8] The theory of the latter includes the following claims: that Luke has with greater sophistication integrated Matthew's fulfillment citations (especially Isa 7:14) into a narrative; created the dialogue between the angel (now named) and Mary; developed in different ways the Matthean motifs of journey and visitors to the child; omitted for literary, theological, and political reasons Matthean material such as the characters of the Magi and the massacre of children by Herod; and reversed Matthew's priorities by pushing Joseph into the background and Mary into the foreground.

These and other theories that assume some direct or nearly direct literary relationship between Matthew and Luke are tantalizing with respect to the study of the two Infancy Narratives.[9] Brodie asks if there are categories of adaptation used in the widespread Greco-Roman practice of literary imitation that would cast light on Luke's possible use of Matthew. Among these modes of adaptation, he discusses "positivization" (turning something negative into something positive) and "internalization" (replacing emphasis on something external by emphasis on the internal.)[10] My reading of Luke's treatment of the conception of Jesus attracts me to the possibility that Luke adapted Matthew's narrative in part along these lines. But it is a possibility that can only be mentioned here and not pursued without distraction from the task at hand, the presentation of this reading. In my opinion, the attempts to prove dependence are so far incomplete and unconvincing.

The majority of scholars accept the two-source theory, or a modified form of this theory, a corollary of which is the independence of Matthew and Luke: Matthew did not know Luke's Gospel, and Luke did not know Matthew's. Their Infancy Narratives are drawn in part from special material, oral or written, peculiar to each of them and heavily redacted.[11] But the similarities and agreements between them indicate that there existed a common, pre-gospel infancy tradition. Although the two-document theory is increasingly under fire,[12] it is still the most plausible and most useful.

The argument that Luke presupposes, hands down, and "refines" the tradition of Jesus' illegitimacy depends on the coherency of explanations of many small and seemingly strange details in his narrative. Luke writes, but with far less directness even than Matthew, of an illegitimate conception of Jesus by Mary. Luke permits rather than requires this proposed reading. But a primary objection must be raised: is it really possible for such an interpretation of Luke 1 to occur to a reader, without a basis in an acceptance of the foregoing analysis of Matthew 1, a text that has preserved the original tradition of illegitimate conception more clearly? I think it is possible, but unlikely. Luke presupposes knowledge of the illegitimacy tradition, and with that knowledge puzzling elements of the narrative fall into place. The contention here, however, is not that Luke 1 should be read in the light of Matthew 1, nor that Matthean insight be imported into the Lucan outlook, nor that the two accounts be harmonized. It is significant to note that in an article several years ago J. A. Fitzmyer expressed the opinion that the present Lucan account *can* be read as *not* about a virginal conception. "When this account is read in and for itself—without the overtones of the Matthean annunciation to Joseph—every detail of it could be understood of a child to be born to Mary in the usual human way."[13]

For Fitzmyer, however, this means conception with Joseph as the biological father of Jesus, an idea not expressly denied in Luke 2. "Every detail" of the narrative includes: (1) Mary's question in 1:34, understood by Fitzmyer primarily as a literary device (the question gives the angel an opening to speak about the character of the child to be born); (2) the statement of Gabriel in 1:35 about the Holy Spirit coming upon and overshadowing Mary, a figurative way of speaking about the child's special relation to God, without implying the absence of human paternity (cf. Gal 4:29); (3) mention in 2:5 of Mary as Joseph's pregnant betrothed, with no hint given about the cause of her pregnancy.

One detail (4) gives Fitzmyer the most trouble. In his genealogy, Luke writes of Jesus "being the son, (as was supposed [or: in the minds of the people; *hōs enomizeto*]) of Joseph" (3:23). In this 1973 article, Fitzmyer discussed the possibility that Luke inserted the phrase *hōs enomizeto* to correct the genealogy in the light of the annunciation scene. This raised the further possibility that Luke *did* want 1:26–38 to be understood in terms of a virginal conception, "a possibility that cannot be excluded." In the long run, however, Fitzmyer held that the Lucan Gospel did not clearly assert the virginal conception.[14]

Some major aspects of Fitzmyer's analysis are accepted here. But my contention is that the phrase in 3:23 simply rules out *Joseph's* biological paternity. The reader who understands Luke 1 to be about a normal conception is thus faced with another alternative: the biological fatherhood of some unnamed person.

Let me hasten to add that arguments against this position of Fitzmyer's, arguments by R. E. Brown and by the scholars who produced the study *Mary in the New Testament*,[15] caused Fitzmyer to change his mind and agree with them that the Lucan text does indeed present the virginal conception of Jesus.[16] He thinks now, however, that "the phrasing of individual verses in the [Lucan] account of Jesus' conception remains ambiguous."[17]

In the following pages we will examine aspects of this discussion, in particular the main question on which this debate turns, the question of whether or not the parallelism between the Lucan stories of John the Baptist and Jesus, which is a step-parallelism,[18] indicates that Luke is thinking of a conception of Jesus "greater than" the conception of John the Baptist, hence, a virginal conception. This is the position of Fitzmyer's critics, the position that he eventually accepted. The aim of this chapter is to support my reading of Luke by analysis of aspects of the marital and legal situation depicted by Luke (section B), the parallelism (section C) and the dialogue between Mary and Gabriel in 1:35, 38 (sections D and E). The aim is also to elucidate and criticize the distinctive theological perspective Luke brings to the tradition of Jesus' illegitimacy. It is a perspective that (like Matthew's) is both brilliant and flawed.

B. THE MARITAL AND LEGAL SITUATION LUKE DEPICTS

Luke writes that in the sixth month of the pregnancy of Elizabeth, Mary, "a virgin betrothed to a man (*parthenon emnēsteumenēn andri*) whose name was Joseph" (1:27), received the angel Gabriel's annunciation: "You will conceive in your womb and bear a son, and you shall call his name Jesus" (v 31). Mary's response underlines her present condition as a virgin, and perhaps also Luke's insistence that she has not had sexual relations with her betrothed husband. She asks (v 34), "How will this be, since I do not have sexual relations with[19] a husband?" (*pōs estai touto, epei andra ou ginōskō*).

1. MARY'S QUESTION (1:34)

a. The Translation

I want to discuss my translation of two words in Mary's question. First, the translation, "How *will* this be?" The verb *estai* can be translated either as "will" or "can." It is true that the usual translation, "How *can* this be?" gives the question a thematic link with Zechariah's question in 1:18 ("How shall I know this? For I am an old man, and my wife is advanced in years"), in that both questions seem to be inquiring about the possibility of conception, under conditions thought humanly impossible. This usual translation also links Mary's question with the final statement of Gabriel to her in 1:37: "With God nothing will be impossible" (*ouk adynatēsei para tou theou pan rēma*). I suspect, however, that this translation is misleading. If possibility or impossibility were clearly the issue, we would expect a verb such as that found in John 3:9: "How can this be?" (*pōs dynatai tauta genesthai*); cf. 3:4. I prefer the translation "How will this be?" since it does not prejudice the reader to think immediately of an event that is considered physically impossible. Gabriel's final statement, I think, refers to God's power to overcome humiliation.

Second, the noun *anēr* can mean either "a man" or "a husband," depending on context. Luke uses it two other times in his Infancy Narrative: Joseph is the man (or husband) to whom Mary is betrothed (1:27; cf. Matt 1:16, 19 where Joseph is spoken of as the husband of Mary),[20] and Anna's husband is mentioned in 2:36. If we translate Mary's remark in 1:34 as "I do not have sexual relations with a husband," this emphasizes not only her virginity but also her interim marital status. She and Joseph are betrothed but the home-taking has not taken place; they have not had and are not presently having sexual relations in this interim (compare Matthew's insistence in 1:25, again with the verb *ginōskō*, that Joseph did not have sexual relations with Mary before the birth of Jesus). This translation would imply too that Joseph will not be the father of the child, and it would awkwardly anticipate Luke 3:23. It would also give us another agreement between the Matthean and Lucan stories of the conception of Jesus: two statements that Mary and Joseph did not "know" each other. Further, the reader might be alerted to the possibility that the conception will be by someone other than Mary's husband.[21]

Against the translation and explanation offered above, it can be noted that "not knowing a man" is a simple statement of virginity in Gen 19:8; 24:16; Judges 11:39; cf. Num 31:17, 35; Judges 21:12. If understood as such a simple statement, the words of Mary would merely echo the description of her in 1:27, a virgin, and be a denial of her experience of sexual intercourse.[22] It is significant that in Luke 1:34, the verb is strangely in the present tense, whereas it is never in the present tense in the Old Testament—in the MT, LXX, or Peshitta—in this particular expression.[23] It does not describe a state resulting from a past pattern of behavior (in which case we would expect the Greek perfect tense, as in the above Old Testament examples). The tense has been regarded as making Mary's objection vague, or stressing the permanence of her virginity,[24] or emphasizing her present condition ("I remain a virgin"), leaving undecided whether this is to be understood as meaning she does not wish, is not able, or is not to know a man. My proposal is that the present tense draws attention to Mary's current marital situation.[25]

b. The Logic of the Question

How are we to understand the logic of Mary's question? It must be insisted that it is useless to ask what was in the mind of the historical Mary when she learned of her pregnancy, since the text is no transcription of the event. But we can inquire about the logic of Luke's narrative. He is telling a story he wants the reader to regard as believable, and he is portraying characters whose actions and reactions (whether described or implied) he wants the reader to take seriously. An "emotional quality" of interaction is presented in the text and should be examined.[26]

Mary's words have nothing to do with being unmarried, since in the Lucan text as it stands she is betrothed, in the first stage of her marriage. (The RSV translation, "since I have no husband" ignores or obscures this fact.) But why would a betrothed woman or girl object to the announcement that she will become pregnant? Some critics have tried to answer that question by claiming that in an original version, Mary either (a) did not object, or (b) was not betrothed. For example, Hubbard[27] remarks that such a question would be strange in the light of v 27 where Mary's engagement to Joseph is noted; but his conclusion is that "Verse 34, therefore, probably represents Lucan redaction of the annunciation tradition." Also noticing an apparent contradiction between v 34 and v 27, Grundmann draws the opposite conclusion: the reference to Joseph in v 27 is secondary, and in the original story the annunciation was to a young unengaged girl.[28] Strong and convincing reasons have been given for taking this whole annunciation scene (vv 26–38) as composed by Luke, with vv 34–35 and 27 always having been part of it.[29] But even if either of these solutions concerning additions were accurate, which I think is not the case, this would still not solve the redactional critical problem of how Luke intends us to understand the story as we find it in his Gospel.[30]

Mary's words also do not describe a premenstrual condition,[31] nor do they express ignorance of how children are conceived or imply a vow or resolve of virginity in marriage (an idea out of harmony with the Jewish mentality of the time).[32] They have nothing to do with an interpretation of Isa 7:14 that led Mary to believe that the Messiah would be born of a virgin (as we have

seen above, there is no evidence for such a pre-Christian interpretation). Each of these options has been carefully refuted.[33]

The angel has announced that Mary will conceive (v 31; cf. v
35), so it is clear that Luke does not think of her as already
pregnant before the announcement. Does he think of her becoming pregnant as the pregnancy is announced (and so ob-
jecting on the basis of her virginity)? This seems to be ruled out
by the future tenses in v 35. Is Luke then presenting Mary as
surprised to think that conception is immediate or already un-
derway (a misunderstanding then corrected by the angel's reference to the future)?[34] It is true that some Old Testament
annunciation scenes concern women already pregnant (Gen
16:11 MT; LXX, cf. Isa 7:14 MT). But the majority, including
the annunciation scenes on which this one is modeled, concern
future pregnancies (1 Sam 1:19; Luke 1:24; cf. *Jubilees* 16), so it
is unlikely the reader would be expected to understand Mary's
question from the perspective of an immediate pregnancy. Does
Luke intend the reader (with Mary) to understand that the pregnancy is in the imminent future, to occur before the home-taking? This last is the most natural interpretation, and one that
allows the pieces of the narrative to fit together smoothly.[35] Mary
objects to the announcement of a pregnancy in the near future,
since she is in the interim period between betrothal and home-
taking, the period during which she does not "know" Joseph.

But many contemporary critics argue for what they call a literary rather than a psychological solution. That is, they think
Mary's question is asked in the light of the annunciation pattern
(see below), to advance the dialogue and give the angel the occasion to explain to the reader how the pregnancy is to come
about.[36] Her question, for example, has been called "merely a
Lucan stage prop for the dramatization of the identification of
the child."[37] It has been claimed that "the answer determines the
question."[38]

The literary versus the psychological are in this case false alternatives. The literary solution here *is* the psychological solution. The question is an essential part of the form *and* of the
story line[39] (which has to do with the situation and reaction of
Mary). The question has also been influenced by the content of
the tradition. Let me repeat: I am not speaking of the psychology

of the historical Mary, but of the psychology of Mary, a character in the narrative. To read Mary's question as only a "literary necessity" in the way that has been suggested is to read it as "empirical nonsense,"[40] *and* as literary nonsense. What is a more natural expectation for a young, engaged woman than that she will become pregnant by her husband? As a betrothed virgin, she is not "someone who seems outside the possibility of childbearing,"[41] but someone on the threshhold of childbearing.

Further, it is extremely important to note that the angel does *not* really explain *how* the pregnancy is to come about. As we will see below, v 35—like the reply to Zechariah in v 19—is primarily a statement of reassurance, urging trust. It is not an explanation of how the pregnancy will happen. The objections of both Zechariah and Mary are indeed overcome, but not with explanations.

2. THE CONCEPTION

a. When?

If we read Mary's question as one of surprise that she will conceive in the immediate future, rather than in the still relatively distant future when she and Joseph will complete the home-taking, the continuation of the narrative indicates that her question is meant as the expression of a correct intuition. The pregnancy apparently is thought to take place in the interval between the annunciation to her and her visit to Elizabeth, who blesses the fruit of Mary's womb (v 42). (Some scholars argue that conception is implied by Luke to take place at the moment of Mary's consent [v 38].[42] But if that were so, we would expect this to have been indicated more clearly.) How long is this interval between the annunciation to Mary and her visit to Elizabeth? The latter scene is introduced by Luke with the vague adverbial phrase, "in those days" (*en tais hēmerais tautais*).[43] As Elizabeth is already six months pregnant when the annunciation to Mary occurs (v 36), and Mary remains with her "about three months" (v 56), leaving before John the Baptist is born, even if we reckon with the notion of a ten-month pregnancy of Elizabeth (see Wisd 7:1–2), the interval between the annunciation to Mary and the visitation must be thought of as a short one.

b. Meta spoudēs

The reader is told further that Mary went to visit Elizabeth *meta spoudēs*, usually translated, "with haste" (v 39), and usually understood to express her haste to share the joy of the two pregnancies or her properly eager reaction to the confirming sign given in v 36, that of Elizabeth's pregnancy. (Compare the reaction of the shepherds in 2:16 to the angelic announcement to them: they hurry [*ēlthon speusantes*] to verify what they have been told.) But *meta spoudēs* is a phrase that merits some pause and study. In the Greek translations of the Hebrew Bible it often has overtones of terror, alarm, flight, and anxiety. It has been called a compact classical and biblical Greek idiom "with a definite import, fraught with psychological and spiritual meaning," conveying the idea of seriousness, gravity, "the innermost condition of a perturbed, thinking mind."[44]

To give a few examples of such use, in Exod 12:11(LXX) the people are told to eat the Passover lamb *meta spoudēs*, ready for flight; in Wisd 19:2(LXX) the Egyptians are said to have expelled the Hebrews *meta spoudēs;* in Ps 77:33(LXX) the days of sinners are spoken of as "consumed in vanity; and their years *meta spoudēs*" (with anxiety); in Dan 13:50 (Theod.) the people return *meta spoudēs* to the place of judgment, after being told they condemned Suzanna as an adulteress on the basis of false witness borne against her. The sense of anxiety may also be present in Mark 6:25, where Herodias's daughter comes to the king to ask for the head of John the Baptist; this is the only other time the phrase *meta spoudēs* appears in the New Testament. There is also a tendency to translate forms of the Hebrew verb *bhl* (which means to be disturbed, dismayed, terrified, as well as to hurry) and equivalents by *spoudazō* or *spoudē*. Job 23:16 (cf. v 14) reads, "The Almighty has troubled me" (*espoudase*); Jer 8:15, "We assembled for peace, but there was no prosperity; for a time of healing, but behold anxiety" (*spoudē*).[45]

Luke uses the adverb *spoudaiōs* in 7:4, where the elders of the Jews beseech Jesus earnestly and urgently to heal the slave of the centurion. Besides using the verb *speudō* to speak of the shepherds coming to Bethlehem (2:16), Luke uses it to speak of Zacchaeus's coming to Jesus (19:5–6); cf. Acts 20:16 (Paul trying to get to Jerusalem by Pentecost); 22:18 (Paul warned in a trance to get out of Jerusalem fast).

My tentative conclusion is this: that the phase *meta spoudēs* in 1:39 may be a clue—a small one, I admit—that points toward a situation of violence and/or fear in connection with Mary's pregnancy, or at least to the idea that she is depicted as reacting with anxiety or inner disturbance to the pregnancy. If it were the only clue, it would be easy to dismiss, but it is not. On the other hand, the phrase could be read to convey terror, fright, or alarm over an unknown mode of conception. Or it is possible that in 1:39 it connotes rather eagerness, zeal, and earnestness (see 3 Macc 5:24; Josephus, *Ag. Ap.* 2.4.42; Rom 12:8, 11; 2 Cor 7:11; 8:7, etc.). The advantage of this traditional interpretation is that a certain parallelism is emphasized between Mary's reaction to angelic revelation and that of the shepherds.[46] In this case, we would have no indication that violence or danger is thought of in 1:39. The reader must judge which is most likely to be Luke's nuance.

It must be stressed that Luke says nothing explicitly about the actual circumstances of the conception of Jesus, in contrast to his comment about the conception of John (1:24). An abrupt conclusion to the scene of the annunciation to Mary has been noticed by some critics. Legrand remarks that when the angel exits in 1:38, "it seems that the narrative breaks off: one does not know what happened to Mary, what were her reactions and those of others; keeping strictly to the text, the reader does not even know if the conception has taken place or how." He holds that the openness of the text has a theological function: Mary is the earthly arrival point of intervention from on high. The dénouement is at this transcendent level; there is nothing to add after the act of faith of Mary (v 38).[47] This suggestion is odd, coming from the critic who proposes that the Lucan annunciation scene is apocalyptic in thought pattern;[48] apocalyptic does not hesitate to enter the realm of the transcendent. Easton speaks of the "delicacy" and "reserve" of the Lucan treatment.[49] I ask if this is delicacy and reserve in the treatment of a miracle, or in the treatment of an embarrassment, even perhaps of a brutality.

3. THE HOME-TAKING? (2:5)

In 2:5 Luke writes of Joseph traveling from Nazareth to Bethlehem with the pregnant Mary, called "his betrothed." It is possible that this is meant to depict the home-taking, if Joseph is thought to be bringing Mary to his hometown, and/or "performing the central and public act which proclaimed the marriage."[50] But then why is she called "his betrothed" rather than "his wife" at this stage?[51] Some critics comment that perhaps here Luke is displaying his ignorance of Palestinian marriage customs, that is, of the two stages of a Palestinian marriage, or simply repeating the description of her in 1:27.[52] Another claim is that the reference here to Mary as Joseph's "betrothed" (as well as to Jesus as the "supposed son" of Joseph in 3:23) are Lucan editorial touches, "designed to bring a conformity with 1:26–39 into material that otherwise shows no awareness of the virginal conception."[53]

But the best explanation is that with the term "betrothed" Luke is emphasizing once again his belief that Joseph was not the biological father of Jesus; the marriage was not a "completed" one, in the sense that it did not involve sexual intercourse. In other words, Luke 2:5 "intimates what Matt 1:25 states."[54] However, Joseph in Luke's narrative, as in Matthew's, assumes the role of legal and public parent of the child (Luke 2:16, 27, 33, 41, 43, 48, 51).

4. DEUT 22:23–27

Does Luke in his account allude to the law concerning the seduction or rape of a betrothed virgin (Deut 22:23–27)? I think that he does.

a. Luke 1:27

There is a verbal closeness between Luke's description of Mary in 1:27 ("a virgin betrothed to a man:" *parthenon emnēsteumenēn andri*) and Deut 22:23 LXX (*pais parthenon memnēsteumenē andri*). The phrase in Luke seems to be derived from the LXX of Deut 22:23.[55] Luke, however, does not narrate or have the angel refer to seduction or rape, and unlike Matthew he does not depict

Joseph wrestling with the application of this law. But there are other clues in the text that point to the possibility that the passage in Deuteronomy runs as a thread through the Lucan story, that Luke is thinking of the passage and not simply describing Mary's marital status. One clue is the tone and aspects of the content of Mary's canticle, the Magnificat, truly appropriate only in the mouth of a character who has experienced injustice and justice, oppression and vindication. Another clue, a linguistic one, is the term *tapeinōsis* in v 48 in that canticle, which I think gives us another allusion to the passage in Deuteronomy.

b. The Magnificat as Mary's Song

Commentators have often remarked on the seeming inappropriateness of the tone and sentiments expressed in the Magnificat, as attributed to Mary.[56] That is, they are thought to be inappropriate in the mouth of a young girl who has just miraculously conceived the Messiah and received the glorious promises of his destiny. There are several reasons for this opinion.

(1) The Magnificat is a song of liberation, personal and social. It praises God's liberating actions on behalf of the speaker, actions that are paradigmatic of all God's actions on behalf of the lowly, the oppressed, the suffering. It has been called "one of the most revolutionary documents in all literature, containing three separate revolutions": moral (v 51), social (v 52), and economic (v 53).[57] The Magnificat trumpets joy in and seems to imply personal knowledge of the accomplishment of God's justice. It is true that Mary's words here might be understood as voicing the joy of all the world's needy (her words "describe the human situation in general"[58]), or of all Israel's needy—those physically and spiritually needy—at the divine response to them in the coming of the Messiah. Mary could also be regarded as the type or representative of all "the poor" who receive God's favor (1:28, 30; 2:14). But still, the song must be considered as an expression of the speaker's praise of God for what has happened to her. In Luke's narrative, what has happened to Mary that would elicit such a hymn?

(2) The tone of the canticle is battle-like, as P. Winter noticed. It may have been originally an old Maccabean victory hymn, or drawn in part from such a hymn.[59] There is a certain violence

about it, and a note of revenge. It has been called "Mary's song of victory," but with the victory interpreted as "spiritual" and the Lucan meaning unexamined.[60] The militancy seems to some a jarring note in a narrative that has apparently been tranquil and joyful up to this point.

(3) With its past (aorist) tenses, the Magnificat stresses salvation accomplished or having come now in a new way, rather than being merely hoped for. Action is concentrated in the present, projecting a tone of finality.[61] The hymn seems to deal with "salvation in retrospect (after the resurrection) rather than the inauguration of salvation." This seems strange coming from a young woman who has just become pregnant but not yet given birth to the Messiah.[62]

(4) The mention of God's mercy in v 54 ("He came to the aid of his servant Israel, mindful of his mercy") appears to find no echo in the story of Mary. It is said to suit her situation only in a generic sense, without any specific application. This stands in contrast to the other two attributes of God mentioned in vv 49–50: power ("He who is powerful," v 49, echoing "the Power of the Most High," v 35) and holiness (God's "name is holy," v 49, echoing the statement that the child to be born will be called holy, v 35). God's mercy figures here, according to this view, because of the pre-Lucan composition of the hymn. Further, God's great deeds of the past are now seen to be manifested in a new form in the conception of Mary's child. Luke can put such sentiments on her lips at this stage in his narrative because he is writing with hindsight and knows that each of the details of the Magnificat can be interpreted figuratively of the career of Jesus himself.[63] The militant tone, the use of aorists, and the mention of God's mercy all acquire new significance from the standpoint of the resurrection faith. But in the immediate context of the Lucan Infancy Narrative and Luke's portrait of Mary, what is their significance?

(5) The Magnificat is a blend of Old Testament allusions, drawn primarily from the prayer and the song of Hannah (1 Sam 1:11; 2:1–10), the once-barren woman whose condition was reversed and who became the mother of Samuel. But Mary was not barren, and her virginity as a betrothed girl is not really equivalent to barrenness (see below). What has Mary in common

with Hannah (other than pregnancy), that the song of the latter should be the principal model of the song of the former?

The allusions to Hannah's song are a primary reason the Magnificat seems much more appropriate in the mouth of Elizabeth, the once-barren woman whose condition was reversed and who became the mother of the Baptist. Hannah figures as a model or type for Elizabeth in 1:5–7, 24–25. The first four difficulties mentioned above would also be eased and the Magnificat seen to fit better into its context if Elizabeth were the speaker intended by Luke. (1) In the Lucan narrative, Elizabeth has been liberated from the stigma of sterility; what was presented as her great need has been met. (2) A tone of triumph and even ferocity against enemies would seem to fit her situation better (cf. 1:25 where she speaks of her barrenness as her reproach or disgrace among men). (3) The aorists can still be understood to express in anticipation the resurrection faith, but talk of great reversal would appear to arise out of Elizabeth's own experience as well. (4) The statement in 1:54 concerning God's mercy does have an echo in Elizabeth's story: in 1:58 her neighbors and relatives, hearing that the Lord had shown his great mercy to her, rejoice with her. In addition, v 48a, with its reference to *tapeinōsis* (a term often applied to a woman's barrenness), may fit Elizabeth better and match her reference to her disgrace in v 25. This important verse 48 will be discussed presently.

There is, in fact, a variant tradition in v 46, which reads, "And Elizabeth said," putting the Magnificat into her mouth. The "Elizabeth" reading is bolstered also by a number of other arguments besides those mentioned above, some of which have to do with an awkwardness in the text as it stands (for example, with Mary the subject of v 46, and her name repeated again as subject in v 56 immediately after the Magnificat). So a minority of critics hold that Luke composed the Magnificat for Elizabeth, not for Mary.[64] But the canticle is ascribed to Mary in the best textual tradition (in all Greek witnesses and almost all versional and patristic witnesses).[65] And a certain disjunction in the text can be explained by the theory that Luke later inserted the Magnificat and Benedictus into his narrative. Also, if Luke meant the Magnificat to be Elizabeth's, why would he omit the antithesis in 1 Sam 2:5 where Hannah says, "the barren has born seven, and she that abounded in children has waxed feeble"?[66]

I think that Luke saw the appropriateness of the Jewish Christian hymn for use as Mary's canticle, and he inserted it as hers in order to communicate the tradition he received: that she had been violated and made pregnant, but that God vindicated her, protecting her and her child,[67] even recognizing and causing to be recognized this child as God's Son and Messiah. Her own experience, in Luke's mind, stands in itself as an anticipation of the resurrection. He is presenting her here as one who was oppressed and liberated, one who triumphed over her enemies, one to whom God was merciful, one for whom there was a radical overturning of social expectations. Hannah's canticle is appropriate as a model for Mary's because Mary, in the tradition Luke inherited, experienced a disaster worse than barrenness: sexual violation.[68]

But in the Old Testament narratives, the violated women sing no canticles, they provide no models of triumphant song. They wail (like Tamar, 2 Sam 13:16–19) or they are mute (Dinah, Gen 34; the concubine, Judg 19:26–28). The aftermath of their stories is revenge, bloodshed, further violation, not divine vindication. Tamar, raped by Amnon, goes away weeping; she is powerless and desolate. Dinah the daughter of Jacob never speaks at all; her rape, thought of as the humiliation and burning shame of her brothers, leads to murder and plunder by those brothers (cf. Judith 9:2–4). In Judges 20–21, the rape of one becomes the rape of six hundred, the concubine's story reenacted, justifying "the expansion of violence against women."[69]

The remarks of Tannehill are apt and trenchant. The Magnificat forces us to compare extremes and so to think of a radical overturning of society, precisely by presenting "God's choice of the lowly mother and his overturning of society as *one* act." In the unique poetic vision of the text, "the mother's personal experience is already a fulfillment of the earth-shaking events which are still to come." The text has a dramatic unity that holds together the small and the great, and a "triangular tension, with the humble, the mighty God, and the oppressive rulers of the world forming the three corners." God's surprising concern for a humble, unimportant, insignificant woman becomes the sign of God's eschatological act for the world. The mother and the baby remain a sign, according to Tannehill, "only so long as we understand them through the tensive unity of the text. We shatter this unity not only when we regard the mother and baby as ordinary but also when we completely remove them from the ordinary, giving them a special, superhuman status." Further, "It is by the power of this sign that we can see signs in our own lives, but the text becomes false to our reality if we take it to be a simple statement of prosaic truth," since the poem lays claim to be a unique vision of the world, rather than an example of what we all know and say.[70]

Read in the context and with the meaning I am suggesting, there are in the poem even more surprises, greater extremes and tension, and a social vision more powerful than Tannehill is aware of. Luke's point is not that the girl who utters the Magnificat is lowly, humble, unimportant, insignificant in comparison to the mighty God. It is rather that she who was humiliated and degraded, and the child whose origin is in humiliation and degradation, were "helped" by God (v 54). This help is "the deed which fulfills Israel's hope,"[71] though a hope never fully voiced before. Even if the Magnificat was drawn by Luke from another, quite different context and inserted into his narrative, maybe even at a later date,[72] it is appropriate to the tradition he is handing on, and a brilliant addition. Its tone and content are compatible with and support the theory proposed here, that Luke alludes to Deut 22:23–27 as the law that applies to Mary's story.

c. Luke 1:47

If it were probable that the Magnificat was originally composed in Hebrew, it might be argued that there is a verbal allusion to Deut 22:27 in Luke 1:47. The former text, it will be recalled, reads, ". . . though the betrothed young woman cried for help there was no one to rescue her" (*wĕ'ên môšîa' lāh;* literally: there was no savior for her).[73] The Lucan verse reads, "my spirit has found gladness in God my Savior" (possibly translating *'ĕlōhîm môšî'î*). The idea in Luke 1:47 (cf. v 54) might then be that even though there was no human savior, God acted as Mary's savior. But it is not certain that the canticle ever existed in Hebrew,[74] and the LXX of Deut 22:27 finds no verbal resonance here in Luke.[75] Luke may be aware of the popular etymology of "Jesus" as "Yahweh saves" (see 2:11, 2:30–31), but there is no evidence of this awareness (which we might press as an allusion to Deuteronomy) in the annunciation to Mary (1:31).

d. Luke 1:48

I think there is, however, an allusion to the law of Deuteronomy in Luke 1:48. It is a common scholarly opinion that in order to link the pre-Lucan, Jewish Christian hymn with his story, Luke composed v 48, or part of it.[76] The verse gives the reason why[77] Mary is proclaiming the greatness of God: "for he has regarded the *tapeinōsis* (a term whose translation I shall discuss) of his servant. For behold, all generations will call me blessed." Luke has picked up the term "servant" or "handmaid" (i.e., female slave) used by Mary of herself in her response to Gabriel (1:38, a verse we will consider below),[78] and he has reiterated and escalated Elizabeth's blessing of her in 1:42. V 48 is also linked to the rest of the canticle by means of the term *tapeinōsis*. Compare v 52b: God has exalted the *tapeinous*. The RSV translates the former term applied to Mary as "low estate," and the latter, "those of low degree."

As Fitzmyer remarks, usually the term *tapeinōsis* means "humiliation," but he and others understand it to refer here to Mary's "humble station." It expresses "her unworthiness to be the mother of the Davidic Messiah and the Son of God."[79] Many interpreters understand both terms primarily in a theological or spiritual sense to refer to those who know themselves "poor" in God's eyes, in need of God's grace and help, the humble ones. It is held that Mary's statement of acquiescence in v 38 epitomizes this attitude. But is there another, fuller sense in which Mary is one whose *tapeinōsis* has been regarded by God?

Grundmann, who argues for the idea of Mary's lowliness here, explains it in this way. "The fact that God chooses the humble handmaiden, the virgin, who is of no account in the eyes of the world, to be the mother of His Son" is the reason for the thankful joy confessed in vv 46–47 and the cause of the honor which she will be paid.[80] Cf. Plummer's reference to Mary's "humble position as a carpenter's bride."[81] Is there, then, a social or economic dimension to the term *tapeinōsis,* intended by Luke? He does speak of her as from Nazareth, a small and obscure village. But in Luke's theological geography, this is the place not of poverty and oppression but of beginnings (cf. Acts 10:37), the village of refusal (Luke 4:16–30), contrasted with Jerusalem, the holy place.

In 2:24 Luke mentions that Mary and Joseph sacrificed birds (not a lamb) at the purification after childbirth, perhaps implying their economic poverty. The law of purification in Leviticus 12 states that the woman is to offer a lamb *and* a young pigeon or a dove. If she cannot afford a lamb, then two young pigeons or doves can be offered. But it is not certain that the alternative offered in Leviticus was still an active custom; possibly everyone offered birds by the time of Jesus.[82] In any case, there is no special emphasis by Luke on Mary's poverty.[83] For what it was worth, her betrothal had incorporated her legally into the Davidic lineage, perhaps into one of the nonaristocratic, lateral branches.[84] It may be true that the Magnificat, with its characteristic stress on the imminent divine reversal of the plight of the poor, reflects the Jewish Christian experience of social and political deprivation.[85] The motif that attention must be paid to the poor, whose plight God will reverse, is an important one in this Gospel. Vv 51–53 are the first instance of this motif, and they alert us, I think, to interpret v 48 as referring to more than (but not less than) an "attitude." To put it another way, v 48 refers to an attitude that arises out of an experience of injustice.[86]

Mary's statement that God "has regarded the *tapeinōsis* of his servant" (1:48) is linked to the preceding Lucan narrative in yet another way. The line is reminiscent thematically of Elizabeth's statement in 1:25: "Thus the Lord has done to me in the days when he looked on me, to take away my reproach among men" (*oneidos mou en anthrōpois*)—the reproach, that is, resulting from her barrenness. It is well known that the inability to conceive, especially as this meant the inability to provide sons for her husband, is spoken of in the Hebrew Bible and elsewhere as a source of tremendous shame for a wife. Barrenness, however, was regarded as less of a shame than conception through adultery or fornication or rape. See Sir 16:3: ". . . to be childless is better

than to have ungodly children." Wisd 3:13: "blessed is the barren
woman who is undefiled, who has not entered into a sinful
union; she will have fruit when God examines souls"; cf. 4:1:
better than the children of adulterers "is childlessness with virtue."

Elizabeth's story is built on the stories of the barren Sarah
(Genesis 16–18) and the barren Hannah (1 Samuel 1–2). In fact,
v 48 of the Magnificat seems to be a strong allusion to 1 Sam
1:11, where Hannah prays, "O Lord of hosts, if you will indeed
look on the affliction of your maidservant (*bāʿŏnî ʾămātekā;* LXX:
epi tēn tapeinōsin tēs doulēs sou) and remember me, and not forget
your maid servant, but will give to your maidservant a son, then
I will give him to the Lord all the days of his life. . . . " See also
Gen 29:32 (unloved Leah names her son Rueben "because the
Lord has looked on my humiliation" [*eide mou Kyrios tēn tapei-
nōsin]); see 4 Ezra* 9:45. Cf. Gen 16:11 (the persecuted Hagar is
told to call her child Ishmael, "for the Lord has given heed to
your humiliation" [*tapeinōsei]*), this last a case not of barrenness
but of oppression.

The link Luke forges between Mary's statement in 1:48 and
Elizabeth's in 1:25, and the general parallel between Elizabeth
and Mary (which we will treat in more detail below) lead me to
think of Mary's statement in terms of humiliation, not in terms
of low estate or humility. The term *tapeinōsis* "regularly suggests
positive humiliation and distress."[87] But in what way could the
reader of Luke's narrative think of Mary as experiencing humiliation?

She was not, of course, humiliated by being barren. And the
attempt to understand the term *tapeinōsis* applied to her by Luke
in terms of her virginity I find unconvincing in the extreme.
Soares Prabhu, for example, argues it would be "shocking" to
the Jews of Jesus' time that God should send his messenger to
a virgin. This is so, in his opinion, because "virginity in the Old
Testament was not a title of honour, but with its implied childlessness in a society where motherhood was a woman's sole glory,
a cause of shame. . . . The sending of the angel to a 'virgin' is
thus part of the paradox of lowliness graced, of creaturely powerlessness made fruitful through the spirit, of a badge of shame
become a sign of consecration."[88] Brown contends (I think

rightly) that with the term *tapeinōsis* in 1:48 Luke refers not to Mary's attitude but to her human status; but then Brown goes on to say that for Luke, "Mary's virginity was like the barrenness of the Old Testament women: both constituted a human impossibility which only the might of God could overcome"; Luke uses the term *oneidos* and *tapeinōsis* "to describe the womb that has not produced the fruit of children."[89]

But the virginity of a betrothed girl was not regarded in a negative, but in a very positive light. It implied that her father had exercised proper care and protection of her and had disciplined her (see Sir 7:24; 26:10–12; 42:9–11), a matter of his honor (22:4). It met the normal expectation of her fiancé and of society in general, and it is anachronistic to regard it as having been otherwise. Mary's virginity, therefore, is not a good parallel to Elizabeth's barrenness. *Lack* of virginity of a betrothed girl could more properly be considered a humiliation—especially if her virginity was lost by seduction or by rape.

Deut 22:24, as we have seen, speaks of the seducer as having violated or humiliated ('innāh; LXX: *etapeinōsen*) the betrothed virgin (cf. v 29, of the rapist of a virgin who is not betrothed). The verb *tapeinoō* is used in the LXX for the sexual humiliation of a woman also in Gen 34:2 (Dinah); Judges 19:24; 20:5 (the concubine of the Levite); 2 Kings 13:12, 14, 22, 32 (David's daughter Tamar); Lam 5:11 (the virgins of Jerusalem); cf. Isa 51:21, 23; Deut 21:14; Ezek 22:10–11. The humiliation of a girl was a moral and social degradation by which she could lose the expectancy of a fully valid marriage, and hence her place in the fabric of society.[90]

My argument is that Luke alludes again to the law in Deut 22:23–27 with his insertion of 1:48 into the Magnificat. He achieves here, then, a double allusion: to Hannah and to the law.[91] The virgin betrothed to a man (1:27) was sexually humiliated. But her humiliation, like the barrenness of Hannah (and Elizabeth) was "looked upon" and reversed by God.

Some hold that the source of the Magnificat was the Jewish Christian circle of Anawim (the unfortunate, poor, lowly, sick, downtrodden, widows, orphans, those totally dependent on God for support, those who represented themselves as the faithful remnant of Israel). These suffered physically as well as spiritually.[92] Luke chose the Magnificat for Mary's hymn because he saw her as one of them, and he composed v 48 with v 52 in mind. The hymn foreshadows what Jesus will do, on the basis of what God has done for Mary. The tradition of illegitimacy does not negate the theology that Jesus came from the pious Anawim, nor does it destroy the images of sanctity and purity with which Luke surrounds Jesus' origins.[93] Rather, Luke uses that theology and those images as the vehicle for his communication of the illegitimacy tradition in order to show that this child and his mother were fully incorporated into Israel. In her Magnificat, Mary preaches as the prophet of the poor.[94] She represents the hope of the poor,[95] but she represents that hope *as a woman*[96] who has suffered and been vindicated as a woman.

5. CONCLUSION

Luke presents essentially the same marital and legal situation that Matthew does. Mary, a virgin betrothed to Joseph, conceives Jesus in the period between her betrothal and the home-taking. By means of his allusions to Deut 22:23–27 and his statement in 3:23 that Jesus was only the "supposed" son of Joseph, Luke indicates that he has taken over a tradition that Jesus was fathered by some unnamed man. The home-taking takes place, but there are no sexual relations between Mary and Joseph before the child is born. Joseph assumes the public role of the legal father of Jesus.

C. PARALLELISM BETWEEN THE STORIES OF JOHN THE BAPTIST AND JESUS

An interpretation of the parallelism between Luke's stories of John the Baptist and of Jesus indicates to contemporary scholars that Luke was writing of a virginal conception of Jesus. In fact, this is the *main* critical argument that has been brought forward in recent years to support this claim with regard to the Gospel of Luke.[97] The argument runs this way. Luke has constructed a step-parallelism, designed to show point by point the superior greatness of Jesus over John the Baptist (cf. the step-parallelism in the promises concerning Isaac [Gen 17:7] and Ishmael [21:17–21]). For example, it is said of the Baptist that "he will be great before the Lord" (1:15), but of Jesus that "he will be great, and will be called the Son of the Most High" (v 32). Gabriel predicts that John "will be filled with the Holy Spirit, even from his mother's womb" (v 15), but that the Holy Spirit will "come upon" Mary, causing Jesus to be "called holy, the Son of God" (v 35). Whereas the Baptist is said to have a prophetic destiny (he will go before the Lord "in the spirit and power of Elijah," v 17; cf. v 76), Jesus' destiny is royal (he will be given "the throne of his father David, and he will reign over the house of Jacob forever; and of his kingdom there will be no end," vv 32–33).

The step-parallelism, according to this view, demands an even greater miracle at the conception of Jesus than that at the conception of John. John's parents, says Luke, are old, and have no child because Elizabeth is barren (v 7). God enables Elizabeth to conceive naturally (vv 13, 23–24). But the conception of Jesus, it is thought, is more extraordinary: it is conception without male sperm. God's "intervention" is greater: Zechariah and Elizabeth are empowered to produce a child, but Mary is empowered to conceive without a sexual partner. The conception that overcomes lack of sexual relations is greater than the conception that overcomes barrenness.[98] To have Jesus naturally conceived "would reverse the pattern of his superiority, since it would mean that there was nothing extraordinary about the manner of his conception."[99] Natural conception would also disappoint the expectation of a greater intervention, since it would mean Jesus was conceived "without divine help."[100] The two questions, "How shall I know this, for I am an old man, and my wife is advanced in years?" (v 18) and "How can this be, since I have no sexual relations with a man?" (v 34)[101] express this step-parallelism "of one-upmanship."[102] (It will be argued below, however, that neither of the "how?" questions is answered directly.)[103] The virginal conception in Luke "is more implied by the contrast with John's miraculous birth to aged parents than by direct affirmation about it, and stands in contrast to the open affirmation of it in Matt 1:18."[104]

In my opinion, step-parallelism is indeed present in the two questions and in Luke's understanding of God's role in each of the conceptions. But what is "greater" in the case of Jesus is not a miraculous manner of his conception, but God's overcoming of the deeper humiliation of his mother. Elizabeth's humiliation was that she was barren. Barrenness was thought to cancel out what was regarded as a woman's main function in life, the bearing of children—especially sons—to her husband. It denied to her "the highest status a woman might normally achieve," with its honor, security, social approval, and the opportunity to exercise authority (over children).[105] Barrenness was a cause of contempt (Gen 16:4–5: Hagar's contempt of the barren Sarai), creating envy and the wish to die on the part of the barren one (Gen 30:1: Rachel envies the fertile Leah and says to Jacob, "Give me children or I shall die"). She is represented biblically as feeling "great anxiety and vexation," provoked and irritated by a rival, fertile wife (see 1 Sam 1:16, 5–7). Barrenness could be a cause for divorce and return of the woman to her father's house (Lev 22:13 speaks of the widowed, divorced, and childless women returning to their fathers' houses; see *m. Yebam.* 6:6). In Sir 42:10, the father's worry that his daughter may be sterile is really worry for himself: he would experience disgrace and have to once more support her if she were released by her husband and sent home. A home and motherhood are promised by God to the barren woman in Ps 113:9.

Childlessness was commonly understood to be the woman's fault. The barren womb is listed in Prov 30:16, along with Sheol, the parched earth, and fire, as things that never say "Enough!" Barrenness was also spoken of as punishment for sin (Lev 20:20–21; perhaps 2 Sam 6:23? Cf. *1 Enoch* 98:5) or at least caused by God "forgetting" the woman (see 1 Sam 1:11). Luke, however, takes pains to inform his readers that both Zechariah and Elizabeth were "righteous before God, walking in all the commandments and ordinances of the Lord, blameless" (1:6), so their childlessness was not the result of sin. Nevertheless, Elizabeth can still speak of her barrenness as "my disgrace (or: reproach) among men" (v 25; cf. Rachel's reaction to her pregnancy in Gen 30:23: "God has taken away my disgrace").

But the humiliation of a betrothed virgin who was seduced or raped, and who became pregnant by someone other than her husband, was far worse. In contrast to the humiliation of the barren woman (see Isa 54:1–3; 1 Sam 2:5), this kind of humiliation was never explicitly promised reversal. The promise-fulfillment theme, so strong in the rest of Luke 1–2, is here topped, shattered, surpassed. The Lucan narrative, against all expectations, challenges the reader to believe that the Holy Spirit was involved in a pregnancy resulting from such a humiliation. Just how Luke expressed his belief that in Mary's case God overcame this second humiliation will be considered in the next section (D), a discussion of Gabriel's words in v 35.

This understanding of the step-parallelism is supported by an analysis of the form of a conception/birth annunciation. Brown lays out the pattern of such an announcement, referring to Gen 16:7–13 (Ishmael); Gen 17:1–21 and 18:1–15 (Isaac); Judg 13:3–23 (Samson); Luke 1:11–20 (John the Baptist); Luke 1:26–37 and Matt 1:20–21 (Jesus). The five steps of this pattern are:

1. The appearance of an angel of the Lord (or appearance of the Lord)
2. Fear or prostration of the visionary confronted by this supernatural presence
3. The divine message:
   a. The visionary is addressed by name
   b. A qualifying phrase describing the visionary
   c. The visionary is told not to be afraid
   d. A woman is with child or about to be with child
   e. She will give birth to a (male) child
   f. The name by which the child is to be called
   g. An etymology interpreting the name
   h. The future accomplishments of the child
4. An objection by the visionary as to how this can be, or a request for a sign
5. The giving of a sign to reassure the visionary

Steps 4 and 5 are missing in Gen 16:7–13 and 2, 4, and 5 in Matt 1:20–21.[106] Similar steps appear in the commission form, which will be discussed below.[107]

But this pattern needs some amplification. Robert Alter, in an article called "How Convention Helps Us Read: the Case of the Bible's Annunciation Type-Scene," analyzes Genesis 18:9–15 (Isaac); 25:19–25 (Jacob and Esau); Judges 13 (Samson); 1 Samuel 1 (Samuel) and 2 Kings 4:8–17 (the Shunammite's son), in an effort to determine the fixed sequence of narrative motifs tacitly understood by the biblical authors and their audiences as one that would be used to convey in most cases the conception and birth of the hero. His notion of a convention of type-scene is in some ways related to various conceptions of fixed and recurrent patterns (*Gattungen*) that have been discussed in biblical scholarship. But Alter argues that the recognition of pattern as literary convention leads to a different understanding of how the patterns actually work. In a literary convention, in contrast to a *Gattung*, culture has been transformed into text, offering a highly mediated, stylized image of social or cultural realities. Focus on this is different from form criticism's tendency to insist on the function performed by text in culture. Also, while the form critic attempts to identify *common* formulas in different texts, Alter, the literary critic, thinks "more significant is the inventive freshness with which formulas are recast and re-deployed in each new instance."[108]

Alter holds that the annunciation type-scene has a tripartite schema:

1. It begins with the statement of the plight of barrenness of the future mother of the hero.
2. Annunciation is made to the barren woman, enabled to conceive through the promise or prediciton of an oracle, a visiting man of God, or an angel.
3. Then the conception and birth are said to occur, in some versions immediately, but in one of the scenes Alter examines (the story of the conception of Isaac) after the intervention of other narrative material.[109]

Alter's five texts include two that are treated also by Brown (Gen 18:9–15; Judg 13) and three that are not (Gen 25:19–25; 1 Samuel 1; 2 Kings 4:8–17), since Brown is only dealing with annunciations that are made by supernatural beings who appear to a visionary. In Gen 25:19–25, the Lord grants Isaac's prayer for his barren wife Rebekah, and then Rebekah, pregnant, goes to inquire of the Lord, receiving an oracular answer but no appearance. In 1 Samuel 1:17, the barren Hannah is told by Eli the priest at Shiloh, "The God of Israel grant[110] your petition which you have made to him." And in 2 Kings 4:8–17, Elisha the prophet tells the Shunammite woman that she will conceive.[111] Brown's texts include two from the Hebrew Bible not treated by Alter (Gen 17:1–21 and 16:7–13), as well as the three New Testament annunciation scenes. Alter has perhaps omitted Gen 17:1–21 (Isaac) since it is a duplication, in a sense, of 18:9–15, and he has omitted Gen 16:7–13 (Ishmael) probably because Hagar was not barren.[112]

If we look at all these texts in the light of Alter's tripartite schema, it becomes clear that in every case, with the apparent exception of Luke 1:26–37, the annunciations occur as response to the plight of a woman. This is not always the plight of barrenness, although that is the case in seven of the ten texts treated by Brown and Alter. The plight of Hagar is not barrennesss; rather, it is her pregnancy that has made Sarah jealous and oppressive. The annunciation to Hagar occurs in the wilderness where she is fleeing from Sarai (Gen 16:4–8). The plight that occasions the annunciation in Matt 1:20–21 is the pregnancy of Mary, which occasions the dilemma Joseph faces and the decision he makes to divorce her.[113] If we consider also Isa 7:10–17, it must be noted that the annunciation by Isaiah to Ahaz of Immanuel's conception and birth is in response to the plight of the nation of Judah of the house of David; so too is the annunciation of Josiah's birth a response to the plight of Israel (because of Jeroboam's apostasy). And in 1 Chron 22:7–10, the promise of a son is in response not to a woman's plight but to a father's inadequacy. Perrot enumerates the diverse themes he finds in the pre-Christian haggada on the infancy of great men; the first of these themes is mention of the lamentable situation in which humanity or the people of God finds itself.[114]

Alter says that since the plight of barrenness is present in all the annunciations he considers, it is safe to assume "that the general configuration of the annunciation type-scene is meant to intimate something supernatural about the birth of the hero. He cannot simply be born as the result of a natural process; instead, his mother must be desperately barren, so that the birth occurs only through divine intervention, with a direct message from above."[115] But Old Testament conceptions by barren and/or aged women were not considered by the biblical writers and their early audiences to be "supernatural" rather than the result of a natural process. These conceptions were intended to highlight dramatically what might be only loosely called the divine "intervention" in *every* conception, as well as to highlight divine fidelity to the covenant(s). Alter does not define what he means by his terms "something supernatural" and "intervention."

But it is another aspect of Alter's anlysis that interests me here. This is the fact that the scenes normally begin with the plight of a woman; the annunciation is a response to that plight. The plight of barrenness is *not* present in all biblical annunciation scenes. Barrenness may be the most common plight, but innovation occurs. In two exceptions I have mentioned, the annunciations are revelations the God "intervenes" to support or protect the endangered pregnant women Hagar and Mary.

In the case of Hagar, who, in a striking reversal of the Exodus motif, is fleeing *to* Egypt but in her annunciation scene is sent back to submit to the persecution of Sarai (Gen 16:9), one must speak of divine support of a minimal and ambiguous sort. God pays heed to her affliction (Gen 16:11; cf. Exod 3:7–8; Deut 26:7). Hagar receives the promise of innumerable descendants (16:10) and is assured of a future through her son. But because she is ordered to submit to further oppression, "Suffering undercuts hope. . . . The divine promise of Ishmael means life at the boundary of consolation and desolation."[116] Still, Hagar names God: "You are a God of seeing" (16:13). Her declaration has a positive emphasis, even if the meaning of this name and of the revelation to her remain unclear. Hagar, however, is not liberated, and in her story God identifies with the oppressor.

In the case of Mary, in Matthew's account her plight is that she is betrothed and pregnant not by the one to whom she is betrothed. She is in danger of being put to shame (or worse), but Joseph is unwilling to choose this way of dealing with the dilemma. He puts her rather under threat of divorce and social ostracism. Her plight is responded to, in that she is freed from this threat and brought under the protection of Joseph in marriage, as a result of the angelic revelation to him. This is the extent of Mary's "liberation" in Matthew's Gospel.

What about the Lucan scene of the annunciation to Mary? Without a discussion of the structure of the two annunciations, to Zechariah and to Mary, Schweizer notices that one significant difference between the two is that there is no description of need in the latter, no persistent prayer of a sufferer. He thinks this is so "because no need exists." A free creative act of God brings Jesus into being.[117] Certainly it is not impossible that Luke innovates to such an extent that there is no plight to which the annunciation is a response, but I think this is improbable. Alter's discussion of the annunciation type-scene suggests to me that "convention" should lead the reader to expect that this annunciation too has a relationship to the plight of a woman. Virginity could not be considered a "plight."[118] And Luke has given no indication that the reader is to think here of the plight of Israel, or of the world. Convention should alert the reader to the allusions to Deut 22:23–27 in 1:27 and 1:48.[119] Luke's innovation is drastic and subtle. As in the majority of Hebrew Bible annunciations, the announcement precedes pregnancy. But (as in Gen 16:7–13 and Matt 1:20–21) pregnancy itself and its occasion will be the cause of the plight. This is only foreshadowed in 1:27 and referred to in 1:48.[120] So the Lucan annunciation is the response to a plight anticipated—a plight is responded to in advance. In a sense, its revelation forestalls the plight. What I mean will become clearer in the following section (D) in a discussion of Gabriel's promise to Mary.

Admittedly, convention also operates here in another way. Because of the fact that the majority of biblical annunciations deal with barrenness, because Luke has so closely paralleled the annunciation to Mary with that to Zechariah, which deals with barrenness, and because of the two "how?" questions in 1:18, 34, the reader is led to expect something physically extraordinary in the case of Jesus' conception.

It should be noted parenthetically that scholars disagree on whether Luke has fashioned the account of the annunciation of the conception of John in dependence on that of Jesus,[121] or whether Luke is using a pre-gospel source that recounted the conception of John in terms of Hebrew Bible models, in imitation of which he fashioned the annunciation of Jesus' conception.[122] I tend to think the latter is the case. The arguments of Schweizer are persuasive: it is unlikely that the story of John was shaped after the story of Jesus. Luke 1:5–24a (25), 57–66 probably originated among followers of John the Baptist who did not recognize Jesus as Messiah, and who awaited only God's final coming, not the Messiah. In Schweizer's opinion, whether it was a pre-Lucan Jewish Christian or Luke himself who expanded the tradition by adding parallel Jesus narratives is hard to determine, as is the extent to which the two accounts had already been assimilated to each other in the oral stage. This process probably antedates Luke, who holds Mary in high esteem but never subsequently refers to Jesus' conception, not even in summaries of the faith. In addition, in the rest of his Gospel Luke actually reduces the parallelism between John and Jesus, depicting Jesus as Elijah and omitting the account of John's martyrdom.[123] It should be added that comparison with the Matthean annunciation shows that the pre-gospel tradition about Jesus had already been cast in an angelic annunciation form.[124] This form is less evident in Matthew 1 than in Luke 1, since in the former it has been merged with the dominant pattern of a dream narrative. Luke expanded the inherited tradition of Jesus' conception by imitating the tradition of John's conception, and thus strengthened the annunciation pattern.[125]

Early Christian and then Lucan imitation of the annunciation story may have brought about an unintended result. Convention operates here in this second way to lead the reader to think of divine "intervention" in the process of conception, or divine empowering in a "supernatural" way (although neither of the terms "intervention" or "supernatural" quite captures the meaning of the narratives about barrenness). Convention operates this way *less* in the Matthean narrative, because the annunciation pattern is less strong there. Further, Matthew has prepared the reader, by his insertion of the names of the four women into his genealogy, and by his presentation of the dilemma of Joseph (which more directly draws the reader's attention to the law in Deuteronomy), to regard Mary's plight in a broader context.

It will undoubtedly seem curious—and even perverse—to claim that convention helps us read Luke in such an unconventional way. But Alter remarks that "many of the organizing conventions of biblical narrative have been forgotten, overlaid with later logics, later ways of producing and deciphering texts," and that an effort of "recuperation" may be necessary, an effort that will be "more or less conjectural" and therefore risky.[126] Convention, then, does not mean *our* conventions, *our* conventional way of reading. A sense of biblical convention can lead to surprising contemporary interpretations. If the annunciation pattern is expanded to include the conventional annunciation *setting*—the plight of a woman[127]—then Luke (and Matthew, and the framers of the Christian tradition before them) can be seen to innovate by employing the pattern in a situation—that of an illegitimate pregnancy—in which it had never been used before in the biblical tradition.

To my mind, this is in fact less surprising and more in line with the possibilities inherent in pre-Christian, Jewish tradition than the very odd claim that the two New Testament texts are about the "virginal conception" of Jesus.

D. LUKE 1:35: GABRIEL'S RESPONSE TO MARY'S QUESTION

1. QUESTIONS AND "ANSWERS"

Gabriel states in Luke 1:31 that Mary will conceive and give birth to a son, whom she will name Jesus and who will "be great and will be called Son of the Most High." To him God will give the throne of David and an endless kingdom. Mary replies, "How will this be, since I have no sexual relations with a husband?" (1:34). Her question, as we have seen, parallels that asked by Zechariah when he is told Elizabeth will bear him a son, whose destiny will be one of prophetic greatness. Zechariah asks, "How shall I know this, for I am an old man and my wife is advanced in years?" (1:18).

Neither of the angelic responses that follow is a direct answer to the question posed by the human participant in the dialogue. Neither response gives information about "how" the respective pregnancies will be accomplished.[128] Rather, the pattern is one of objection followed by reassurance and the giving of a sign, or (in the case of Zechariah) doubt followed by rebuke, and (in the case of Mary) hesitation followed by reassurance.[129] Luke 1:18 echoes Abraham's question in Genesis 15. When Abraham is told he will possess the land before him, he asks, "O Lord God, how am I to know that I shall possess it?" (15:8). The response given him after the covenant ceremony, given in deep sleep, dread, and darkness, is more of a direct answer than the one given to Zechariah. Abraham is given a preview of the history of his descendants: their sojourning, their descent into Egypt, their oppression, their exodus, and their return to the land. But Zechariah is given only the statement of the messenger's authority: "I am Gabriel; and I stand in the presence of God. I have been sent to speak to you and announce to you this good news" (1:19). Then the sign is given: because he did not believe, he will be mute until the promise is accomplished. The essence of this angelic response is: You should have trusted. It can be read as a rebuff to Zechariah's challenge.[130]

The response to Mary's question is crucial to our interpretation of this entire passage. She is told, "The Holy Spirit will come upon you (*epeleusetai epi se*) and the power of the Most High (*dynamis hypsistou*) will overshadow (*episkiasei*) you. Therefore, the child to be born will be called holy, Son of God." Elizabeth's pregnancy is the sign mentioned, to show "nothing is impossible for God" (*ouk adynatēsei para tou theou pan rēma;* vv 36–37). Reaching back again into the story of the conception of Isaac, this line answers the question the Lord asked Abraham when Sarah laughed, "Is there anything impossible with God?" (Gen. 18:14 LXX: *me adynatēsei para tǭ theǭ rēma*). What is the essence of this second angelic response? It is this: You should trust; you will be empowered and protected by God. The reversal of Elizabeth's humiliation shows that nothing is impossible for God. Mary's trust is contrasted with Sarah's laughter.

There is a striking similarity between this dialogue of Gabriel and Mary in Luke 1 and that of Jesus and Nicodemus in John 3. In both cases, the questions asked are about biology, about how births or begettings are to come about. But both answers given are on another level, the spiritual, and both mention the role of the Spirit.[131] Jesus tells Nicodemus, "Truly, truly, I say to you, unless one is begotten from above (or: born again; the Greek *gennēthēnai anōthen* is capable of both meanings), he cannot see the kingdom of God" (3:9). Nicodemus questions, "How can a man be born when he is old? Can he enter a second time into his mother's womb and be born?" (v 4). The dialogue proceeds by way of Nicodemus misunderstanding, a kind of progression common in the Fourth Gospel. Nicodemus correctly understands part, but only part, of the meaning of *anōthen*. As far as that word means "anew" or "again," it is correctly paraphrased by "a second time." But to think of a second entry into and emergence from the womb of a human mother is to ignore the fact that *anōthen* means also (and here perhaps primarily) "from above." Because Nicodemus understands what has been said to him in purely human terms, and the human not as a parable, he misunderstands.[132] Jesus' reply concerns those "begotten of water and the Spirit" (v 5–8). Vv 7–8 are a denial that one can really understand what "begotten of the Spirit" involves, in terms of the when or the how.[133] (There is an important difference between the Lucan and Johannine passages here: the latter is not speaking about a spiritual begetting or birth that coincides with the biological;[134] but the former, in a sense, is.)[135] When Nicodemus questions again, "How can this be?" (v 9), the response of Jesus, like that of Gabriel to Zechariah, concerns the trustworthiness of the witness who has access to the heavenly world and must be believed (vv 10–15).

The Lucan narrative should not be interpreted through the lens of typical Johannine misunderstanding (note that there are no wordplays or double meanings in the Lucan scene). But the curious similarities between these sections of Luke's annunciation to Mary and John's conversation between Nicodemus and Jesus suggest some connection in the remote reaches of pre-gospel tradition. These similarities help us to see that Luke is not writing a simple question-and-answer dialogue.

2. "To Come Upon" and "to Overshadow"

The angel speaks to Mary in synonymous parallelism (v 34bc): the Holy Spirit is the power of the Most High (cf. 24:49; Acts 1:8), and its coming upon Mary is an overshadowing. But the verbs have difference nuances. The first verb implies Mary's empowering, and the second promises protection.

The first verb, "to come upon" (*eperchesthai*), is used only by Luke among the evangelists. He uses it seven times, four (or possibly five) to speak of something dreaded or overpowering assailing a person: Luke 11:22 ("But when one stronger than he assails [*epelthōn*] him and overcomes him. . . .");[136] 21:26 ("men fainting with fear and with foreboding of what is coming on [*eperchomenōn*] the world"); Acts 8:24 (Simon the magician's request, "pray for me to the Lord, that nothing of what you have said may come upon [*epelthē*] me"); 13:40 ("beware, therefore, lest there come upon [*epelthȩ*] you what is said in the prophets"). Cf. James 5:1 ("Come now, you rich, weep and howl for the miseries that are coming upon [*eperchomenais*] you").

Only once elsewhere in the New Testament (again by Luke) is the verb used of the Spirit, in Acts 1:8, where the risen Jesus promises the Spirit at Pentecost: "but you shall receive power (*dynamin*) when the Holy Spirit has come upon (*epelthontos*) you." There are important associations between this verse and Luke 1:35. Suffice it to say here that in his first volume, the Gospel, Luke depicts the Spirit "coming upon" an individual, Mary, in power. Her own empowerment is implied and then illustrated in the continuation of the narrative, as Mary becomes the prototype of the believing disciple in her response (1:38), and the first powerful proclaimer of the good news in her Magnificat. As a consequence of the Holy Spirit's coming upon Mary, the child to be born of her will be "holy." In his second volume, Acts, Luke's Jesus promises the Holy Spirit will "come upon" his assembled followers; as a consequence, they will be empowered to be his witnesses "to the ends of the earth," empowered to proclaim Jesus as God's holy one (3:14; 4:27, 30) and to enable others to receive the Holy Spirit. Luke's use of a verb that he usually associates with danger and dread emphasizes the notion of the Spirit's humanly uncontrollable power. His use of it again in Acts 1, in the scene that is meant to evoke the annunciation to Mary, shows that this power comes to empower.

In almost all instances of the verb *eperchesthai* in the LXX, the connotation is negative, often of an attack. Affliction, plague, curse, enemy troops, evil, robbers, and destruction are said to "come upon" people (see, for examples, Gen 42:21; Lev 14:43; Judg 9:57; 1 Kings 30:23; 2 Kings 19:7; 22:1; Job 21:17, etc.). The verb carries the notion of onrushing, overpowering vitality where it is used in a positive sense: for the coming of an ecstasy from the Lord, giving the power to fight oppression "as one man" (1 Kings 11:7); the coming of God in great strength (Job

23:6); the coming of salvation (Bar 4:9) or joy from God (4:36). In one pre–New Testament text in which it is used for the Spirit of God, it is used in an eschatological sense, in terms of eschatological reversal of wilderness and fertile field (Isa 32:15–16). In only one instance is *eperchesthai* used in what looks like a (violent) sexual context, Hos 10:11 LXX: God warns, "I will come upon (*epeleusomai*) the fairest part of her neck; I will mount Ephraim" (depicted as a heifer). But this one text is not enough evidence for us to hold that sexual sense is intended in Luke 1:35. This interesting verb, then, is well chosen to carry in the annunciation scene the notion of tremendous and even dangerous power, power to overturn destinies, in God's justice.

The second verb, *episkiazō*, must be discussed at a little greater length. It used in the New Testament in Acts 5:15, where Luke reports that people "even carried out the sick into the streets, and laid them on beds and pallets, that as Peter came by at least his shadow might fall on some of them." This use of the verb is very literal, and aids us in understanding Luke 1:35 only in the sense that we find here in Acts a similar connection between shadow and power used for the good. The tradition transforms Peter "into a man filled to his very shadow with miraculous power, by aid of which he directly manifests the divine omnipotence,"[137] by healing.

Episkiazō is used again in the account of the Transfiguration (Mark 9:7; Matt 17:5; Luke 9:34). In the Lucan version, a cloud overshadowed (*epeskiazen*) the three disciples with Jesus, with whom Moses and Elijah had appeared in glory, speaking of his "departure which he was to accomplish at Jerusalem." The disciples "were afraid as they entered the cloud. And a voice came out of the cloud, saying, 'This is my Son, my chosen; listen to him' " (9:34–35). There are a host of apocalyptic and Exodus associations in this scene, but whatever else the cloud may symbolize, here it is the context for revelation of the divine Sonship of Jesus, linked only in Luke's transfiguration scene to Jesus' exaltation through suffering, his "departure" in death, burial, resurrection, ascension, his journey to liberation.[138] Again the sense of overshadowing may be literal, but the literal may symbolize a certain obscurity that protects from the full impact of such a revelation.

But in Luke 1:35, the sense is figurative, denoting God's presence to Mary.[139] This figurative sense can be elucidated by an examination of the appearance of the verb and of shadow imagery used for the presence of God in the LXX and elsewhere. It is presence of a specific kind: protective presence. This needs to be stressed, because in contemporary Western literature and film, overshadowing and shadow imagery have primarily an ominous, menacing connotation. We think of the shadow of dangerous empty streets, of crime, of loneliness, confusion, of nuclear armaments deployed and nuclear clouds, of shadows on X-rays, of aging and death. Like Luke 1:35, Eliot's line, "Come in under the shadow of this red rock" has to be carefully explicated.

Three of the four uses of *episkiazō* in the LXX concern the presence and power of God. Exod 40:35 speaks of the cloud of the glory of the Lord overshadowing the tabernacle in the wilderness; because of this overshadowing, Moses was not able to enter the tabernacle. The passage continues: "And when the cloud went up from the tabernacle, the children of Israel prepared to depart with their baggage. And if the cloud did not go up, they did not prepare to depart, until the day when the cloud went up. For a cloud was on the tabernacle by day, and fire was on it by night before all Israel, in all their journeyings" (vv 36–38; cf. Num 9:18, 22; 10:35 [*skiazō*]).[140] The overshadowing of the cloud, then, is a sign that Israel may rest, encamped; the movement of the cloud directs the journey to freedom. Many critics claim that in Luke 1:35 there is an allusion to this text in Exodus; along these lines, Mary would be understood as the tabernacle that God overshadows.[141] The allusion should not be pinned to this one text; but even if it is, the point must be made that God's presence signified by the cloud in Exodus protects, refreshes, directs, liberates.

There is no mention of the tabernacle, however, in Ps 90 (91):4 or in Ps 139 (140):7. The first text promises that God "will overshadow (*episkiasei*) you with his shoulders, and you will trust under his wings; his truth will cover you with a shield." (Cf. Deut 33:12: "The beloved of the Lord will dwell in confidence, and God overshadows [*skiazei*] him always, and he rested between his shoulders.") The second psalm text is the prayer, "O Lord

God, the strength (*dynamis*) of my salvation; you overshadowed (*episkiasas*) my head in the day of battle." These texts are about God's protection, God's presence in danger and affliction with the one who trusts. In Wisd 19:7–8, "the cloud [here without the Tabernacle] was seen overshadowing (*skiazousa*) the camp and dry land emerging where water had stood before, an unhindered way out of the Red Sea and a grassy plain out of the raging waves, where those protected (*skepazomenoi*) by Your right hand passed through as one nation, after gazing on marvelous wonders." The fourth LXX use of *episkiazō* is in Prov 18:11, which reads, "The wealth of a rich man is a strong city; and its glory casts a broad shadow" (*mega episkiazei*). This could be understood to imply that the rich man is fortified and protected by the wide extension of his power and influence.[142] The shadow (*skia*) of God's cloud on Mount Zion (Isa 4:5–6),[143] of God's wings (Ps 56 [57]:1), of God's hand (Isa 51:16) and of God's anointed (Lam 4:20) are all symbols of divine protection.[144]

The Syriac and the Christian Palestinian Aramaic versions translate (*episkiasei* in Luke 1:35 by *naggen 'al* (*af'el* of *gnn*, "cover over," "overshadow").[145] The fact that this verb is used in a number of other important New Testament passages, translating quite different Greek verbs (e.g., in John 1:14; Acts 2:26; 5:15; 10:44; 11:15; 2 Cor 12:9) indicates that it was "already established at a very early date in Syriac traditon as a technical term for a specific type of salvific activity on the part of God."[146] This verb appears in the Peshitta Old Testament with God as subject (2 Kings 19:34; 20:6; Isa 31:5; Jer 17:17; Zech 9:15; 12:8; Job 3:23; Wisd 5:16[17]; Sir 34:16; 2 Bar 48:18; 71:1) and with God's hand as direct object (Exod 33:22; Job 1:10; Ps 138:8)— all passages in which the idea of divine protection is uppermost. See also Wisd 19:8, where God's hand is the subject of the verb, and *4 Ezra* 7:122, where the subject is "the glory of the Most High" and the object "those who have lived in chastity." In the Targums the Aramaic verb *'aggên* is found at Exod 12:23, where the context is again that of salvific protection, as well as at Gen 7:16; 15:1; Exod 32:22; Num 10:34; Jonah 4:6, where the context is the same. Even if *'aggên* is best translated as "cover over" or "overshadow,"[147] rather than as "protect," still its connotation is that of protection or defense. My point is that the translators of the Syriac versions of Luke 1:35 chose a verb, *naggen 'al*, which captures this connotation of *episkiasei*—a connotation I think Luke intended.[148]

In my judgment it is also correct to see with Daube a connection between Luke 1:35 and Ruth 3:9 (Ruth's request to Boaz, "Spread your skirt over your maidservant"; LXX: *peribaleis to pterygion sou epi tēn doulēn sou*). Cf. Ruth 2:12 (Boaz's prayer that Ruth will be recompensed by "the God of Israel, under whose wings you have come to take refuge"; LXX: *pros hon ēlthes pepoithenai hypo tas pterygas autou*).[149] The connection is simply one of the motif of protection. But Ruth 3:9 is not alluded to in Luke 1:35, and is not the passage that explains Luke's choice of a verb.[150]

We have seen that Ruth 3:9 was read as having sexual connotations.[151] Is the "overshadowing" in Luke 1:35 open to such an interpretation? Daube claims that Luke, as an innovator or as one following a later-suppressed tradition, read Ruth 3:9 (with 4:12–13) as having to do with some sort of miraculous begetting by God.[152] But there is no evidence that the story of Ruth became the basis of a quasi-sexual interpretation of the verb "to overshadow," much less of belief in a conception without human paternity. Luke 1:35 is less open to sexual interpretation than Matt 1:16, 20.[153] Luke's linking of God's protection and divine sonship brings this New Testament text in line with an important motif in the Hebrew Bible. As McCurley remarks, "It is the role of protection and deliverance rather than sex and procreation which defines Yahweh as Father in regard to king and people."[154]

3. Virgin Daughter of Zion, Virgin Israel

This analysis of Gabriel's words to Mary in Luke 1:35 (as well as the analysis of 1:48, given above) may have some bearing on the question of Marian symbolism in the Lucan narrative. It has been proposed that Luke is evoking the image of the virgin daughter Zion or of virgin Israel in his presentation of Mary, twice called a virgin in 1:27. The first word of the angel to her, *chaire*, appears only four times in the LXX, addressed twice to the daughter of Zion (Zech 9:9; Zeph 3:14; cf. Lam 4:21 [daughter of Idumea; the next verse, 22, addresses the daughter of Zion whose iniquity (*anomia*) has come to an end]; Joel 2:23 [children (*tekna*) of Zion]). The term "virgin" does not appear in these passages from Zechariah, Zephaniah, or Joel, but it is present all through the book of Lamentations. See 5:11 ("they humbled [*etapeinōsan*] the women in Zion, the virgins in the cities of Judah"); 1:4, 15, 18; 2:10, 21. Lam 2:13 resounds as the question other Daughter of Zion passages answer: "Who shall save and comfort you, O virgin Daughter of Zion?" Zeph 3:14–20, an oracle of eschatological consolation for the afflicted, debilitated, rejected Jerusalem, is especially interesting in its similarity to Luke 1:28–33. This similarity has led some critics to suggest Luke's story was composed with the passage from Zephaniah in mind.[155] This text is as follows:

Rejoice (*chaire*), O daughter of Sion;
cry aloud, O daughter of Jerusalem;
rejoice and delight yourself with all your heart,
O daughter of Jerusalem.
The Lord has taken away your iniquities (*adikēmata*);
he has ransomed you from the hand of your enemies.
The Lord, the King of Israel, is in the midst of you.
You shall not see evil any more.
At that time the Lord shall say to Jerusalem,
Be of good courage, Sion;
let not your hands be slack.
The Lord your God is in you.
The Mighty One (*ho dynatos*) will save you.
He will bring joy upon you, and will refresh you
with his love;
and he will rejoice over you with delight
as in a day of feasting.
And I will gather your broken ones.
Alas! who has taken up a reproach (*oneidismon*) against her?
Behold, I will work in you for your sake at that time,
says the Lord.
And I will save her that was oppressed (*ekpepiesmenēn*),
and receive her that was rejected (*apōsmenēn*).
And I will make them a praise,
and honored in all the earth.
And (their enemies) will be ashamed at that time,

when I will deal well with you,
and at the time when I will receive you.
For I will make you honored
and a praise among all the nations of the earth,
when I turn back your captivity before you,
says the Lord.

As Brown points out, "the ravaging of nations and cities by foreign conquerors is often compared to the rape of a virgin, and so most of the specific references to Israel or Zion as a virgin portray her in a state of oppression" (Amos 5:2; Isa 23:12; 37:22; Jer 14:17; 31:3–4 [38:3–4 LXX]). Sometimes she is portrayed as well lusting after foreign lovers and untrue to God (Jer 18:13; 31:12; 46:11). A. Mintz comments well that the serviceableness of the image of Jerusalem in Lamentations as an abandoned, fallen woman "lies in the precise register of pain it articulates. An image of death would have purveyed the false comfort of finality; the dead have finished with suffering, and their agony can be evoked only in retrospect. The raped and defiled woman who survives, on the other hand, is a living witness to a pain that knows no release." In the rhetoric of Lamentations and elsewhere, she is not held to be entirely innocent of complicity in her fate. It is implied that in her glory Zion conducted herself with easy virtue and gave no thought to her end (1:8), "so that what began as unwitting, voluntary promiscuity, suddenly turned into unwished for, forcible defilement."[156]

For Brown, the echoes of the despoiled virgin passages concerning Zion and Israel in the Hebrew Bible are inappropriate as background to Luke's description of Mary. In the Magnificat she is to be identified with those of low estate and the poor; "but she is not oppressed or violated, and is totally faithful (1:45) and obedient to God's word (1:38)."[157] My thesis, however, is that in the tradition Luke inherited and wished to transmit, Mary *was* oppressed and perhaps violated. But I find no clear indication that the Christian annunciation tradition had any implication of her disobedience or infidelity. The Lucan account is careful to avoid any hint of this, and the Matthean, squarely facing the danger of such a charge, appears to acquit Mary.

In my opinion, echoes of the virgin daughter Zion or Israel passages are quite possibly present in Luke. I think they are thematic as well as linguistic,[158] and not confined to only one Old Testament passage. Luke means to evoke the powerful image of the woman oppressed and violated, told finally that her violation is at an end, told to rejoice and proclaim her deliverance. But the image is not a perfect one for Luke; he attempts to evoke the oppression and violation of the virgin without the fallenness usually associated with this image. Mary's oppression can then be seen to parallel the barrenness of Elizabeth, a condition considered without sin.

In line with the promise of protection that is transmitted by Gabriel in 1:35, the virgin daughter symbolism may evoke as well the promises that God will comfort, defend (Isa 23:12 LXX; 37:22), and even "rebuild" his daughter (Jer 38:3–4 LXX). Here may be another aspect of the step-parallelism. As the human agony preceding the birth of Jesus is greater than that preceding John's, so (it is implied) the relief from and reversal of that agony will be greater. Mary's Magnificat echoes and answers the lament of Jerusalem: "Behold, O Lord, my humiliation (*ide Kyrie tēn tapeinōsin mou*), for the enemy has magnified himself" (*emegalynthē;* Lam 1:9). "My soul magnifies (*megalynei*) the Lord . . . for he has regarded the humiliation (*epeblepsen epi tēn tapeinōsin*) of his handmaid" (Luke 1:46, 48).

4. PROMISES CONCERNING THE CHILD

As a consequence of the Holy Spirit "coming upon" and "overshadowing" Mary, the child to be born "will be holy, the Son of God." How is this promise to be understood? The first stage of Gabriel's announcement (vv 32–33) emphasizes Jesus' Davidic descent and his royal destiny. Although the term "messiah" does not appear, these verses suggest that he will fill the role of Davidic Messiah. And more: in v 32, although we have no example in pre-Christian Jewish literature in which the expected Messiah is given such a title, Gabriel says Jesus "will be called the Son of the Most High." This title is paralleled in v 35 by the title Son of God. V 35 complements rather than contradicts vv 32–33.[159]

In a still unpublished Aramaic fragment from Qumran (4Q246), there are some striking parallels to Luke 1:32–33, 35.

In this document, it is said of someone that he "shall be great upon the earth . . . he shall be called [son of] the [g]reat [God], and by his name shall he be named. He shall be hailed (as) the Son of God, and they shall call him Son of the Most High." Destruction reigns "until there arises the people of God." It (or he) will give rest to all, will possess an eternal kingdom, judge the earth with righteousness, and be honored by all. The Great God will be its (or his) help, giving peoples into its (or his) power.[160] It is not clear to whom the text (which does not mention David) refers. The figure may be the son of an enthroned human king, possibly heir to the throne of David; but there is no indication he is messianic. Since detailed discussion of this text must await its full publication, its primary help now for interpreters of Luke 1:32–33, 35 is that it shows that these verses do not exhibit two competing christologies—Palestinian and Hellenistic—as some scholars think. The double theme of Davidic and divine sonship appears in Rom 1:3–4; but there a contrast appears (between flesh and spirit of holiness) which is not present in Luke 1:32–25.[161]

5. DIVINE BEGETTING?

Most critics comment that we have in Luke 1:35, as in Matthew 1:18, 20, a statement about divine begetting, but in Luke without the verb *gennan*.[162] If the parallelism of the verse is respected, the "coming" of the Holy Spirit explains why the child is called holy, and the "overshadowing" by the power of the Most High explains why the child is called Son of God. These divine actions are considered to really (not figuratively) beget the child. "Jesus' conception *is to occur by* the coming of the holy Spirit upon Mary and the power of the Most High overshadowing her (1:35); as a result Jesus will be the Son of God" (emphasis mine).[163] The Holy Spirit is regarded as "the generating cause of Jesus."[164]

But I am not so sure that Luke is thinking of divine begetting, of the *conception* occurring *because of* the coming and overshadowing. More likely, he is thinking of divine protection of the woman who will conceive (or, at the most, of divine empowerment of human begetting). He may have, in fact, intentionally avoided using *gennan* as an active verb or as a theological passive in 1:35.[165] In Acts 17:27b–29a Luke refers to human beings as the *genos* of God (quoting Aratus). But in 17:26, with his use of the verb *to make* (instead of *to beget*) alluding to Gen 1:26–27; 5:1–3, Luke preserves the transcendence of God and avoids the notion that God begets, probably because of its possible sexual connotations.[166] In Luke 1:35, the coming and the overshadowing explain the nature and destiny of the child and his special relationship to God. The emphasis is not on God causing the child's physical existence (in some contrast to Matt 1:18, 20).[167]

In any case, in Luke as in Matthew, there is no implication that divine begetting would be understood sexually, in terms of God or the Holy Spirit mating with Mary. As we have seen, neither of the verbs Luke uses carries that connotation. Moreover, the Jewish traditions drawn on so heavily in both Infancy Narratives neither prepare the reader for such an interpretation, nor allow it within the context of a Jewish understanding of God. Most contemporary scholars, therefore, understand Luke, like Matthew, to be speaking of a new creation.

The claim is made that the coming upon and overshadowing by the Holy Spirit may carry overtones of the Spirit's "hovering" (MT: *měraḥepet;* LXX: *epephereto*) over the waters, over the formless void (Gen 1:1–2), producing life. Mary's womb represents this void. Conception is thought to take place without intercourse, without human paternity, so that the child will be totally God's work.

But allusions to the creation stories in Genesis are as difficult to find in Luke's Infancy Narrative as in Matthew's.[168] Luke does trace Jesus' genealogy to Adam, "the son of God" (*tou theou*) in 3:38. This creates a link between the heavenly announcement at Jesus' baptism that he is God's "beloved Son" (3:22) and the episode that follows the genealogy, that of the testing of Jesus as God's Son (4:1–13: "If you are the Son of God . . ."). What does Luke mean by tracing Jesus' genealogy to Adam and then to God?[169] Some scholars consider this to be evidence that he is thinking of the creation of Adam in Genesis as he writes of the conception of Jesus. Mackey, for example, argues that the literal impact of Luke 1:35 is that the coming of the Spirit at Jesus' conception makes that a virginal conception and makes the conceived God's Son, but Mackey has difficulty in understanding what exactly is being conveyed. Ruling out the idea that the Holy

Spirit acts as the male principle in the conception of Jesus, he hazards a guess that Luke is thinking of the Spirit supplying

what was necessary to the embryonic Jesus by an act such as creation out of nothing. Jesus' being God's son *as a result of this act* (see Luke's "therefore") could then mean only what Luke meant when he calls Adam "the son of God" in his genealogy of Jesus (Luke 3:38)—for to call Adam God's son there presumably refers to the belief that Adam was created by God (out of nothing, or out of "dust") and not derived in the normal way from parents.[170]

Or, to put it in a different way: the title Son of God, used for Adam in 3:38 and for the risen Christ in Acts 13:33, may be used for one who lives because of God's direct, creative intervention; and thus these texts are used to illuminate Luke 1:35.[171] Neither Genesis nor Luke links the creation of Adam with the action of God's Spirit.[172] Further, the verbs *to come upon* and *to overshadow* are never used in a creation setting. And Jesus is not created out of nothing but is born of a woman.

Adam may be mentioned in the Lucan genealogy not in order to underline the manner of Jesus' conception in an act of new creation, but for other reasons, none of them mutually exclusive.[173] Luke may be stressing the unity of the whole human race, descended from a common founder, a belief the Greeks did not have. He may be showing Jesus' relation to humanity's whole history as well as to the whole history of his people. Calling Adam "Son of God" perhaps emphasizes the divine origin of the human race, (a popular Hellenistic philosophical view known to Luke) rather than (or, as well as) the divine origin of the individual Jesus.[174] Luke may here envision Jesus' relation to all humanity as Son of God. The Adam-God relationship is indeed like that of Jesus and Joseph, in that neither Jesus nor Adam was sexually begotten by his "father" in the genealogy—Joseph and God. When Luke adds the phrases "as was supposed" in 3:23 at the beginning of his genealogy, and "of God" at 3:38 at the end of his genealogy, he calls attention "to more than one kind of sonship-paternity in the genealogy."[175] What about the creative aspect of God's fatherhood of Adam: does it have any bearing on God's relationship with Jesus? Luke can speak of Adam as God's son, think of Adam as "made" by God's creative power (see Acts 17:24); but this creative activity to Luke's mind "makes" all of humanity from one [human, Adam] (17:26). Luke seems to be thinking not of how Adam is different from all his descendants except Jesus, but of how having Adam as ancestor makes all (including Jesus) one.[176]

For the above reasons, mention of the Holy Spirit in Luke 1:35 and of Adam in 3:38 seems too slim a support for the new creation theory as an explanation of Gabriel's words in 1:35. Instead, I think Luke is insisting that the involvement of the Holy Spirit in this pregnancy means that the quality and power of holiness will be extended to this child. Luke knows and uses elsewhere the tradition of Jesus as "the holy one of God" (4:34; par. Mark 1:24), and of Jesus as "the holy and righteous one" (Acts 3:14), as God's "holy servant" (or: child [pais]; Acts 4:27, 30), the holy one who was nevertheless executed as a criminal (Acts 2:27; 13:35). We have seen that earlier Jewish tradition, which associated God with human begetting, still considered illegitimate children as bearing the curse of their parents. The involvement of the Holy Spirit means also for Luke that this child, recognized and nurtured by no biological father, will be Son of God.

Luke is undoubtedly aware of the early christological formulation and thought pattern exemplified in Rom 1:3–4, containing the four elements: Son of God, power, Spirit of holiness, and Davidic descent.[177] The first three elements were early associated with the resurrection of Jesus and are found here in Luke 1:35 (the fourth element appears in vv 32–33). What Luke has done is to push the christological affirmation back to Jesus' conception, affirming that Jesus was holy and was Son of God "not only at his conception, but through his conception."[178] Matthew also retrojects this christology. But he has not in his Infancy Narrative said anything about the holiness of Jesus, nor has he explicitly linked the divine Sonship of Jesus with the action of the Holy Spirit. These are distinctive Lucan interpretations of the tradition he inherited.

6. CONCLUSION

The words of Gabriel in Luke 1:35 "could tolerate the meaning that the Spirit's role would be one of endowing the child with a special character suiting him to bear the title Son of God."[179] If v 35 is treated by itself, several critics find it possible to interpret it of an ordinary human conception. Taylor, for example, argues there is much that is attractive in such an interpretation. "The words may be said to speak of the Holy Ghost who should come upon Mary to inspire and preserve the purity of her soul in the act of conception.[180] They may speak, that is to say, of God's use of His own appointed agencies." Taylor regards this interpretation as untenable, however, since in his opinion and that of others it would be necessary to regard Mary's protest in v 34 as a later, post-Lucan insertion, an option he correctly rules out.[181] But v 35 cannot be treated in isolation, if the aim is to understand Luke's intention. The interpretation I have offered above of Mary's words in v 34 and their logic is compatible with an interpretation of v 35 as concerning a biologically normal conception.

How v 35 is understood turns on how the parallelism of the two conceptions in Luke 1 is understood. For those who think that the step-parallelism in the two announcements demands a miraculous divine intervention and has to result in a conception more extraordinary than John's—hence in a virginal conception—the words of Gabriel in v 35 express that meaning, virginal conception, or are fully compatible with it. Due to the creative power of the Spirit, the child will be no man's son at all; rather, he will be Son of God. Divine paternity replaces human paternity. New creation replaces sexual begetting. The child to be born, then, holy and Son of God, will be as extraordinary and unique as his origin.

But as I have interpreted the parallelism, no such leap is necessary—from (a) enabling conception in the barren woman to (b) creating a fetus in a virgin, dispensing with the role of the male. Both conceptions (by Elizabeth and by Mary) are due to sexual intercourse, and both are empowered by the creative activity of God. But here in 1:35 the terms "holy" and "Son of God" do carry special meaning. This child will be holy because the Holy Spirit will come upon his mother, and she will experience divine protection and empowerment even in a situation deemed unholy. This child, unholy in human estimation, will be holy before God. Like "every male that opens the womb," he will be called holy to the Lord (2:23). That is, he will be considered sacred, will be set apart and consecrated to the service of God.[182] The child will be called the Son of the Most High and Son of God because the power of the Most High will overshadow his mother. He will enter the world as Son of God because God says so: God in effect declares him to be son, accepts him as son, anticipating 3:22.[183] Divine paternity, then, does not replace human paternity. Fitzmyer was correct to argue that the two verbs used in v 35 "are, at most, figurative expressions for the mysterious intervention of God's Spirit and power which will be responsible for the divine and messianic character of this child. The figurative use of these verbs here obviously does not exclude the idea of a miraculous conception; but they do not say it either, least of all in an exclusive sense implying no human intervention."[184] The promises to Mary of empowerment and protection and the promises to her son are intertwined, embedded in each other.

In Greco-Roman biographies, stories of miraculous or marvelous conceptions functioned to explain the hero's later greatness. In a similar way, the story Luke told, of divine involvement in Jesus' conception, set the stage and provided an explanation for Jesus' extraordinary earthly life. Jesus was what he was because of this involvement. The whole structure of Luke's presentation of the life of Jesus resembles in some significant ways the biography of an immortal,[185] or (in broader terms) the Greco-Roman superstar paradigm.[186] Luke's Jesus has an extraordinary conception, lives the life of a benefactor of humanity, dies a martyr's death, and is translated into the heavens. His work is continued in the work of his disciples and followers. "There is no way a Mediterranean person could have missed [Luke's presentation] as a portrayal of Jesus in the mythology of the immortals. . . . If the converts in Luke's church came from the Greco-Roman world where philosophers were sometimes described as divine men who became immortals, then the Lucan picture of Jesus is intelligible."[187]

It is widely held that Luke himself was a Gentile Christian (that is, one converted to Christianity from paganism, not from Judaism).[188] His writings are evidence that he received a good Hellenistic education, was acquainted with Hellenistic literary techniques and patterns, as well as with the literary traditions of the Greek Bible. He was challenged to interpret the significance of Jesus the Jew probably for a Gentile Christian audience (or one that was predominantly Gentile Christian) in a predominantly Gentile setting.[189] Luke intended to show his readers how similar as well as how dissimilar Jesus was to the heroes and immortals from antiquity of whom they knew. The extraordinary conception of Jesus in Luke is no miraculous conception such as those found in traditions about divine begetting in non-Jewish literature roughly contemporaneous with the New Testament narratives and/or possibly available to the evangelists. With his choice of verbs in 1:35, Luke guarded against an interpretation of Jesus' origin as the result of a *hieros gamos*. But with his close, causal association in this verse of the action of the Holy Spirit with the holiness and divine Sonship of Jesus ("*therefore* the child to be born will be . . ."), Luke stressed the divine dimension of Jesus' origin, character, and destiny. So-called pagan "parallels" provided a context in which Luke grasped and presented the specialness of Jesus. But, as we will see in chapter 4, evocation of the "parallels" led to interpretations of his narrative (and Matthew's) that Luke did not foresee or intend.

E. MARY'S CONSENT (V 38)

1. LUCAN INNOVATION

Mary's response to Gabriel's message is consent: "Behold, I am the handmaid (or slave: *doulē*) of the Lord; let it happen to me according to your word" (*genoito moi kata to rēma sou*).[190] This element of consent is quite odd in an annunciation narrative. In none of the ten Old Testament texts classified above as annunciation scenes does the recipient of the message finally give consent. Nor is consent given by Joseph in Matthew 1, or by Zechariah in Luke's other annunciation scene. Two texts are interesting to compare to Luke 1:38 in this regard. In 2 Kings 4:16 the Shunammite woman expresses disbelief or fear of believing when Elisha tells her that she will conceive: "No, my lord, O man of God; do not lie to your maidservant" (LXX: *doulē*). The reaction of Hannah in 1 Samuel 1 comes closest to Mary's reaction in Luke: to Eli's prayer or blessing that the God of Israel grant her petition, she replies, "Let your maidservant (LXX: *doulē*) find favor in your eyes." Then she "went away and ate, and her face was no longer sad" (v 18). Belief or hope in Eli's words has relieved her anguish. But this is not consent.

Attention should be drawn in this regard to the words of Ruth to Boaz (Ruth 3:9): "I am Ruth your handmaid (LXX: *doulē*); therefore spread your wing over your handmaid" (*doulē*). What appears in both Old Testament passages is the linking of a woman's self-understanding as servant or slave with the image of her as protected. The difference is that Ruth calls herself Boaz's handmaid and says "therefore" protect me, while Mary receives a promise of protection and then calls herself the Lord's handmaid. But, as we have seen, it is not likely Luke is directly alluding to or building on the story of Ruth. Moreover, Ruth in 3:9 is simply responding to Boaz's startled question "Who are you?" And she is requesting, not consenting.

2. THE COMMISSIONING OF MARY

Several critics have noted the the dialogical style of the Lucan annunciation to Mary echoes aspects of prophetic commissions or calls.[191] Hubbard analyzes a wide range of Hebrew Bible pericopes of commissioning and isolates seven formal components: (1) introduction; (2) confrontation between the deity/commissioner and the commissioned; (3) reaction to the presence of the holy by way of an action expressing fear or unworthiness; (4) commission; (5) protest, the claim that the commissioned is unable or unworthy to accomplish the commission, or questioning of the word of deity/commissioner; (6) reassurance by the deity/commissioner; (7) conclusion, more or less formal, most often the statement that the one commissioned starts to carry out the commission.[192] The reaction and the protest are the two elements that appear with the least frequency, but one or the other is usually found in a commissioning account.

Hubbard reads Luke 1:26–38 as the commissioning of Mary to be the mother of the Messiah. He lays out the structure of the passage, with a two-stage commission, in this way: (1) introduction vv 26–27; (2) confrontation v 28; (3) reaction v 29; (4) reassurance v 30; (5) commission vv 31–33; (6) protest v 34; (6)

commission v 35; (7) reassurance vv 36–37; (8) conclusion vv 38–39 ("Mary accepts her role and the angel departs").[193] For Soares Prabhu, the Lucan story is a call narrative in which a birth oracle—with its triple proclamation of the conception and birth, the name-giving, and the future destiny of a child to be born— *replaces* the commissioning. More accurately, I think, the birth oracle *is* the commissioning, as he recognizes when he speaks of Mary's "call."[194] But in my opinion, Mullins's analysis most deftly captures the Lucan blend of the annunciation and the commission forms.[195] (1), (2), (3) are as Hubbard lays them out above. But for Mullins the other elements of the scene are as follows: (4) commission vv 30–33: the prediction of the birth of Jesus and commission to call his name Jesus; (5) protest v 34; (6) reassurance vv 35–37: in response to Mary's protest in v 34, Gabriel promises the presence of the Holy Spirit, a holy child, and Elizabeth's child as a sign; (7) v 38: Mary accepts the commission, the angel departs.[196] So where Hubbard sees Mary's commission in two separate stages, Mullins sees one stage, reading vv 35–37 as I have, as a reassurance. These verses function mainly as a promise to Mary that she will be invested with divine power and protection, and as a reprise of the message of vv 30–33 only in that description of the nature of the child and of his relationship with God (the christology) is advanced and the description enhanced.

This scene can indeed be seen as a commissioning of Mary to be mother, and Mary is presented as accepting the commission with faith. Like the disciples who are said to leave all and follow Jesus (see 5:11; 18:28–29), her response is immediate and unconditional. But Luke's Mary voices here more than her consent to motherhood. She has just heard from Gabriel what amounts to a postresurrection proclamation of Christian faith (in 1:32, 33, 35), and in this sense (at the level of the written gospel, not of history) she is the first to hear and believe the good news. She is depicted by Luke as the ideal disciple, the one who hears the word of God and does it (8:21: "My mother and my brothers are those who hear the word of God and do it"; cf. 8:15: those in the good soil are "those who, hearing the word, hold it fast in an honest and good heart, and bring forth fruit with patience"). In other words, she "meets the criterion of the escha-

tological family which Jesus will call together."[197] Luke will make
clear that her blessedness rests on her hearing and doing rather
than on the fact of her biological motherhood (11:27–28). It is
in the scene of the annunciation to her that he begins to make
this point.

Too much should not be made of a distinction between a commission to keep the word, and a commission or sending to relay
the word.[198] Mary's Magnificat does relay the word, if not in a
public sense. One could say that without an explicit commission
to preach, she preaches as though she were commissioned. The
child's mission (cf. Jer 1:4–5) is given along with that of his
mother. The form of this pericope is a distinctively mixed one,
and analysis of both elements of that mixture (and of the ways
Luke innovates with those elements) elucidates the text in significant ways.

3. CONSENT TO MIRACLE?

The presence and wording of Mary's consent may be reasons
(not always articulated) behind the strong opinion that "Luke
intends to tell us about a miracle. There is no question about
that."[199] This is so because the consent in 1:38 is reminiscent of
sayings of Jesus linking the miraculous actions of God to the
suppliant's faith, sayings that (like Luke 1:38) contain some form
of the verb *ginesthai*. These sayings, however, are all Matthean
and have no Lucan parallel; Matt 8:13 ("be it done for you as
you have believed"); 9:29 ("according to your faith be it done to
you"); 15:28 ("O woman, great is your faith! Be it done for you
as you desire"); 18:19 ("if two of you agree on earth about anything they ask, it will be done for them by my Father in heaven");
21:21, par. Mark 11:23 ("If you say . . . 'Be taken up . . .' it will
be done"). Matthew shapes his miracle stories as conversations
climaxing in Jesus' sayings about faith, to illustrate the principle
that faith and miracle belong together.[200] But Luke's treatment
of the miracles in the ministry of Jesus does not exhibit these
traits, which in turn cannot be used to interpret the Lucan annunciation story. Luke does believe that miracles are related to
faith,[201] though to have experienced a miracle is not the same
thing as having faith. He may have the most positive attitude of
the evangelists toward miracles.[202]

4. CONSENT AND FAITH

It may be objected that Mary's consent in 1:38 is prime evidence against the theory proposed here—that Luke inherited and passed down a tradition of the illegitimate conception of Jesus, alluding to the law in Deut 22:23–27, which concerns the seduction or rape of a betrothed virgin. That law, and the situation I think is implied in Luke, as in Matthew, have to do with sexual relations without the woman's consent or without her full consent. How can we hold that Luke presents Mary as consenting to such a situation, or God as asking for her consent? Admittedly, this objection is extremely important, perhaps the most important one that can be raised. But raising it leads us to further insight into the peculiarities of the Lucan narrative, peculiarities that in fact can serve to support my reading.

First, notice that although Mary is consenting in 1:38 to a future pregnancy and motherhood, she is not depicted as consenting to the act that will cause the pregnancy. That act is never mentioned or discussed. As we have seen, her question "How?" remains unanswered, as does Zechariah's question in the previous scene. Gabriel's response in v 35 sidesteps her question: Gabriel does not specify how Mary will become pregnant, but promises the presence of the Holy Spirit, especially in terms of divine empowerment and protection of her.

Second, the objection requires us to look more carefully at the elements of the commissioning form found in the pericope. Mary's verbal acceptance, her consent, is a Lucan innovation when we read the scene as a commissioning as well as when we read it as an annunciation and as a blend of the two forms. In none of the twenty-seven Hebrew Bible commissionings, none of the ten nonbiblical accounts, none of the fifteen other commissionings in Luke-Acts, and of the nine other New Testament commissionings analyzed by Hubbard are the commissioned ones depicted as assenting verbally and directly to their commission.[203] (The near-exception that proves the rule is Isaiah's volunteering for service in Isa 6:8: "Behold, here I am, send me." But he has not yet been directly commissioned. Jacob's consent to his commissioning in Gen 28:20–21 is really more of a bargain: Jacob "made a vow saying, 'If God will be with me, and will keep me in this way that I go, and will give me bread to eat and clothing to wear, so that I come again to my father's house in peace, then the Lord shall be my God. . . .' ") Neither is consent expressed in the commissionings in the apocalyptic tradition that Hubbard mentions: Dan 10:2–12:4; *1 Enoch* 14–16; *Test. Levi* 2–5; *2 Esdras* 14; *2 Baruch* 1–5.[204] Also, the disciples in the gospels do not verbalize their consent to the call of Jesus.[205] In each of the stories of the call to discipleship, where the commissioned one's consent is dramatized, this is simply by means of the statement that he or she began to act in obedience to the commission.[206]

So Luke is again innovating, here by injecting an unexpected element into his narrative and in fact climaxing the narrative with this element. What is the point of this Lucan innovation? Is it merely a way of underlining belief in Mary's conscious and active faith, her model discipleship? Surely this is his intention, and it is the effect he achieves. And it is consistent with Luke's protrait of Mary during the ministry of Jesus and after the resurrection. Mary is a believer for whom God's word is enough.

But why does Luke innovate in this way, that is, why is his portrait of her so positive? He may have inherited a positive tradition, which placed Mary in the early church community. The basic affirmation in Acts 1:14, that she belonged to the early church, is "scarcely the product of [Luke's] wishful thinking."[207] A positive depiction of her as a believing disciple is given also in the Fourth Gospel's crucifixion scene; this is corroborating evidence of a development in the assessment of Mary in the pregospel period, an assessment that found its way quite differently into the gospels of Luke and John. On this tradition, Luke based his redaction of the ministry accounts in which Mary appears (see his redaction of Mark 3:20–21, 31–35),[208] and the tradition also influenced his Infancy Narrative. This positive tradition may reflect belief in the innocence of the mother of the Messiah. Luke's presentation can also be seen as his attempt to further defuse the illegitimacy tradition[209] by making Mary one whose pregnancy is God-empowered, God-protected, and by making her the first disciple. Focusing directly on her, and perhaps attempting to rehabilitate her from charges of scandalous immorality, he deals with the story of the conception of Jesus quite differently than Matthew does.

5. THE ANNUNCIATION AND THE AGONY

But there is more to understand here. Mary's response in 1:38, that it may happen to her according to Gabriel's (and therefore God's) word, corresponds to the prayer of Jesus just before his arrest, the prayer that God's will be done (22:42: "not my will but yours be done"). In Luke's account, only the verb *ginomai* links the two sayings linguistically (in Luke 1:38 *genoito*, the aorist optative; in Luke 22:42 *ginesthō*, the present imperative).[210] The connection I see is thematic and dramatic as well. Luke's Mary consents fully and with courageous trust at the beginning of the Gospel, as Jesus later will near the end, to an obscure future. The Latin Vulgate translation strengthens this connection, rendering 1:38 as *fiat mihi secundum verbum tuum*, and 22:42 as *non mea voluntas sed tua fiat* (cf. *fiat voluntas tua* in Matt 6:10). Soares Prabhu[211] laments the Vulgate translation of 1:38 as having led to translations that falsely suggest a resigned and submissive acceptance on the part of Mary, rather than a tone of joy and earnest desire. The resignation in 1:38, however, is apparent to other commentators.[212] The element of joy critics find in v 38 is read backwards from Mary's next words in Luke, the opening line of her Magnificat (1:47: "My spirit has found gladness in God my Savior").

But it is better to hold separate these two scenes, between which the pregnancy occurs in Lucan silence. If, however, Mary's consent in 1:38 is read as a statement of passive submission and resignation, then how can the change of tone and new energy found in her Magnificat be accounted for? We must look more carefully at the scene in which two women meet. Between the annunciation to Mary and her Magnificat occurs Mary's visit to Elizabeth, her greeting of Elizabeth, and Elizabeth's response. Visual artists have long recognized the dramatic importance of this woman-to-woman scene. The critic may recognize here in Luke's narrative an empowerment and illumination of Mary through Elizabeth's confirmation of the promise, and her bonding with Mary. Elizabeth pays tribute to and affirms Mary's faith, her trust in God's promise.[213]

The annunciation and the agony are the Gospel's central and critical moments of choice and decision. "By her lucid and unconditional acceptance of her 'mission,' Mary, like her Son, makes herself authentically 'servant,' in one of those great self-constituting decisions that give shape to a human life."[214]

But if Luke did intend a connection between the two scenes, it seems that he has obscured it by omitting from the second the saying in Mark 14:36 ("Abba, Father, all things are possible to you" [*panta dynata soi*]). This could have evoked for the reader Gabriel's words in Luke 1:37 ("nothing will be impossible with God" [*ouk adynatēsei para tou theou pan rēma*]). Perhaps Luke has shifted this idea backwards from the scene of the agony as he found it in Mark to the annunciation scene, and worded it so that it becomes more clearly an answer to the question asked of Abraham in Genesis 18:14, and a motivation to total trust. Even though Luke, according to the two-source theory, had access to the Gospel of Mark, in this section of his passion narrative he may be following another source,[215] which did not contain the saying in Mark 14:36.

Another aspect shared by the two Lucan pericopes, the annunciation and the agony, merits our attention. This is the appearance in both of an angel. In many manuscripts, some ancient, there is the statement that during Jesus' prayer "there appeared to him an angel from heaven, strengthening him. And being in an agony he prayed more earnestly; and his sweat became like great drops of blood falling down upon the ground" (22:43–44). Opinion is divided about the authenticity of these verses.[216] If they are authentic, the presence of an angel may be Luke's way of signaling a connection between the two pericopes. If they are not authentic, the presence of the angel may indicate that a later interpolator saw some connection. Angels appear in Luke's Gospel only in his Infancy Narrative, in the scene of the agony, and at the empty tomb.[217] In the annunciation to Mary, Gabriel promises empowerment and protection; in the scene of the agony, the angel strengthens.[218] Both human characters are facing the major crises of their lives. And only in these scenes are characters depicted as expressing total acceptance of God's will.

If Luke does intend the scene of Jesus' agony to evoke the scene of the annunciation to Mary, it can be argued that we have another indication that in spite of the joy and calm of this annunciation scene (recognized by artists down through the centuries), there is an underlying note of struggle. Joy and calm do not come cheaply in Luke, even here. And Mary's consent no more condones violence than Jesus' consent condones the execution of the crucifixion. Consent is to God's protection/salvation, not to the humiliation from which God protects/saves. Consent is to empowerment in the midst of humiliation. These passages depict the two great moments in the New Testament of human acceptance of the divine will to overcome: in Jesus' case, God's will to overcome death; in Mary's case, God's will to overcome sexual humiliation. Jesus' agony facing death was one that Luke could openly write about; Mary's agony was one that he could not or would not. Luke's dilemma here is that he cannot have Mary consent with foreknowledge, precisely because in his understanding of the tradition he is trying to pass on, the conception occurs against her will, and she is innocent of complicity. In constrast, Jesus in his agony knowingly faces arrest and death, as Luke tells it. Jesus, of course, is also victimized against his will; his death is an execution, not a suicide. But it is easier to present the innocent martyr not resisting his death than to hand down the tradition about the innocent woman Mary and her illegitimate pregnancy.

6. MARY AS SERVANT OR SLAVE

Mary's response in 1:38, her characterization of herself as the servant or slave (*doulē*) of the Lord, may be the text most responsible for the understanding of her by some as a passive, colorless character, the antithesis of a liberated woman—ecclesiastical statements to the contrary.[219] Her person and fate have been regarded as subsumed into that of her son, her own will, autonomy, and initiative abdicated. She is seen as subordinated to God, his representatives, and her own son. Is Mary's consent Luke's way of setting her up as a model, *the* model, for submissive feminine behavior, and of articulating an acceptance of patriarchal belief in female inferiority, dependency, and helplessness?[220]

She calls herself a slave, a term referring to those of the lowest social position within the Israelite, Jewish, and Christian communities.[221] The slave was commonly believed to exist on a lower level of humanity and was unable to own property or have a family or a genealogy in the proper sense. A slave had no rights at law and, regarded as ethically inferior, was subject to cultic obligations and the law only to a limited extent. Slavery is service that is not a matter of choice but subjection to the alien will of an owner.

The term *doulē* (feminine) always and everywhere carries associations that *doulos* (masculine) does not: associations of sexual use and abuse.[222] Slavery (whether a literal socioeconomic, historical reality or a religious metaphor) means something different for women and for men. A male slave in a man's world has a different experience in any age, from a female slave in a man's world. She sinks lower, and the very boundaries of her personhood and her bodily/psychic safety are more endangered. Gentiles understood *doulē kyriou* in Luke 1:38 as "slave of her master," an interpretation that some scholars think may have given rise to the slander that Mary was a concubine.[223] Familiarity with the words of Luke 1:38 should not desensitize us to their shock value in a world where slavery was a recognized fact of everyday life, even though the pious in Judaism had begun to refer to themselves as God's slaves (see below). That shock and distaste can be felt by those today who recognize the slavery that exists in our own world.

Because of Greek rejection of and scorn for slavery, the Greek usage of the word group, with few exceptions, had no connection with the religious sphere. But in Judaism and the mystery religions, slavery came to describe the relationship of dependence and service in which human beings stand to God. Already in the Holiness Code we find the source of this religious idea in the biblical framework: Yahweh speaks of the poor Israelites who should not be enslaved: "For they are my slaves, whom I brought forth out of the land of Egypt; they shall not be sold as slaves" (Lev 25:42). The paradox is a strange one: the God who sets slaves free, frees them to be slaves to God. There is an enslavement to the God who liberates slaves. But of fundamental importance here for real social revolution are the insights that each person among the people of Israel was originally a slave who had been set free; and that the real "ruler" is one who frees the oppressed and yet is a servant. Changes in existing conditions "are understood as a liberation wrought by God's servanthood."[224]

New Testament talk of slavery can also emphasize the unconditional nature of human responsibility to God, describing an inescapable state of affairs. Slaves were integrated into the Christian community, regarded as standing in the same relationship to Christ as the free members (see Philem 16; 1 Cor 12:13; Gal 3:28; Col 3:11). But in spite of the baptismal tradition found in Gal 3:26–28, the institution of slavery was not repudiated in the New Testament. (Only) in Christ, who took the form of a slave (Phil 2:7), there was no slave or free. The language of slavery and servanthood to God was appropriated to convey belief in the spiritual freedom of Jesus and the Christian from the powers of the world.

Luke's choice of the term *doulē* in 1:38 and 1:48 (cf. 2:29)[225] surely is intended to have a positive dimension. It must be seen in connection to Jewish use of the honorary title *doulos,* usually in the phrase *doulos theou* (slave of God), for a few outstanding men of Israelite history: Moses (Mal 4:4; Josephus, *Ant.* 5.39; see Rev 15:3); Joshua (Josh 24:29; Judg 2:8); Abraham (Ps 104:42); David (Ezek 34:23; 37:24; Ps 88:3); Isaac (Dan 3:35); the prophets (4 Kings 17:23); Jacob = Israel as the people of God (Isa 48:20; Ezek 28:25; cf. Isa 65:9; Josephus, *Ant.* 11.90, 101 on the Jews) and *doulē* for one woman, Hannah (1 Sam 1:11). Luke means to associate Mary with these figures, believed to have been totally committed to God. He associates her also with Jesus, whom he portrays as among the disciples as one who serves (*ho diakonōn;* 22:27) but whom he does not call *doulos.*

Luke 1:38, 48 are also linked by the term *doulē* to the citation of Joel 2:28–32 in Acts 2:17–18: "And in the last days it shall be, God declares, that I will pour out my Spirit upon all flesh, and your sons and your daughters shall prophesy, and your young men shall see visions, and your old men shall dream dreams; yes, and on my menservants (*doulous*) and my maidservants (*doulas*) in those days I will pour out my Spirit." Luke adds, "and they shall prophesy" (as Mary does in her Magnificat). These associations with the term *doulē* show us the powerful religious context Luke means to evoke in 1:38. We can be certain that he means her consent to be an expression of her freedom and courage. But how is this to be understood within the context of the story he tells? As Ruether remarks, servanthood langauge changes its meaning radically in different contexts.[226]

In the traditional interpretation of Luke 1, involving a virginal conception, Mary's consent is read as consent to the miracle that will preserve her "purity," her sexual innocence and inexperience. This is seen to have religious value, in that her virginity is the "void" in which God's new creation is brought into existence; her consent provides the opportunity for this "action" of God and is a response to the grace of God. Mary's description of herself as a slave of the Lord would express the "vessel's" sense of powerlessness and nothingness.

But within the context of the interpretation offered here, Mary's consent is to a conception whose origin, she has protested, can or will not be marital relations with Joseph.[227] She assents even though her question about how the pregnancy will come about is not answered. She consents, in other words, in ignorance of her specific fate, but in trust that she will be empowered and protected by God.[228] Awkwardly, Luke makes Mary a victim of forces unknown to her. Having her call herself the slave of the Lord expresses the powerlessness and suffering of the victim, but also her inner freedom from human "masters."

F. CONCLUSION AND RESPONSE

Luke, like Matthew, hands down the tradition of the illegitimate conception of Jesus. The basis of this statement is (a) the fact that Luke's first chapter can be and has been read as being about a pregnancy that occurs in a normal, nonmiraculous fashion; and (b) Luke's subsequent statement (3:23) that Joseph was only thought to be the father of Jesus. Thus Luke presupposes on the part of his reader some awareness of the tradition of Jesus' illegitimacy, and he discreetly confirms this awareness.

Once we realize this, several small details in the text fall into place and are seen to support and interpret the tradition. For example, Luke alludes to Deut 22:23–27 and refers in the Magnificat to Mary's "humiliation." Mary's question about how the pregnancy will occur goes unanswered, but she is promised divine empowerment and protection. My claim is that this reading explains the details of the text better than, or at least as well as, the traditional interpretation.

At first glance my reading of Luke is less pursuasive than the reading of Matthew presented in chapter 2. This is so because in at least four ways Luke has obscured and nearly obliterated the tradition of illegitimacy that he inherited. (1) He has reinterpreted it primarily with the help of Septuagint and Baptist birth-annunciation models. These are less adequate (although more obvious) vehicles for the tradition than the stories of the four women alluded to in Matthew's genealogy, and perhaps even than Isa 7:14. These primary models Luke uses stress that God enables the barren woman to conceive, and thus they are an opening toward the idea of a supernatural, miraculous, or extraordinary conception. In contrast, Matthew's insertion of the names of the four women into his genealogy, evoking their stories, stresses God's siding with the oppressed woman within the normal workings of history. Matthew also uses the annunciation form but integrates it with these and other Hebrew Bible traditions in such a way that it does not evoke so strongly the stories of barren women conceiving.

(2) Luke has adapted the annunciation form, blending it with a commission form, and added to it the unusual element of Mary's consent. This element of consent makes it almost—but not totally—impossible for the reader of this Gospel alone to understand that this pregnancy is illegitimate and perhaps the result of violence done to Mary. The important narrative moment of her consent to the pregnancy undercuts the tradition in a serious fashion, and it is that aspect of the New Testament narratives most responsible for the Christian erasure of the tradition. If the illegitimacy tradition concerned an act in any way against Mary's will (as it may have), then Luke's choice to dramatize her consent appears to deny the tradition, or at least to whitewash it.[229] But that impression is not the whole story. I

think Luke is trying to present the tradition in such a positive fashion that he comes close to denying it.

Mary's consent serves two related purposes. First, it illustrates Luke's belief in the holiness of the mother—something the Matthean narrative did not do. Second, it partakes of that impulse that operated in the fashioning of the Mount of Olives tradition. In consenting to the will of God, Jesus is not suicidal, nor is his impending execution condoned or attributed directly to the will of God. Similarly in Luke 1, Mary's consent to this pregnancy neither acquiesces in nor condones a crime; no evil is attributed to the will of God. But here is consent without an agony, because it is consent to conception without any statement of the means or situation in which it takes place. Only clues are left in the text to help the reader face that situation. Luke's allusion to Deut 22:23–27 is light, and no effort to interpret or apply the law is depicted. Mary is cast in the role of the first Christian disciple: she is one who responds with alacrity to the will of God, who learns only slowly the suffering that her response demands, and who matures by pondering and attempting to understand.

(3) Attention has been drawn to the images of sanctity and purity with which Luke surrounds Jesus' origins, and to the theology that Jesus came from the pious Anawim, who fulfill all legal and cultic obligations and who accept Jesus (contrast the rejection at Nazareth; 4:16–30). Those images, if understood superficially, do create a narrative atmosphere of delicacy, restraint, and "perfection" that threatens to smother the illegitimacy tradition and the prophetic dimension of Luke's work. In addition, if the tradition is to be grasped, the reader must initially resist the dominant mood Luke creates of joy and serenity. Ultimately, those images and that mood can be seen as ways of interpreting, not negating, the tradition.

(4) Further, the structure of Luke's presentation of the life of Jesus in his Gospel as a whole would lead the reader of Gentile Greco-Roman background to see Jesus—with some reservations, of course—as an immortal, and possibly to understand his conception in terms of a *hieros gamos*. In his presentation, Luke intended primarily to appeal to readers of this background (which was likely his own). He took the risk that Jesus' origins would

be misunderstood, for the sake of communication with that audience.

Luke took the risk of misunderstanding also, I think, because he aimed to defuse the inherited tradition of illegitimacy. The potential scandal of Jesus' origins, like the scandal of his death, was toned down by Luke in an effort to convey the "good news," power, and respectability of the Christian message. There is a similar tendency in the Lucan Passion Narrative. The Lucan Jesus goes to his death healing (22:51), forgiving (23:34), comforting others (23:43). Luke omits the Marcan cry of abandonment (Mark 15:34) and has Jesus die peacefully citing Ps 31:6, entrusting his spirit into the hands of God his Father (Luke 23:46).[230] This Jesus is not a victim, not out of control, and not subject to fear, terror, or doubt; on the contrary, he is the almost superhuman martyr who practices virtue and single-hearted dedication to God. About the crucifixion, C. K. Barrett writes, "The fact is that Luke stands far enough from the historical Jesus to have digested the raw, perplexing traditions which stand in Mark in all their crudity and offensiveness, and to have made them something less scandalous, and more easily assimilable."[231] According to Käsemann, "the Cross of Jesus is no longer a scandal but only a misunderstanding on the part of the Jews which the intervention of God at Easter palpably and manifestly corrects."[232] Conzelmann finds "no trace of any Passion mysticism" and thinks no direct soteriological significance is drawn by Luke from Jesus' suffering and death.[233] Fitzmyer admits that Luke has no story of "the Cross" in a Pauline or Marcan sense and that Luke attaches more saving significance to the resurrection than to the cross; still, only Luke depicts Jesus as a suffering Messiah (24:26), and this depiction is Luke's way of presenting the saving significance of Jesus' death.[234] So also the "raw, perplexing traditions" of Jesus' illegitimate origin are transmuted Luke 1 in a scene of serenity, even triumph. For Luke, Jesus' and Mary's persons have absorbed the scandal (2:34–35).[235]

This understanding of Luke's first chapter thus causes us to revise our understanding of other parts of this Gospel and/or to find that they throw light on Luke's intentions and methods in chapter 1.[236] Only a few further suggestions can be sketched here.

In his second chapter,[237] Luke picks up the major theme of the first: great joy in this child, now spoken of as "a savior . . . Christ the Lord" (2:11), "the Lord's Christ" (2:26), "a light for revelation to the Gentiles and for glory to [God's] people Israel" (2:32). A note of anxiety and anguish is also struck in this chapter, in the words of Simeon to Mary: "Look, this child is marked for the fall and the rise of many in Israel, to be a symbol that will be rejected—indeed, a sword shall pierce you too—so that the thoughts of many minds may be laid bare" (1:34–35).[238] Luke may intend this saying to refer to the scandal of Jesus' origins, the suffering caused by hostile rumor. The note of suffering is sounded again in the transitional final scene, the story of the search for the twelve-year-old Jesus by his parents and of their lack of understanding of his words "How is it that you sought me? Did you not know that I must be in my Father's house?" These are words that reveal a new aspect of Luke's belief concerning the identity of Jesus: not the belief in his divine sonship, nor the belief that it entails a special destiny, but the belief that this destiny (as well as his origin) involves the disruption of ordinary patriarchal family relationships.[239]

As we have seen, Luke's portrait of Mary is consistent, from the first to last mention of her: she is the disciple, the believer, esteemed for hearing the word of God and doing it (11:27–28). This portrait seems to prefigure the miniature portraits of other women throughout the Gospel. Luke's positive treatment of women has often been highlighted and analyzed.[240] He has been called the strongest "feminist" among the evangelists, the one who most reflected the open attitude of Jesus toward women. A large number of Luke's stories deal with the vindication of women. Through Mary and through his other women characters like the sisters Martha and Mary (10:38–42), Luke shows that "Faithful discipleship, not biological motherhood, is the eschatological calling of women."[241] Further, the discipleship of women is presented more favorably than that of men.[242] Parallel to the contrast between Mary's trustful response to the angel and Zechariah's mistrust in chapter 1 is the contrast between the believing women and the disbelieving men at the conclusion of the Gospel (24:9–11).

But at the same time, there is a Lucan restriction of the role of women, a playing down of their apostleship.[243] Aspects of this are prefigured by the restriction of Mary's role in Luke 1. (a) As Mary is an evangelist and prophet without an explicit commission to preach the word, so the women at the end tell the eleven and all the rest about the empty tomb, although they themselves receive no commission and no appearance of the risen Jesus (cf. the appearance to women in Matthew, John, and the Marcan Appendix).

(b) In Acts as in the Gospel, the role given to women has been criticized as stereotypically passive, reflecting a church situation or hierarchical ideology similar to that reflected in the Pastorals near the end of the first century C.E.[244] Mary's role is also often characterized as passive.[245] Luke may intend her consent in 1:38 to be an expression of her active, free choice and courage, and he may see her as much more than just a passive instrument of God. It must be noted that the Lucan Mary is not "merely the means of Jesus' birth."[246] Her life is not at Joseph's disposal as his property, nor does she obey him. She is evaluated in terms of her relationship not with him, but with God.[247] Joseph is not depicted as her protector or the agent of her liberation. And in the Magnificat (which is not the song of a victim) she proclaims that liberation with tough authority. But it remains true that Mary reacts to the revelation rather than acts on her own with independent initiative. Once it is seen that Luke is working with the illegitimacy tradition, his avoidance of the possible themes of a woman's anger, struggle, and protest, in favor of the themes of protection, trust, and gratitude can be judged to confine the character of Mary in a personal powerlessness that only God can break. As Legrand remarks, "From the apocalyptic point of view, receptivity is the only 'virtue' that counts."[248] Unfortunately, it is also often the main one from a patriarchal point of view.

(c) Luke sees and seizes the opportunity to begin the story of Jesus with what he considers a perfect response to the word and promise of God, a response of human incomprehension and trust, the response of the woman Mary. God takes the initiative,

Mary obeys. As part of his espousal of a new social order based on service and humility, Luke has Mary identify herself as the slave of the Lord, a statement that expresses a certain androcentric insensitivity to the perennial condition and needs of women,[249] and, I think, an ignorance of authentic feminine spirituality, to which the master/slave relationship is foreign. In the body of the Gospel, we find women exercising another form of self-sacrifice: Luke emphasizes the ministry of women as one of providing financial aid and support to Jesus and to the male disciples.[250] In short, Luke does not imagine women as fully disciples of Jesus in his ministry.

Luke, I think, is not really interested in the discipleship of Mary in itself; rather, the use of this motif is one of several strategies to defend her honor. Burrows rightly notices that Luke 1–2 was written by "one who was zealous for [Mary's] honor."[251] Luke's aim was a bold one, which we might say succeeded all too well. The Lucan annunciation to Mary is a scene too conventionally beautiful and too indirect to properly convey the illegitimacy tradition. Its subtlety borders on deception. It is not fully the story of a woman for women, but a story told by a man's world for a man's world.

Still, this Lucan scene in which a betrothed virgin is visited by the angel of God and told of her forthcoming pregnancy and God's empowering protection of her is the only biblical instance of God's direct interest in a woman who conceives illegitimately.[252] Natural and ordinary notions of greatness are called into question, making this "the essential Gospel story in miniature"[253]—much more so than we have realized.

4. The Pre-Gospel Tradition and Post-Gospel Traditions

Albert Schweitzer asks, "Who knows the laws of the formation of legend? Who can follow the course of the wind which carries the seed over land and sea?" And "why should whatever is incomprehensible to us be unhistorical?"[1] Both questions are worth pondering in connection with the topic of traditions concerning the conception of Jesus. This chapter will attempt to reconstruct and analyze the tradition the evangelists inherited and to trace different branches of its development. How and why did the tradition of illegitimate conception become one of a virginal conception?

A. THE PRE-GOSPEL TRADITION

Although "the laws of the formation of legend" at present escape us, New Testament scholarship does try to comprehend what lies behind a text and how communities and individual writers shaped the traditions they received. In the case under study here, it is agreed by most scholars that the general outlines of the pre-gospel tradition can be reconstructed by analysis of the elements of the story of Jesus' conception which are common to Matthew and Luke. On the basis of the two source theory, it is assumed that these elements appear independently in each gospel and are taken from a prior tradition, oral or written.[2] The attempts to derive the Matthean and Lucan accounts from a common written source are extremely unconvincing. The common and partly theologized source that lies behind Matthew and Luke is probably oral. It may be "meagre and remote,"[3] but it is well worth investigating.

1. COMMON ELEMENTS

While the differences between the Matthean and Lucan narratives are drastic, "more drastic than anywhere in the canonical gospels,"[4] the common elements are many. In the previous chapter,[5] these common elements are listed. Several more common elements can be seen now on the basis of the interpretation of the narratives given above. Both Matthew and Luke allude to the law in Deuteronomy 22:23–27 concerning the seduction or rape of a betrothed virgin. Both intend to hand down the prior tradition that Jesus was conceived illegitimately during the period of Mary's betrothal. Neither evangelist casts blame on Mary or accuses her of wrongdoing. Matthew presents Joseph as wrestling with his obligations against the background of this law and finally, in obedience to the word of the angel, completing the home-taking with her. The resolution of this story implies that Mary is not at fault in this pregnancy. Luke presents Mary herself as making a leap of faith and consenting to her pregnancy and her child's future as the will of God. Analysis of these elements of the narratives lead me to conclude that both evangelists want the reader to regard Mary as innocent of cooperation in seduction, that is, adultery. They are leading the reader to think (however obliquely) of her rape, not seduction. References in Matthew 1:21 to the meaning of the name of Jesus ("he will save his people from their sins") and in Luke 1:47 to God as savior ("my spirit rejoices in God my savior"; cf. 2:11) may be subtle allusions to Deut 22:27 ("though the betrothed young woman cried for help there was no one to save her"). Cf. the reference to Mary's "humiliation" in the Magnificat (Luke 1:48; see Deut 22:24, 29). As we have seen, the Gospel of Luke and Acts stress Mary's perfect discipleship; but in Matthew, this stress is absent. The apologetic motif, of response to rumor and of refutation of what is regarded as calumny, is more highly developed in Luke than in Matthew.

Did the evangelists inherit a tradition in which it was clear that Mary was raped during the period of her betrothal? Or are they (independently of one another) correcting an earlier tradition and/or rumor about her as seduced and an adulteress? I find it impossible to decide between these two alternatives.

In both accounts, the biological father is absent and unnamed. He plays no role at all, but this absence and silence do not mean he does not exist. That Joseph did not "know" Mary, and vice versa, is expressed in Matt 1:25; Luke 1:34. The activity of the

Holy Spirit is clearly not thought to "merely enhance normal marital relations."[6] Joseph becomes the child's legal father, incorporating him into the Davidic line. There is a strong theme of protection of the woman and child (in Matthew, by Joseph; in Luke, by the Holy Spirit overshadowing).

The role of the Holy Spirit in this conception is worded quite differently in the two gospels. The angel in Matt 1:20 insists to Joseph that "the child begotten (*to . . . gennēthen*[7]) in her is through the (or a) Holy Spirit." The angel in Luke 1:35 predicts to Mary, "The (or a) Holy Spirit will come upon you, and the power of the Most High will overshadow you; therefore the child to be begotten (or: born; *to gennōmenon*[8]) will be called holy, the Son of God." Even without the notion of the virginal conception, we can regard as correct the statement that both evangelists point to a higher causality in the conception of Jesus, to God's power "from above" giving humanity this child. Both evangelists present the faith conviction that *in* his human origins, the child will be God's, because the Holy Spirit is ultimately responsible for his conception. The pregnancy is no accident or mistake, but divinely ordained.

The conception, the very existence of Jesus, is seen as the keeping of God's promises to Israel, promises of divine presence and salvation (Matt 1:21, 23; cf. Isa 7:14) and of dramatic reversal of the deepest human inadequacies, deprivations, and humiliations (Luke 1:51–53). In the tendency to stress the intrinsic connection of Jesus' conception with the story of Israel, and to stress continuity between the conception and what will follow in each gospel, the Infancy Narratives are correctly said to be the place where the scriptures of Israel and the gospel most directly meet. They are the place where the evangelists strain to radically reinterpret, reapply, and appropriate ancient traditions. In this the Infancy Narratives are similar to the New Testament Passion Narratives (although the older traditions prepare the reader less for the tradition of an illegitimate conception of the Messiah than for the tradition of his meaningful death). Scandal was dealt with as foreshadowed in the Scriptures. Luke makes the transition from Old Testament to Gospel more smooth with his web of allusions, while Matthew makes it more obvious with his direct quotations.

In both accounts, the recipients of revelation are alone and are depicted as troubled and pondering (Joseph, before the dream; Mary, during the communication by the angel; cf. Luke 2:19, 51). The major figures in each narrative respond with consent in obedience to revelation. In both stories, the presence of God is emphasized (Matt 1:23: "Emmanuel, which means God with us;" Luke 1:28: "the Lord is with you"). Both Infancy Narratives foreshadow danger (Matthew presenting the endangered Mary in his first scene and following the annunciation with the scenes of the Magi tricked by Herod and of the murder of innocent children; Luke by the saying of Simeon regarding the child and his mother).

Finally, neither gospel is understood fully unless it is read from the perspective of its Infancy Narrative, which introduces the reader to the belief that God has provided humanity with this Messiah humanly conceived.

2. A RECONSTRUCTION

What can be said of the shape of the pre-gospel tradition of Jesus' conception?[9] The fact that both evangelists make use of an angelic annunciation indicates that the early tradition took such a form. It was the vehicle for the message that a virgin who was betrothed had been seduced or raped and impregnated by someone other than her fiancé; for the message that the child so conceived was conceived through the power of the Holy Spirit, and was of Davidic descent through Joseph. The annunciation form itself was a well known literary pattern from the scriptures, and so a natural medium for Christians of Jewish descent to have used for their reflections. The angelic announcement to Joseph in Matthew 1 occurs in a dream;[10] but the dream format was probably not part of the original annunciation tradition. In Luke the announcement to Mary occurs while she is in a waking state; if it is meant to be a vision, no visionary elements are depicted; perhaps it is best to consider it a revelatory insight.

The basic content of the angelic message in both New Testament narratives is now cast in the language of early Christian creedal affirmation, and involves christological insight that was earlier associated with the resurrection and the baptism of Jesus and finally seen as appropriate to his conception. But the original, traditional content may have been simply the statement that this child's conception was effected through the Holy Spirit and, perhaps, that his destiny was one of great importance for "his people" Israel.

Which of the ways of speaking about the involvement of the Holy Spirit, Matthew's or Luke's, is likely to be earlier? Matthew's way is simpler, and in v 18 he reminds the reader of the strange ending of his genealogy in 1:16 and of the mention of the four women.[11] As we have seen, Matthew's formulation in v 20 in the angelic message could be translated without reference to the Holy Spirit of God, reading simply, "that which is begotten in her is of a spirit which is holy" (*ek pneumatos estin hagiou*), in implied contrast to "of a spirit which is unholy or impure" or in contrast to "of fornication" (*ek porneias*).[12] V 18 shows that the clause has been understood, however, as a reference to the Holy Spirit; the older clause remains embedded like a fossil in the narrative. Since both evangelists speak of the Holy Spirit of Christian tradition in connection with Mary's pregnancy, that connection is traditional. Luke's more elaborate saying, stressing the protection of the Holy Spirit, has been regarded as a Lucan version of an early Christian christological formula, and it is clearly in Lucan vocabulary and style.[13] The Matthean statement in v 18, then, may be closer than the Lucan to the way the pre-gospel tradition worded its faith.[14]

Who was the central figure and recipient of the angelic annunciation in the original tradition, a man or a woman?[15] Annunciations in the Hebrew Bible are to both men and women, so convention cannot help us decide this point. The annunciations to Zechariah and to Mary may be an instance of the Lucan tendency to pair scenes to men and to women; and his focus on Mary is part of Luke's general interest in women. Matthew's schema, of the discovery of the pregnancy of Mary and the dilemma this causes, is a less awkward way of preserving the tradition of illegitimacy than is Luke's announcement to Mary before the pregnancy; but focus on Joseph is necessary to Matthew's interest in Torah interpretation. If the revelation in the original was to Mary after she became pregnant, then Matthew has kept the time frame but changed the recipient, and Luke has done the opposite. Matthew has all but erased Mary from his narrative, writing of an announcement to Joseph and of his problem of how to treat her, in the context of his own "righteousness." Luke, according to this theory, has also changed the tradition radically, securing Mary's consent before pregnancy— an element that is clearly secondary and designed to stress her innocence.

If the tradition followed the hypothetical full form of an annunciation of birth, this would have been its outline.

1. Description of plight: Mary, betrothed to Joseph of the house of David, is seduced or raped during the time of her betrothal and made pregnant
2. The appearance of an angel of the Lord: to Mary or to Joseph
3. Fear or prostration of visionary confronted by this supernatural presence
4. The divine message
   a. The visionary is addressed by name
   b. A qualifying phrase describing the visionary
   c. The visionary is urged not to be afraid
   d. You are (or your betrothed wife is) pregnant
   e. You will (or she will) give birth to a son, who is begotten through the Holy Spirit
   f. The name by which the son will be called
   g. Etymology of the name
   h. The future accomplishments of the child; note that in Matt 1:21 the etymology = the future accomplishments, unless the meaning of the name is intended to be: He (Yahweh) saves
5. An objection by the visionary as to how this can be, or a request for a sign; (we should remember that a child so conceived was regarded as bearing the sins of his parent[s], and cursed. How then could the Holy Spirit be involved in this pregnancy?)
6. The giving of a sign to reassure the visionary[16]

However, the early Christian tradition may have been fairly minimal, more minimal than such a full account, since the two evangelists feel free to compose narratives that are so very different from one another. Perhaps the tradition was only oral[17] and only contained these elements:

1. The plight
2. The (angelic) revelation, concerning
    d. Pregnancy, involving the Holy Spirit (and, behind this, the notion of a spirit which is holy, as opposed to unholy)
    e. The birth of the child
    f. The name to be given the child, and perhaps
    g. Its etymology or some other statement about the future importance of the child[18]

Originally the involvement of the spirit which is holy may have meant simply that the pregnancy was good, even a "holy" event, was divinely willed.[19]

We can imagine such a minimal tradition gradually taking on the other elements of an angelic annunciation, becoming more specific in terms of the future predicted for the child, a future already known and believed in retrospect. The use of the annunciation form for the revelation, evoking the stories of the Hebrew Bible, communicated the belief that the story of Jesus was rooted in the history of Israel. "So much does information depend on form, and spirit on style, that in orality one could almost say that the form is the soul of the message."[20]

3. Historicity

A historical nucleus may be extracted from the details both gospels have in common, details that may come from the previous tradition.[21] The situation drawn from the tradition and described in the narratives, of Mary conceiving in the interim between betrothal and home-taking, is historically correct. There is no clear reason why Christians would have invented this potentially damaging information. The insistence of both evangelists that Joseph was not Jesus' biological father should also be understood as insistence on historical fact.[22]

Can we draw any conclusions about how the conception occurred? The allusions to Deut 22:23–27 in the New Testament narratives are faint pointers to an answer; in the pre-gospel tradition clearer reference may have been made to Mary's seduction or rape. Do these allusions pertain to a historical occurrence? Why else would they be present? It appears that the evangelists and the framers of the tradition before them found the allusions to Deuteronomy helpful in defending Mary against a charge or rumor that she freely chose a sexual partner other than the man to whom she was betrothed. As we have seen, both New Testament narratives, read through the lens of this law in Deuteronomy, do not cast blame on Mary; they force us to recognize that illegitimacy does not necessarily imply sin on the woman's part, even from a patriarchal standpoint and within the confines of a patriarchal culture. But the possibility cannot be ruled out that the historical truth on this point may be found in the charge or rumor (of willing fornication, of Mary's free choice in this matter), and not in the pre-gospel tradition and New Testament narratives. The evidence from other sources will be considered below. The question must remain an open one historically. New Testament criticism cannot take us behind the reconstructed pre-gospel tradition here.

There may have been an irregularity about the birth of Jesus, in that he was born noticeably early after his parents came to live together. Public knowledge of early birth, however, would not have been enough to make public the circumstances of Jesus' conception or to ground a rumor or charge of illegitimacy. On the one hand, premature births surely occurred fairly frequently in antiquity (even if many babies so born did not survive), and these births were surely quickly forgotten.

On the other hand, if the birth was too early to be regarded as premature,[23] the normal assumption of outsiders would be that conception occurred because of sexual intercourse between Mary and Joseph during the time of their betrothal. This would not be scandalous behavior, especially since, as we have seen, the rules governing intercourse during betrothal were apparently not uniform geographically and throughout the first century c.e. In Galilee it was considered only "bad taste and the unusual thing" for the betrothed to have sexual intercourse before the home-taking.[24] Unless there was some public repudiation of the child by Joseph (which is highly unlikely, since Jesus is called his son in traditions from the ministry[25]), it is difficult to think of early birth being the basis for later scandal and for such significant defensive writing as the gospels (and the pre-gospel tradition) may be.[26] Seduction or rape or willing fornication would be known of only if one of the three parties intimately involved (Mary, Joseph, or the unnamed man) told of it, or if it was witnessed. In the absence of a trial or hearing, and in the absence of any punishment or repudiation, suspicion of illegitimacy—whether sincere or prompted by the desire to discredit Jesus—could thrive only on the admission of someone involved.[27]

The pre-gospel tradition did not break with the theological notion that divine begetting enables, presupposes, does not eliminate human paternity. But—either because the name of Jesus' biological father was unknown, or because those who handed on the tradition preferred to omit it—this tradition appears to have been silent regarding the name of this man. If the tradition did name him, both Matthew and Luke independently of one another erased his name. But the confusion of names in later materials, which we will treat below, may tell against this last alternative. In any case, and whatever the historical circumstances of the conception, the pre-gospel tradition did break with an important sociological prejudice: that of accounting a child conceived illegitimately as inferior, doomed, cursed. This break, this defiance of social expectations, is illustrated by the historical action of Joseph, who accepted the child into his family. To what can we trace this action of Joseph's? Common decency, the desire to avoid scandal, concern for the fate of his betrothed wife and the child to be born, careful interpretation of the options open to a Torah-abiding man? Matthew's Gospel traces it to a revelation, to divine aid. Luke's Gospel deals not at all with this aspect of the story.

4. PROVENANCE

It is likely that the basis of the tradition does stem from the family of Jesus, probably from Mary or from the brothers or sisters of Jesus rather than from Joseph, who does not appear in any story of the ministry. This basis is simply the report that Jesus was illegitimately conceived.[28] Perhaps also from family circles comes the ancient affirmation that the child was begotten of a spirit that was holy, not unholy, and the insistence that his mother was blameless. The name of Jesus may have been given the child in the family because of a belief that God indeed "saved" Mary in the situation she endured. But further interpretation of the illegitimacy, an interpretation that comes from the pre-gospel period, probably does not stem from the family. Minimal as that interpretation seems to have been, it is difficult to reconcile it with the evidence we have that the family of Jesus was not among his followers during his ministry (John 7:5; Mark 3:21, 31). Whatever the role of Mary in the formation of the tradition, we have to keep in mind that during the ministry she apparently did not have any clear understanding of who Jesus was or what he was to do; her presence in the early Christian community in Jerusalem (Acts 1:14) may be reliable, but this does not tell us when her faith began. The explicit theological/ christological interpretation, linking the begetting of Jesus with the Holy Spirit and predicting the child's future greatness for his people in some way, may have come from an early Christian prophet, female or male, perhaps a member of a charismatic circle, acquainted with the use of Spirit terminology to express divine sonship (see Gal 4:6, 29; Rom 8:15; John 3:5–6) and to express the accomplishment of Jesus' relationship with God in his resurrection and baptism. The actual speaking contexts are lost to us.[29]

Women would have had a special interest in and understanding of the early tradition about Jesus' conception.[30] "Oral transmission is controlled by the law of social identification," with traditions passed down by those whose existence the tradition verifies and whose social needs it meets, by those to whom the tradition is true to life or true to hope, even if, in the wider male-dominated society, it is socially unacceptable and subversive.[31] If Schüssler Fiorenza and others are correct about the important and influential roles of women in the following of Jesus and in the early church—and I think they are—we would reasonably expect that some of these women made significant contributions to the oral and perhaps the written tradition and were among the anonymous shapers and framers of the Jesus story. This is not to deny that "all early Christian writings, whether written by women or by men, more or less share the androcentric mind-set and must be analyzed and tested critically as to how much they do so."[32] But where we find ourselves reading portions or levels of the New Testament as though we were reading subversive women's literature, literature that seems to communicate at least in part the experience of women, this impression may not be an illusion. We may indeed be in touch with the contributions of women. The illegitimacy tradition may be one such contribution: women may have been involved in its creation, and in assuring it was not forgotten or at first (at the gospel level) totally distorted. It is, of course, impossible to be cerain that this was the case. At any rate, discovery of the illegitimacy tradition does permit "a glimpse of the egalitarian-inclusive practice and theology of early Christians."[33] In the post-gospel Christian community the tradition apparently ceased to overcome the social threshold to communal reception.

If the story of how and when Jesus was conceived was family tradition, it is unlikely it would have been communicated to many. Rather, it would naturally have been kept secret.[34] But leakage and rumor were possible, especially in the hometown, and its spread can be easily imagined during the ministry and afterwards, especially on the lips of those who did not accept either the claims Jesus made or those his followers made for him.[35] Early Christian theologizing (perhaps in more than one stage, as oral communication passed through "the feedback loop"[36]), on the basis of the core of that story and to counter rumor, produced the traditions used by Matthew and by Luke. Given the nature of the case, it is not surprising that the belief that Jesus was begotten through a spirit that is holy, or through the Holy Spirit, does not appear in any of the so-called kerygmatic passages of the New Testament.

The appearance of the tradition, with its theological and christological components, in the gospels of the eighties does not indicate the lateness of the tradition. Because of its traumatic nature and its potential damage to the Jesus movement, and because of its faith demand, the tradition was a difficult one to communicate. Once communicated, however hesitantly, it was bound to cause strong audience reactions. Misunderstanding, ridicule, rejection, and slander surely followed in its wake. Reference to rape or seduction, much less to willing fornication, perennially is met with the certainty that the woman involved is to blame, and illegitimacy often connotes inferiority or worthlessness, if not evil. Those offended by the tradition became inadvertent carriers of it, in that both New Testament Infancy Narratives respond to rumor and to these reactions,[37] as well as to the inherited Christian tradition, which they confirm and transform.

Both evangelists also tame or blunt the tradition of Jesus' illegitimacy, making it hard for the reader to experience the grief and danger of the historical circumstances. But if in writing they hoped to still the rumors and end the dialogue over this issue, to lessen audience interference and censorship, they failed, as we will see in the following sections. The oral tradition continued to have a life, or lives, of its own. And the New Testament texts themselves were open to a variety of interpretations, far beyond the control of their authors.

B. OTHER EVIDENCE OF THE ILLEGITIMACY TRADITION

I have claimed that transmitted in the New Testament Infancy Narratives is the tradition of the seduction or rape of Mary in the period of her betrothal to Joseph, and of her illegitimate pregnancy. The core of this tradition was transmitted in family circles and became increasingly public in the pre-gospel period. During this time it was given positive theological and christological interpretation, but this interpretation was challenged. Do we find outside the Infancy Narratives, in the New Testament or elsewhere, any corroboration of the existence of this tradition? And if so, do we find other responses to it, responses quite different from those made in the New Testament Infancy Narratives? The answer to both of these questions is yes. In the first four texts to be examined—John 8:41; *Acts of Pilate* 2:3; Mark 3:6; *Gospel of Thomas* 105—the tradition of Jesus' illegitimacy appears, independent of the New Testament Infancy Narratives in all but the second text. These passages have all been examined before by scholars, but the preceding analysis of the New Testament Infancy Narratives casts them in a different light. It is important to be aware of some of their details as we attempt to look at the spectrum of this tradition.

There is no evidence in the Pauline writings of Paul's knowledge of the illegitimacy tradition. Paul insists on Christ's involvement with sin, on his becoming the redeemer in sinful flesh, evoking Christ's solidarity with sinful humanity. This daring picture of the earthly Jesus may be based on Jesus traditions Paul received, but we cannot be sure that one of these traditions was that of Jesus' illegitimacy.[38]

1. JOHN 8:41

The charge of Jesus' illegitimacy is implied in John 8:41.[39] In 8:31 a debate begins between Jesus and "the Jews who had believed in him." These are believers at least in their own view, possibly (at the Gospel level[40]) conservative Jewish Christians who strongly resent the Johannine community because of its high christology and its admixture of Samaritan elements.[41] By v 48, Jesus' dialogue partners are called simply "the Jews."[42]

The debate concerns authentic sonship. These opponents are descendants of Abraham, yet Jesus questions whether they are slaves or free sons (v 37) and even implies they are not Abraham's true children (v 39), since they seek to kill him. (In Johannine eyes, descent through the flesh from Abraham would not guarantee that those Jewish Christians who insist on it are the true and free seed of Abraham; cf. Matt 3:9, par.) Finally Jesus charges that the devil is their father (v 44). The pedigree of these Jews is invalid. They are physically descended from one father but imitate the works of another. "The Jews correctly perceive that this double paternity is, in fact, an accusation of spiritual illegitimacy."[43] For their part, the Jews argue that as descendants of Abraham they have never been in bondage to anyone (v 33), that Abraham is their father (v 39), that they have one father, God (v 41). It is a debate of escalating hostility on both sides, ending with the Jews' attempt to stone him after he has made the startling statement, "before Abraham was, I am" (vv 58–59).

In the midst of this argument, the opponents say, "*We* were not born of fornication" (*Hymeis ek porneias ou gegennēmetha*), the emphasis on "we" implying "but you were," that is, implying that Jesus was illegitimate.[44] The Jews meet Jesus' challenge to their religious or spiritual legitimacy by a challenge to his physical legitimacy. The suggestion of Jesus' illegitimacy here is subtle and is drawn from pre-gospel tradition.[45] The broad Gospel context supports this reading of the verse, rather than the reading that it means simply that Jesus is not a true son of Abraham or of God.

The following chapter, 9, begins as an antithesis to the claims of Abrahamic ancestry in 8:31–59. "By rejecting the validity of the hypothesis that sins or curses brought about by parents or ancestors affect their children or descendants, the preceding argument, that merits or blessings brought about by an ancestor (Abraham) affect his descendants (the children of Abraham) is rejected as well."[46] From this perspective in chapter 9, we can see also, as a sort of subtext in chapter 8, the implicit rejection of the belief that biological illegitimacy involves a curse on the offspring (see 8:46: "Which of you convicts me of sin?").

The placement in most witnesses of the non-Johannine interpolation about the woman caught in adultery but released (John 7:53–8:11) may support the theory that there is an implication of illegitimacy in 8:41.[47] It is possible that the interpolator knew the tradition of Jesus' illegitimate conception during the period of Mary's betrothal to Joseph, understood the implication of illegitimacy in 8:41, and prepared for it by the story concerning Jesus' own attitude toward a woman in the plight of being accused of adultery. But this must remain conjecture.

The author of the Fourth Gospel meets the implication that Jesus was "born of fornication" indirectly. It is swept aside by the claim made throughout this Gospel that physical and spiritual birth are two separate realities (the first having no bearing at all on the second),[48] and by the Johannine theme of the incarnation of the preexistent Son, a statement of which climaxes the conflict in 8:58.[49] Johannine theology does not rule out belief in a normal, human conception and birth of Jesus; in fact, the christological paradox of this Gospel seems to demand it.[50] But no real interest is shown in the manner of his conception, which is irrelevant to his divine Sonship.

2. THE ACTS OF PILATE

The *Acts of Pilate* 2:3 presents the charge before Pilate of "the elders of the Jews" that Jesus was "born of fornication."[51] Other

"Jews that stood by, devout men" deny that he "came of fornication," saying, "for we know that Joseph was betrothed to Mary,
and he was not born of fornication." This second group is said
(by Annas and Caiaphas) to be proselytes and disciples of Jesus,
meaning "born children of Greeks," who have become Jews;
however, they insist they are not proselytes but children of Jews
"who were present at the betrothal of Joseph and Mary" (2:4).
This work, whose origins are in the second century, is dependent
on the Gospel of Matthew in many places but draws also on the
Fourth Gospel (see 3:1–2). It is possible that this discussion of
Jesus' origin involves a reading of John 8:41 as well as of Matthew's Infancy Narrative.

The logic of the discussion is unclear: if the second group of
witnesses was present at the betrothal, then all they could witness
to was that the betrothal took place, that Joseph did not re-
nounce Mary at that stage. Scheidweiler seems to be speaking
about betrothal, not completed marriage, when he comments,
"If this reference means anything at all, then the thought behind
it must be that if Mary before her marriage had entered into
relations with anyone else, then even if the consequences were
not yet visible in her bodily constitution there would at least have
been a rumor in circulation about it, and in that case Joseph
would have renounced the marriage. In this way, then, the
mother of Jesus is defended against the reproach of pre-marital
intercourse."[52] The author of *The Acts of Pilate* does not make
any distinction between betrothal and home-taking, perhaps because he was unfamiliar with this Jewish custom and read Matthew 1 in the light of that unfamiliarity. The question of Mary
becoming pregnant during the period of betrothal (as in Matthew and Luke) is never raised. The position of the second
group of Jews, who defend Mary, seems to be that Joseph was
the father of Jesus.

This passage is therefore not a witness independent of the
New Testament to the tradition of Jesus' illegitimacy. It may be
evidence of dispute among Jews and Jewish Christians, or Jews
and Gentile Christians, over the reading of Matthew 1. Some
read it (with John 8:41 or with reliance on pre-gospel rumor) as
evidence that Jesus was born of fornication; some read it as evidence that Joseph was Jesus' father.

3. MARK 6:3

In Mark a hint of the illegitimacy charge is found in the phrase used of Jesus, "son of Mary." Like John, Mark deals with the charge indirectly. His tactic is to emphasize the distance between Jesus and his family; they are "outside" the eschatological family of disciples. This is Mark's way of stressing that physical birth and descent are of no importance in terms of entrance into the reign of God. Both John and Mark, then, deal with the charge of illegitimacy by responding: it does not matter. As we have seen, Matthew and Luke, in their Infancy Narratives, use quite different tactics in handling the illegitimacy tradition. They too pass it down, but they incorporate it into theologies of remarkable originality.

In Mark 6:3, those who heard Jesus teach in the synagogue in "his own country," "were astonished, saying, 'Where did this man get all this? What is the wisdom given to him? What mighty works are wrought by his hands! Is not this the carpenter, the son of Mary and brother of James and Joses and Judas and Simon, and are not his sisters here with us?' And they took offense at him." The phrase "son of Mary," is unusual, since a man was normally (for formal and informal purposes) identified by his father's name. This is the only place in the New Testament where Jesus is identified by his relationship to Mary. No mention is made here of his father, and Mark never mentions Joseph at all in his Gospel.[53]

Does this simply illustrate Mark's lack of interest in Jesus' origins? Or is the phrase identifying Jesus in Mark 6:3 a simple descriptive statement, not a formal genealogical identification, indicating that Joseph is dead and Mary a widow (cf. 1 Kings 17:17; Luke 7:12), and/or that the villagers in this scene are informally mentioning his relatives who are present and known to them?[54]

The fact that Matthew changes Mark here to identify Jesus through his father (Matt 13:55; "Is not this the son of the carpenter? Is not his mother called Mary?"), and the history of the textual changes of Mark 6:3 alert us to look more closely. See also the equivalent questions in Luke 4:22 ("Is not this the son of Joseph?")[55] and John 6:42 (at Capernaum: "Is not this Jesus the son of Joseph? Do we not know his father and his mother?"). It is probable that the Marcan phrase is a slur on Jesus' parentage. His father is unnamed because there is doubt about who his father is. This designation is so abusive and shocking that only Mark has had the courage to repeat it.[56]

The mention of Jesus' brothers and sisters in 6:3 is considered by some to militate against the connotation of illegitimacy. "One can scarcely consider all of them to have been illegitimate; and Jesus is being put together with them in order to emphasize his ordinariness."[57] The Marcan text, however, calls only Jesus "the son of Mary." If he were illegitimate, and the brothers and sisters were the children of Mary and Joseph, they would be only his half brothers and sisters, and the phrase "son of Mary" could mark this distinction. Furthermore, there is at least some question whether those spoken of as his brothers and sisters are to be identified as his blood brothers and sisters (the normal meaning of the Greek terms) and children of Mary, or whether they should be considered Jesus' cousins, or perhaps his half brothers and half sisters, as children of Joseph.[58] In this case, the slur would not apply to them.

Is there any evidence, other than the absence of the phrase in the other gospels, and the copyists' difficulties with it, that Mark 6:3 is a slur? There is no certain evidence that the practice of identifying an illegitimate son by the name of his mother prevailed in first century Judaism. The examples in the Hebrew Bible and in early rabbinic literature of a man identified through his mother do not clearly demonstrate that this was a customary way of designating illegitimate children or sons of prostitutes.[59] But it is a later Jewish legal principle that a man is illegitimate when he is called by his mother's name, for a bastard has no father.[60] There is no proof that this principle was operative in the first century C.E. and no proof that it was not. But it is significant that in Samaritan and Mandaean usage the designation *son of Mary* did have the pejorative sense, of Jesus' illegitimacy.[61] In Samaritan Chronicle II, for example, Jesus is said to be illegitimate because Joseph had sexual relations with Mary before the betrothal, an act regarded (strangely) as adultery (vv 2b, 16). He is called "the son of Mary" (vv 58, 92).[62] Information about Jesus' illegitimacy is reported to have come from "the Judaists" (v 2) and from "the Pharisaic community, that is, the Judaists related to him" (v 58).[63]

"In view of the genealogical system there is some *a priori* logic to the suggestion that the phrase 'son of Mary' was a deliberate insult" reflecting on the legitimacy of Jesus.[64] The following considerations support the suggestion that insult is intended. (1) The phrase is spoken during an incident in Jesus' hometown. Accepted by Joseph as part of his family, he would have been known publically and officially and formally as the son of Joseph, as other texts make clear (e.g., Luke 3:23). But the memory of Jesus' illegitimacy would persist, certainly within his family circle, and not unlikely among some in his hometown.

(2) In Mark 6:3 and in John 8:41, the charge appears on the lips of those who do not fully comprehend Jesus or are hostile to him. Matthew and Luke, I have argued, accept a tradition of Jesus' illegitimacy that had already been theologically interpreted, presume knowledge of the illegitimacy tradition on the part of their readers, and respond in their different ways to what they consider misunderstanding or slander. What we have in the Marcan and Johannine charges may be examples of the core tradition before it was given a positive interpretation, or of denials of that interpretation.

(3) Mark did not repeat the phrase in 6:3, with its implications of illegitimacy, without understanding it as an insult,[65] or without providing any hint in his Gospel as to how the charge should be met.[66] He met the charge not by dismissing it, but by, in a sense, dismissing the mother and brothers of Jesus. Note that only Mark (6:4) mentions Jesus' "own kin" as those among whom a prophet has no honor. In 3:31–35, Mark has Jesus distance himself from them and contrast them with his "real" family of disciples, even before the charge of illegitimacy has been uttered. Jesus' mother and brothers are depicted as "standing outside" and asking for him. When Jesus was informed of this, he asked, " 'Who are my mother and my brothers?' And looking around on those who sat about him, he said, 'Here are my mother and my brothers! Whoever does the will of God is my brother, and sister, and mother.' " The eschatological family of Jesus, made up of those who do the will of God, "is not identical with the biological, physical, or natural family (mother, brothers) consti-

tuted by human relationship. How sharp is this contrast? . . . The least it seems to mean is that the physical family has no real importance in the new standard of values established by the proclamation of the kingdom; the family that really matters to Jesus is the eschatological family."[67] In this family that really matters, just as in the biological family of Jesus in Mark, there is no earthly father (cf. Mark 10:30). The human "fatherlessness" of illegitimacy becomes in this context almost a sign of the eschatological "fatherlessness" of those whose real father, it is implied, is God (cf. Matt 23:9). The discipleship of equals replaces the ties of the patriarchal family. What Robinson calls "the gap in both Jesus' and the Christian's spiritual family" is filled by God.[68]

Mark's placement of 3:31–35 at the end of the unit 3:20–35 reveals his own redactional theology, sharpening the meaning of 3:31–35. Jesus' natural family misunderstands him; under the impression that he is out of his mind, they try to seize him (v 21). Their misunderstanding is paralleled by that of the Jerusalem scribes (v 22), who think Jesus is possessed. For Mark, Jesus' natural family is replaced by his eschatological family. Neither Matthew nor Luke retains this assessment of Mark's: both omit Mark 3:19b–20.[69] Mark's Jesus leaves his mother behind, since she is seen by the Evangelist as a representative of the natural family ties, which can constrict spiritual freedom,[70] and also as a scandal that must be overcome.

Mark's negative picture of Mary, including her in the unbelief of the relatives, is toned down in Matthew to at least a neutral picture, and in Luke it is offset especially by the positive depiction in chapters 1–2. While that negative picture in Mark may well not be historical,[71] the apparent tension between Jesus and Mary, her misunderstanding of his work, and his disengagement from her during his ministry have been regarded as motifs in the Synoptics and in the Fourth Gospel[72] that have high claims to historicity, since they stand in contrast to "later pious legends about Jesus' relations with his family."[73] These themes can be read to offer further support to the theory that Jesus' illegitimate conception is historical, and is a tradition used in the New Testament Infancy Narratives.[74]

David Flusser's remarks are worth quoting here: in spite of the danger of glib psychologizing, there is "a psychological element in the life of Jesus that we may not ignore: his rejection of the family into which he was born," an experience that he applied to others as well (see Luke 18:28–30). "Jesus knew that uncompromising religious commitment was bound to break family ties, all the more as he was certain that the end was in sight. . . . An emotion-laden tension seems to have arisen between Jesus and his family, and it would appear to have been this psychological fact—the background to which I do not know—that powerfully contributed to his personal decision that was so decisive for mankind."[75] While that background might be forever unknown, or might be explained in various ways, I want to offer the historicity of the tradition of his illegitimacy as one explanation.

4. THE GOSPEL OF THOMAS

In the apocryphal *Gospel of Thomas* there is an enigmatic saying that has some relevance to this discussion, saying 105: "He who knows the father and the mother will be called the son of a harlot."[76] If the reference is to Jesus, it may mean that he who recognizes his father (God; cf. John 8:55) and mother (the Holy Spirit[77]) is (nevertheless) said (by his opponents) to be the son of a harlot.

The *Gospel of Thomas* was almost certainly composed in Greek in the second century or earlier. It probably contains some sayings that are more primitive than their parallels in the New Testament or are a development of more primitive forms.[78] Logion 105 may draw on the pre-Marcan and pre-Johannine tradition of the illegitimacy of Jesus, even though the slur would go beyond those in John 8:41 and Mark 3:6 (and *Acts of Pilate* 2:3). Here Jesus is not only regarded as illegitimate, but his mother is regarded as a prostitute or whore.[79] Both accusations, however, could have existed at the same time.

To summarize our findings so far: John 8:41 and Mark 6:3 are the only New Testament passages outside the Infancy Narratives that can be cited as evidence that the memory of Jesus' illegitimacy was alive and made public either during the ministry of Jesus or during the period of the writing of these two gospels (John is traditionally dated in the nineties, Mark in the sixties). They are a negative reaction either to the core of the tradition, the fact of his illegitimacy, or to the early stage of the theological interpretation of that tradition. They tell nothing specific of the circumstances of Jesus' conception. *Acts of Pilate* attempts a narrative specification: Jesus was conceived before the betrothal; but the author of this work denies the charge. *Gospel of Thomas* 105 moves beyond the simple claim of Jesus' illegitimacy to the claim that his mother was a harlot. The next example of the illegitimacy tradition we will examine is the story told by Celsus's "Jew."

5. ORIGEN'S *AGAINST CELSUS*

In all of the passages discussed above, with the exception of the *Gospel of Thomas,* the charge of illegitimacy, or hint of the charge, comes from Jews.[80] We turn now to the charge developed into a story[81] as it appears in Origen's *Against Celsus* I. 28, 32, 39, 69, written about 248 and making use of the anti-Christian work of the pagan philosopher Celsus, *True Doctrine,* written around 178 c.e. This latter work in turn probably drew on other, possibly Jewish, sources. Celsus presents his criticism of Jesus here not as his own but as that of a Jew, speaking to Jewish, not Gentile, believers (2:1), and using arguments chosen to appeal to them.[82]

Celsus's tale can be reconstructed: It was Jesus himself "who fabricated the story of his birth from a virgin" (*Against Celsus* 1:28). But see 1:39: "When hated by her husband, and turned out of doors, [his mother] was not saved by divine power, nor was her story believed." (This may mean that the story of a virginal conception comes from the mother of Jesus. Or it may mean that a story of seduction or rape was not believed.) Jesus had come from a Jewish village where he had been born of a "poor country woman who earned her living by spinning." This woman was corrupted or seduced and became pregnant by another man, a soldier named Panthera (1:69),[83] and "was driven out by the carpenter to whom she was betrothed, since she was convicted of adultery" (1:32). While she was wandering about in disgrace she secretly gave birth to Jesus. When Jesus grew up he went to Egypt, and because he was poor, he hired himself out as a workman and "there tried his hand at certain magical powers on which the Egyptians pride themselves; he returned full of conceit because of the powers, and on account of them gave himself the title God" (1:28).

What is the relationship of this story to the New Testament Infancy Narratives?[84] In book 1, "the Jew" seems to follow in part Matthew's Gospel (although in 1:34 Origen reproaches him for quoting selectively, omitting the reference to Isa 7:14). Some of the details are the same as those in the New Testament: the mention of a virgin, of the carpenter (Matt 13:55), conception during the period of betrothal, the rural setting, Jesus' presence in Egypt, mention of magic, the title Son of God. Most important, here is the explicit statement that Mary was corrupted and made pregnant by a man not her betrothed husband, an implicit aspect of the story of Jesus in the New Testament accounts.

Other details of Celsus's report seem to be deliberate revisions of aspects of the New Testament stories: the husband rejects his wife and turns her out (divorces her?) after she is convicted of adultery. This seems to directly contradict the story Matthew tells, of Joseph's acceptance of Mary and his decision not to subject her to the law. We must reckon, however, with the alternative possibility, that Matthew is revising an earlier story of rejection. But this alternative is less likely for two reasons: (1) Jesus was known during his ministry and by the compilers of the two New Testament genealogies as the son of Joseph. If the story of rejection of his mother were early, we would expect it to leave some trace in the body of the gospels. (2) The rejection story may have been suggested not only by Matthew's Infancy Narrative, but by the absence of Joseph during Jesus' ministry and by such texts as Mark 6:3; John 8:41.[85] Also significant is the insistence that Mary was not saved by divine power, which may contradict a subtle use of Deut 22:27 in Matt 1:21 and Luke 1:47. The statement that her story was not believed (*Against Celsus* 1:39) should perhaps be seen in the light of the statement that she was convicted of adultery (1:28).

Other details in the account by Celsus appear to be either polemical embellishments of the New Testament stories or elements drawn from independent, parallel tradition. The biological father of Jesus is named and is given an occupation (as is his mother). The name Panthera is probably not derived from *parthenos* (virgin),[86] not the name of one of Jesus' ancestors[87] and not a name invented for the purpose of the story. Unless Celsus was using rabbinic material, which is unlikely, the name must have come to him from nonrabbinic Palestinian tradition. There is no way to determine for sure whether the name dropped out of early material as it was used by Christians or was added to it as used by Jews; but as this is not the only name given to the biological father of Jesus, the latter may be the case. Panthera was a common Greek proper name, found in many Latin inscriptions of the early Empire, especially as a surname of Roman soldiers.[88] An inscription found on an epitaph in Germany, for example, mentions a Sidonian archer, Tiberius Julius Abdes Pantera, who was transferred in 6 C.E. from Syria.[89] In some rabbinic passages that survived Christian-imposed censorship,[90] Jesus is referred to as "the son of Pantera"—sometimes as illegitimate—and these will be examined below. Celsus mentions Jesus' presence in Egypt as an adult and his expertise in magic. And he also attributes the story of Jesus' origins to Jesus himself (1:28) and to Mary (1:39, a story not believed, perhaps an acknowledgment of family tradition).

Origen's responses to the story of "the Jew" are surprising. He first gives it as his opinion that "all these things worthily harmonize with the predictions that Jesus is the Son of God" (1:28). He appears to accept Celsus's portrait of Jesus and Mary as outsiders *par excellence*, "quintessential aliens," conceding everything but the conclusion that Jesus' claim to the title of God is unwarranted.[91] Jesus, "with all these things against him" has yet been able to shake the whole world (1:29). His reputation is victorious over "all causes that tended to bring him into disrepute," not only those things Celsus has enumerated, but also the shame of the crucifixion (1:30).

In 1:32, however, Origen calls the stories of Mary's adultery and rejection "blindly concocted fables," invented to overturn the story of Jesus' miraculous conception by the Holy Spirit. Inadvertently opponents have preserved the fact that it was not by Joseph that the virgin conceived Jesus. It is not reasonable, Origen argues, that he who did so much for the human race should not have had "a miraculous birth, but one of the vilest and most disgraceful of all." Jesus' great soul merited a body in conformity with its character; whereas a body produced by an act of adultery such as that between Pathera and the virgin would have produced "some fool" to do injury to humanity, a teacher of wickedness (1:33; cf. 6:73).

Further (1:34), the prophets predicted Jesus' birth from a virgin, though Celsus from ignorance or unwillingness did not cite Isa 7:14. Origen knows of disputes concerning the translation of that text, knows that some claim the Hebrew term ʿalmâ found there means "young woman," and not "virgin" (cf. Justin, *Dial.* 43; 67). He responds that the term ʿalmâ occurs with the meaning "virgin" in Deut 22:23–26, the text concerning the seduction or rape of a betrothed girl, and he cites this passage at length. I have argued that this text lies behind and is alluded to in the New Testament Infancy Narratives. Is Origen merely "in his conscientiousness" striving for a philological parallel,[92] any philological parallel, and hitting on this one? Or do we have evidence of his knowledge of the importance that text may have had in discussions of Jesus' conception? If the latter is the case, he has not gone on, on the basis of an application of the law in Deuteronomy, to dispute the charge of adultery leveled by Celsus's "Jew" but has left the matter hanging. It has been noted that, as far as we know, Origen was the first theologian to ponder deeply the question why Christ had to be born of a *betrothed* virgin. His answer, given elsewhere, is that it was possible only in that way to protect her from the suspicion of adultery, and that moreover in that way Jesus' birth was concealed from the devil.[93] But he does not bring up these points in dispute with Celsus. Most intriguing is the fact that the word ʿalmâ does *not* occur in the passage in Deuteronomy that Origen quotes; instead, the term bĕtûlâ and other terms are used. Origen's argument would not have convinced anyone who knew the Hebrew Bible. Is it an unwitting mistake,[94] and/or a trace of pre-gospel tradition?

In 1:35 Origen asks, What kind of sign would it have been for Ahaz, if a young woman who was not a virgin gave birth? Also, he remarks, it is more "appropriate" that the mother of Immanuel be still a pure and holy virgin and not one who has had intercourse with a man, conceiving normally. Isaiah was looking into the future with his prophecy, which was not fulfilled in his time. Origen turns in 1:37 to support belief in the virginal conception by the statements that vultures[95] conceive without sexual intercourse; that even the Greeks admit that the first men must have been produced without intercourse but from the earth; that Christians are not the only ones who have recourse to miraculous conception narratives (though the story of Jesus' conception is compared only by buffoons to Greek fables such as those about Danae and Melanippe; cf. 6:8). Some of the arguments advanced by Celsus are deemed lacking in seriousness and not worthy of attention, such as the argument that it is improbable that the god would have intercourse with Mary since she was of such low rank, or that Mary was not saved or believed (1:39). Finally, in 1:69, Origen quotes Celsus's opinion that the body of a god would not have been so generated as Jesus' was. Origen agrees, since Celsus disbelieves the accounts of Jesus' conception by the Holy Spirit and believes he was begotten by Panthera, who corrupted the virgin.

The evidence afforded by Celsus's story and by Origen's responses to it is puzzling. Both seem to be drawing on gospel materials, and on pre-gospel tradition or tradition parallel to the gospels, which offered a fuller and more explicit account of the illegitimate conception. It is impossible, however, to be sure whether certain details like the name Panthera belonged to the earliest tradition. Origen himself seems curiously aware of and even open to aspects of the illegitimacy tradition; but he takes his stand on belief in a miraculous conception.

We turn now to the illegitimacy tradition as preserved in Jewish literature.

6. RABBINIC LITERATURE

In the opinion of some, the rabbinic material that may concern the origin of Jesus, and the later medieval legends of the *Toledoth Yeshu,* which will be discussed below, are simply part of the literature of heated controversy, polemic, and defamation. More than passing reference to this literature can be regarded as an imprudent waking of sleeping dogs, a potential cause for setback and complication in ecumenical relations between Jews and Christians. But this first opinion is an oversimplification: these materials contain important historical information (about the rabbinic understanding of the christology of the primitive church and of the gospels, and perhaps of the historical Jesus).[96] I hope that the second opinion is wrong: discussion of this issue, inclusive of the voices and interests of women, can serve to improve ecumenical relations.[97]

a. Tannaitic Period (to 200 C.E.)

BEN PANTERA TEXTS

In the first set of texts that should be mentioned, Jesus is referred to as "the son of Pantera" (Yeshu ben Pantera), and this designation is placed in the mouths of rabbis of the Tannaitic period.[98] These texts do not discuss Jesus' origins, explaining how he is the son of Pantera, nor do they call Pantera a soldier. Rather, several record a difference of opinion between two Tannaim regarding the permissibility of healing in the name of Jesus son of Pantera (*t. Ḥul.* 2.22, 23; *y. Šabb.* 14d; *y. 'Abod. Zar.* 27b). This tradition may be as early as the beginning of the second or end of the first century C.E. Another passage (*t. Ḥul.* 2:24) concerns "heretical" teaching told in the name of Yeshu ben Pantiri by a Galilean to Rabbi Eliezer, one of the leading figures of the first generation at Jamnia, who was about 50 years old in 70 C.E. Rabbinic tradition would never have invented such a story about Eliezer had there been no basis for it. It is regarded by Smith as the first appearance of this name generally given by Jewish tradition to Jesus' father.[99] It is possible that Pantera was given simply as a family name of Jesus, with no connotation of illegitimacy or of mockery, but it is more likely that the name is somehow associated with the story told by Celsus's "Jew."[100]

M. YEBAM. 4:13

Another text of interest here from the Tannaitic period is *m. Yebam.* 4:13, which has been mentioned above in chapter 2.[101] "Rabbi Simeon ben Azzai said: I found a family register in Jerusalem and in it was written, Such-a-one (*plwny*) is a bastard through [a transgression of the law of] thy neighbor's wife, confirming the words of Rabbi Joshua." The word *plwny* (such-a-one, so-and-so, or a certain person) is thought by some to be a reference to Jesus, veiled and cautious because of Christian activity or Christian hostility.[102] This text has been called by S.

Krauss "the earliest authenticated passage ascribing illegitimate birth to Jesus."[103] However, this is not certain. *M. Abot* 3:12 warns that "if one exposes his fellowmen to humiliation publicly he has no portion in the world to come"; this might be sufficient reason for the Tanna to avoid the name of the person he had in mind.[104]

If the passage is about Jesus, Mary is referred to as married ('*št'yš*) rather than betrothed (contrast Celsus; but betrothal, as we have noted, was the equivalent of marriage in many respects). It is possible the law referred to is Deut 22:23–27 (see v 24). No details are given about the transgression, except that it was punishable by death. The finding of Rabbi Simeon ben Azzai is said to confirm the opinion of Rabbi Joshua, who argued that a *mamzēr* was the offspring of any union "for which the partakers are liable to death at the hands of the court."[105] We have discussed above the possibility that there is some link between this text and the gospel tradition. Unless this passage does refer to Jesus, we have no certain evidence that the Tannaim ascribed an illegitimate birth to him.

KALLAH 51A

Another rabbinic text should be mentioned here, tractate *Kallah* 51a, although it did not originally refer to Jesus.[106] It is important because it was later applied to Jesus, and a portion of the *Toledoth Yeshu,* which will be treated below, is obviously based on it. The text is as follows:

"An impudent one." R. Eliezer says: [it means] an illegitimate child. R. Yehoshua says: a son of a *niddah* [a menstruating woman]. R. Akiba says: an illegitimate child [who is also] the son of a *niddah.* Once, when the elders were sitting at the gate, two children passed in front of them. One covered his head and the other uncovered his head [the latter gesture a sign of disrespect]. The one who uncovered his head R. Eliezer designated "an illegitimate child"; R. Akiba said, "an illegitimate child *and* a son of a niddah." They said to R. Akiba: "How have you the audacity to contradict the words of your colleagues!" He answered them, "This I shall prove." He went to the mother of the child and saw her sitting in the market, selling peas. He said to her, "My daughter, if you tell me this which I inquire of you I shall bring you to the life of the world to come." She replied, "Swear it to me." R. Akiba vowed with his lips but disavowed in his heart. Said he to her: "This is your son, what is the fact concerning him?" She answered, "When I entered the bridal chamber I was a *niddah* and my husband remained apart from me; but my friend[107] came to me, and by him I had this son—it resulted that the child is illegitimate *and* a son of a *niddah.*" They said: Great was R. Akiba, for he put his teachers to shame. In that hour they said: Blessed be the Lord God of Israel who has revealed his secret to R. Akiba ben Joseph.[108]

The tractate that contains this passage is of later composition than most of the Talmud, but the persons in the story are Tannaim of the end of the first and beginning of the second century. The last sentence (which suggests "that there is here a 'hidden' mystery, and that something of great importance has been 'revealed,' and that the story is not merely concerned with the origin of some street-child"[109]) is regarded as a later addition, since the narrative already has a conclusion. At whatever point the conclusion was added, the story was thought to refer to Jesus. The chronology is mistaken, as in *b. Šabb.* 104b; *b. Sanh.* 67a (see below). The rabbis mentioned could not have seen Jesus as a child (although some might have spoken to Mary).[110] Neither Jesus nor Mary is mentioned by name.

Four things about this passage are significant: (1) as a reference to Jesus, it is a description of him as a *mamzēr;* (2) it insists that his father was a family friend; (3) it says this information came from his mother (cf. Origen, *Against Celsus* 1:39); (4) the story is connected to a divine revelation of a secret.

BEN STADA TEXTS

References to a "son of Stada" (ben Stada) are attributed to rabbis of the Tannaitic period. Rabbi Eliezer, for example, is said to have discussed ben Stada bringing magic spells from Egypt in scratches on his flesh (*b. Šabb.* 104b; *t. Šabb.* 11:15; *y. Šabb.* 12:4 [13d]). The original ben Stada may have been a Jew who advocated some cult involving the worship of deities other than Yahweh, was entrapped by Jews in Lydda, condemned by a rabbinic court, and stoned. Jesus was nicknamed Ben Stada, since he also was accused of introducing the worship of other gods. Therefore it is often difficult to tell to whom the "Ben Stada" passages refer[111] (*t. Sanh.* 10:11; *y. Sanh.* 7:16 [25c,d]; *y. Yebam.* 16:5 [15d]; *b. Sanh.* 67a). In the last passage, he is identified with Jesus, hanged (crucified) on the eve of Passover.

b. Amoraic Period (200–500 C.E.)

BEN STADA, BEN PANTIRA

In *b. Šabb.* 104b and *b. Sanh.* 67a, ben Stada is identified with ben Pandira, and Mary, a hairdresser, is said to have been an adulteress. But there is debate:

Was he then the son of Stada? Surely he was the son of Pandira? Rabbi Hisda[112] said, "The husband was Stada, the paramour was Pandira." [But was not] the husband Pappos ben Judah? His mother was Stada. [But was not] his mother Miriam the hairdresser? [Yes, but she was nicknamed *Stada*]—as we say in Pumbeditha,[113] "*s'tat da* [i.e., this one has turned away] from her husband."[114]

There are attempts to explain the dual name (the husband was Stada, the lover was Pandira; Stada is the [nick]name of the mother, not the father). There is also chronological confusion; Pappos ben Yehuda lived a century later, in the time of Akiba. He may be mentioned because Pappos may be a short form of Josephus or Joseph, and/or because he was so jealous of his notorious wife that he would not let her leave the house (see *b. Giṭ.* 90a; *t. Soṭa* 5.9). Mary is apparently confused with Mary Magdalene: the word for hairdresser is *Mĕgaddĕlā'*.[115] It is also possible that Mary is given the nickname of Stada, not only because she was regarded as an adulteress, but because Mary Magdalene was thought to have been a great sinner.

Many scholars correctly dispute the historical accuracy of the identification of ben Pandira with ben Stada.[116] But the reference to Jesus in the minds of the rabbis of this period is clear and important. If R. Eliezer did refer to Jesus as ben Stada, perhaps the name Stada referred to his mother. The derivation *sṭt d'* would be possible in Palestine no less than in Babylonia; that is, Mary would have been known in the early period as one who went astray from her husband, committed adultery. But we have no rabbinic evidence from the earlier period for this meaning.[117] The reference here to ben Pandira as her lover is the only evidence in the Talmud that assumes an act of adultery on the part of Mary.[118]

PESIQTA RABBATI 100B–101A

In about the middle of the third century, Rabbi Ḥiyya ben Abba (a Palestinian Amora of the third generation) instructed his pupils on how to refute "the whore's son" (*br' dznyt'*) if he told them there are two gods. The expression, "the whore's son" has a double meaning, referring to Jesus in person (as illegitimate) and to his supposedly dualistic teaching (that is, he is a "son of heresy").[119] Mary is nowhere else in Palestinian rabbinic sources referred to as a harlot.[120]

7. THE TOLEDOTH YESHU

The *Toledoth Yeshu* or "Life of Jesus" is a booklet of which there are nearly a dozen versions, based on rabbinic sayings and Christian sources and perhaps on ancient parallel traditions. It reflects relations between Jews and Christians over the centuries and Jewish views on Christianity. It is not read much now, although at one time it had a wide circulation in Hebrew and Yiddish and was studied during the nights of *Natal* (Christmas). Klausner remarks, "Our mothers knew its contents by hearsay—of course with all manner of corruptions, changes, omissions and imaginative additions—and handed them on to their children."[121] Although the earliest Hebrew recension of this work was not made before the tenth century, the Aramaic original may be from the fifth century,[122] and the work may contain "fossils of old tradition," motifs that go back to the second century.[123]

The *Toledoth* is often regarded as worthless (as well as embarrassing) from a historical standpoint. According to Solomon Schechter, it is purely apocryphal in character, neither meant nor ever taken by the Jews as real history. "All the so-called Anti-Christiana collected by medieval fanatics, and freshed up again by modern ignoramuses, belong to the later centuries, when history and biography had already given way to myth and speculation."[124] The *Toledoth* has been called a classic example of Jewish defamation and parody of the New Testament.[125] The old view is that it is a medieval compilation of those myths and fragments of folklore that grew up as a reaction to persecution.[126] However, without denying the presence of elements of distortion and animosity and substitution, an examination of the material concerning the origins of Jesus shows that it is much more than this.

The most widely known version (printed by Wagenseil in 1681) can be summarized as follows:[127]

In the year 3651 [about 90 B.C.E.],[128] in the days of King Jannaeus, a great misfortune befell Israel, when there arose a certain disreputable man of the tribe of Judah, whose name was Joseph Pandera.[129] He lived at Bethlehem, in Judah. Near his house dwelt a widow and her lovely and virginal daughter named Miriam. Miriam was betrothed to Yohanan,[130] of the royal house of David, a man learned in the Torah and God-fearing.

At the close of a certain Sabbath, Joseph Pandera, attractive and like a warrior in appearance, having gazed lustfully upon Miriam, knocked upon the door of her room and betrayed her by pretending that he was her betrothed husband, Yohanan. Even so, she was amazed at this improper conduct and submitted only against her will. Thereafter, when Yohanan came to her, Miriam expressed astonishment at behavior so foreign to his character. It was thus that they both came to know of the crime of Joseph Pandera and the terrible mistake on the part of Miriam. Whereupon Yohanan went to Rabban Shimeon ben Shetah and related to him the tragic seduction. Lacking witnesses required for the punishment of Joseph Pandera,[131] and Miriam being with child, Yohanan left for Babylonia.

Miriam gave birth to a son and named him Yehoshua, after her brother. This name later deteriorated to Yeshu. On the eighth day he was circumcised. When he was old enough the lad was taken by Miriam to the house of study to be instructed in the Jewish tradition. One day Yeshu walked in front of the Sages with his head uncovered, showing shameful disrespect. At this, the discussion arose as to whether this behavior did not truly indicate that Yeshu was an illegitimate child and the son of a *niddah*. . . . It was discovered through Rabban Shimeon ben Shetah that he was the illegitimate son of Joseph Pandera. Miriam admitted it.[132] After this became known, it was necessary for Yeshu to flee to Upper Galilee. . . .[133]

He gathered about himself three hundred and ten young men of Israel and accused those who spoke ill of his birth of being people who desired greatness and power for themselves. Yeshu proclaimed, "I am the Messiah; and concerning me Isaiah prophesied and said, 'Behold, a virgin shall conceive, and bear a son, and shall call his name Immanuel.'" He quoted other messianic texts, insisting, "David my ancestor prophesied concerning me: 'The Lord said unto me, thou art my son, this day have I begotten thee.'"[134]

In all the versions, Miriam is described in a favorable light.[135] All the versions concur that when it became known that she was raped, the husband ran away, and the infant was born to his lonely mother.[136] As in the story told by Celsus's "Jew," two sources are given for the information about Jesus' origins: (1) Jesus himself, telling that he is born of a virgin (here citing Isa 7:14) and is son of God (here citing Ps 2:7); (2) Mary, here admitting that Jesus was illegitimate.[137] We must ask if this last point is invention (based on the fact that the mother's testimony in a matter like this is the most important), or whether this is an authentic memory.

It is misleading to state simply that medieval Jews interpreted the Christian claim that Joseph was not the father of Jesus to mean that Jesus was illegitimate. The relation to older Jewish tradition is clear at many points (for example, the name Pandera, Jesus the son of a *niddah*), as is the relation to Christian tradition (for example, birth in Bethlehem; the betrothed husband of Mary a man learned in the Torah and God-fearing; the rape or seduction of Mary), and perhaps the trace of parallel tradition (the father of Jesus a neighbor; lack of witnesses). The explicit mention of rape may be drawn from pre-gospel tradition.

It is misleading also to reconstruct the history of tradition as Goldstein does in this way:

The earliest record, as we reconstruct it, tells of a natural birth of Jesus by Joseph and Mary.[138] The Jews, and the early Jewish Christians too, believed it, for nowhere in the New Testament is there any Jewish accusation of illegitimacy. When, however, Jesus was interpreted as not only the Messiah but also the Son of God it was stated emphatically that Joseph was not the father. "Who, then, was the father?" asked those who could not accept the Divine Sonship. Various answers were given; one of these is recorded in Toledoth Yeshu.[139]

Views such as this oversimplify and distort the history of the tradition concerning Jesus' origins. The earliest record does not name Joseph as Jesus' father, and there is evidence in the New Testament of a Jewish charge of illegitimacy.

The earlier rabbinic teachers probably knew more about the origins of Jesus than they cared to report or had occasion to express. It may be true that, "If for one reason or another they did not care to speak about these things publicly and explicitly, it would be futile for us to attempt to find out what they knew about them. We cannot make them talk now."[140] Further, all the information they did give may not have been preserved; some of it may have been eliminated either by Christian censors or by Jews for fear of censors, or by negligence or accident, or even because Jewish editors did not think the material worth preserving. The *Toledoth*, the fullest story we have of the Jewish understanding of Jesus' origins, even though it is a product of later times and incorporates later elements, may well give us some idea of the story or stories behind the fragmentary rabbinic traditions, and even behind the New Testament Infancy Narratives.

8. CONCLUSION

The pertinent results of this survey of Jewish materials can be summed up briefly. The Jewish tradition of Jesus' illegitimacy is a strong one. While we have no absolutely certain evidence from the Tannaitic period (first and second centuries C.E.) that he was regarded by the rabbis of that time as illegitimate, the use of the name ben Pantera (and variants) for him is very likely connected to the name and story found in Origen's *Against Celsus*. The saying about the scroll found in Jerusalem containing the genealogy of an illegitimate person is probably a reference to Jesus. In the Amoraic period (200–500) there is solid evidence for the belief in his illegitimacy, with some of these rabbis identifying ben Pantera with ben Stada. The material in tractate *Kallah* is late, and there is no way of knowing exactly when the story about the *mamzēr* and son of a *niddah* was thought to refer to Jesus and Mary. In the Amoraic ben Pantera-ben Stada materials, and in *Pesiqta Rabbati* 100b–101a the reference is clear.

In only two of the Jewish traditions is the mother of Jesus clearly regarded as the guilty party: as a whore (*Pesiqta Rabbati* 100b–101a; cf. *Gospel of Thomas* 105; Tertullian, *De Spectaculis* 30:6), and as one who "turned aside" from her husband (part of the Amoraic ben Pantira-ben Stada texts). In some of the texts, her role is ambiguous (*m. Yebam.* 4:13; *Kallah* 51a; parts of the ben Pantira-ben Stada texts; cf. John 8:41; Mark 6:3; *Acts of Pilate* 2:3). She is said to have been raped or seduced in the *Toledoth*, as implied in the New Testament Infancy Narratives and in the story of Celsus's "Jew" (where she is "corrupted" and convicted of adultery, her story not believed).

This tradition of illegitimacy is not simply "a demonstration of how seriously the Jews took the gospel narratives of Jesus' irregular birth."[141] There are elements that cannot be explained as elaboration of the New Testament narratives, and possibly there is reliance on sources independent of these narratives, supporting the historicity of an illegitimate conception.

It appears, therefore, that the tradition of Jesus' illegitimacy in Jewish literature did not simply originate as a reaction to (and distortion of) a Christian claim that Jesus was conceived without a human father,[142] although that claim, which I have argued does not appear in the New Testament, did play a role in the polemic between Christians and Jews. Basically, I think, the Jewish tradition involves a correct reading of some elements of the New Testament narratives, and a studied ignoring and/or contradiction of other elements, most importantly the role of the Holy Spirit. This may also be a living extension of an early stage of the pre-gospel tradition of the illegitimacy of Jesus.[143]

We have been inquiring here not about what Dalman called "the logic of Jewish unbelief" (since God has no son, while Jesus—as the Christians themselves admit—is not Joseph's son, it follows that he is born of Mary out of wedlock),[144] but about the twists and turns in the development of a legend or legends based on a potentially tragic historical event. That one believed to be the Messiah should have been illegitimately conceived is perhaps incomprehensible to some, but not for that reason unhistorical.

C. THE VIRGINAL CONCEPTION

1. THE ORIGIN OF THE DOCTRINE: HYPOTHESES

If the virginal conception of Jesus is not historical and is not the creation of the authors of primitive tradition or the authors of the New Testament Infancy Narratives, where does it come from, and why does it appear? I do not know the answers to these questions. To explore them would necessitate another full study, concentrating on New Testament apocrypha, early Gnostic, Jewish Christian, and patristic thought. The investigation would be difficult, since the late first and early second century literature is fragmentary, and much of the literature of the

Christian "losers" has not been preserved. In particular, I suspect that clues may be provided by study of the origin and development of such figures as Sophia (who conceives without a male partner or without his consent) in the *Apocalypse of Adam, The Thunder, Perfect Mind,* and elsewhere;[145] the redeemer Illuminator in the *Apocalypse of Adam* (described by the third kingdom as originating from a virgin womb [7:9]);[146] and the virgin-mother Spirit (who is the counterpart and consort of the Heavenly Father) in the *Gospel of Philip*.[147]

This present study is incomplete without the suggestion of a few working hypotheses: (1) The belief in a virginal conception is primarily a Gentile product. It developed when the New Testament Infancy Narratives, or aspects of the pre-gospel infancy tradition, were heard or read against the background of predominantly Gentile religious heritages and sensibilities and without enough of an ear for the subtle Old Testament allusions and Jewish sensibilities. The tendency in Greco-Roman literature to create for great men tales of miraculous births influenced the writing and reading of the New Testament narratives. In some non-Jewish descriptions of such births, the god takes the role of the husband or lover in intercourse[148] or assumes another form.[149] Even when the stories are of pneumatic conceptions, where the spirit (*pneuma*) or power (*dynamis*) of a god is mentioned,[150] these seem to be forms of sexual intercourse. This sexual element means that even though there is the notion of "double paternity" (divine and human),[151] and thoughts of divine and human participation in conception were not always mutually exclusive in the non-Jewish literature,[152] the tendency was to regard divine paternity as *replacing rather than enhancing* human paternity in the biological act of conception. The absence of sexual undertones in the New Testament treatments of the role of the Holy Spirit in the conception of Jesus stands in contrast to most descriptions of the role of the gods. But the notion of replacement or cancellation of the role of the human male in the post–New Testament doctrine of the virginal conception is the result of pagan influence on the reading of the Matthean and Lucan texts. Both texts lack direct statements of Jesus' illegitimacy and insist Joseph was not his biological father. No biological father mentioned became read as no biological father.

Conception without a human father was eventually regarded as appropriate, finally as necessary.[153]

(2) The belief in a virginal conception also draws on Jewish thought patterns. Held in check by Christian acceptance of Jewish monotheism and of the Jewish and Gentile philosophical notions of divine transcendence, patristic speculation and reasoning about the nature of the role of the divine in this conception steered fairly clear of sexual imagery[154] and eventually fastened on the explanation that Jesus' conception was like a second creation (and Mary the antithesis of Eve), an explanation that remains dominant today. The development of the doctrine may also have been influenced by the Jewish story in 2 *Enoch* 23 of the conception of Melchizedek, even though this is not a story of a *virginal* conception and may be about the appearance of a superhuman being, not the conception of a real human being (see below).

(3) The doctrine is the product of deafness to and denial of the story of the plight of a woman and a child. Luke, and, to some extent, Matthew bear a large measure of responsibility for the deafness and the denial, since their narratives each alter the focus of the pre-gospel tradition, defuse it, and develop it further theologically and Christologically. In Matthew, the woman's plight and salvation are seen primarily as they have impact on the life of a man and his decisions. In Luke, the woman is center stage, but the anguish of the event is muted to a whisper and all but overwhelmed by strains of triumph and joy. The knowledge of the illegitimacy tradition, which they presumed on the part of their readers, was not handed on clearly. The earliest Mariology was swamped by Christology. Ironically, the story lived on and was elaborated in polemical and sometimes patriarchal directions by those Jews who did not accept growing Christian claims and sought to discredit Mary and Jesus.[155] Unlike the story of the crucifixion, which drew on the tradition of the martyrdom of the righteous, the story of seduction or rape and illegitimate pregnancy had no strong defensive tradition on which to draw.

(4) Belief in the virginal conception is strangely linked to contemplation more of the Fourth Gospel than of the Matthean and Lucan narratives. Gentile Christian belief in the incarnation of

a divine being in the womb of Mary resulted from reading Matthew and Luke in the light of the Johannine prologue, from harmonizing the conception Christology with the stronger and apparently more appealing incarnational Christology. See, for example, *Epistula Apostolorum* 3: "We believe that the word, which became flesh through the holy virgin Mary, was carried (conceived) in her womb by the Holy Spirit, and was born not by the lust of the flesh but by the will of God, and was wrapped (in swaddling clothes) and made known at Bethlehem."[156]

(5) It was primarily in debate with Gnostics that the doctrine of the virginal conception took shape. Von Campenhausen speaks of controversy on two fronts: on the one hand with those Jewish Christians and Gnostics who held that according to his physical origin Jesus was the son of Joseph and a natural human being, and on the other hand with those Gnostics who developed purely docetic Christologies, holding that the Christ was a superhuman being like an angel, who joined with or appeared in a human body.[157] To these latter thinkers, "any birth, even a birth from a virgin, seemed to bring Christ into too intimate relation to the world."[158] Interest and emphasis in early patristic writings lie above all not in the *manner* of his conception, but (against the first front) on the preexistence of the divine Son, and (against the more powerful second front) on the *reality* of his human conception.[159] In the combat against Gnostic docetism, concessions were made to Gnostic views on sexuality and thought patterns, while conception by the virgin Mary was insisted upon as essential to Jesus' true humanity. (Only later, with Athanasius, did virginal conception become a sign of his divinity.[160]) The Gnostic texts from Nag Hammadi provide new evidence that must be taken into account in the attempt to understand the early stages of belief in a virginal conception. In the light of these five hypotheses, but without the time and space to test them, we turn to a brief look at some early statements of this doctrine.

2. EARLY STATEMENTS

Examination of the New Testament Infancy Narratives and of the history of their early interpretation shows that in the first two centuries C.E. there were four competing understandings of the origin of Jesus Christ: (1) he was illegitimate; (2) he was the son of Joseph; (3) he was virginally conceived; (4) he was not humanly conceived or born at all. Several good studies exist on this fourth belief, the virginal conception in the early church, such as those by H. von Campenhausen, J. G. Machen, A. Hoben, T. Boslooper, and R. E. Brown.[161] The reader is referred to these for fuller treatment.

It took over a hundred years for belief in the virginal conception to become the dominant Christian view. It is claimed that by the year 200 C.E. "the virginal conception of Jesus was 'in possession' as a Christian doctrine."[162] Attention to the New Testament apocrypha and to the writings of the early Fathers of the Church show that it was known and accepted by Christians of various origins and many places during the second century. There are, however, puzzling instances of silence that may indicate ignorance or rejection of the doctrine. Among the "Apostolic Fathers," only Ignatius (writing around 110–115) is thought to mention it. In the next few pages we will look at a selection of passages that illustrate the points mentioned above and communicate a sense of the complexity of the development of the doctrine.

a. Early Patristic Evidence

IGNATIUS OF ANTIOCH

The earliest statements are brief and somewhat ambiguous. Ignatius bishop of Antioch holds that Jesus was "both of Mary and of God" (*Ephesians* 7:2) but also that he was "according to the dispensation of God conceived in the womb by Mary, of the seed of David, but of the Holy Spirit" (18:2; cf. *Smyrnaeans* 1:1: he was "truly of the seed of David according to the flesh, and the Son of God according to the will and power of God . . . truly born of a virgin"; *Trallians* 9:1: he "was descended from David, and was also of Mary"). Fitzmyer notices that the phrase "truly born of a virgin" is significant, "but it still has not clearly enunciated virginal conception."[163] Ignatius may be drawing on a tradition such as that found in Rom 1:3 in his statements about the seed of David,[164] but it is impossible to know how he understands this phrase. Do he (and his readers) suppose Mary to have been a descendant of David, as Justin later did? Or is he unthinkingly combining traditions? In *Ephesians* 19:1 he remarks that "the virginity of Mary was hidden from the prince of this world, as was also her offspring, and the death of the Lord; three resounding mysteries which were wrought in the silence of God."

It is uncertain whether Ignatius relies on Matthew's Infancy Narratives or on independent tradition.[165] If Ignatius does rely on Matthew, he shows us that Matthew 1 was read with emphasis on Mary's virginity, on Davidic descent, and on divine begetting, and apparently without any awareness of an illegitimacy tradition. If Ignatius relies on pre-gospel tradition, this might be on the early theological interpretation of Jesus' conception (an interpretation I have suggested did not come from but was added to family tradition), perhaps somehow floating free from the illegitimacy tradition.

Whatever his sources, if Ignatius is writing of a virginal conception, he is assuming it, not arguing for it.[166] The emphasis he lays on the conception and birth of Jesus is antidocetic, and to him the humanity of the conception is more important than the conception by a virgin.[167] Whatever Ignatius understands by Mary's virginity, he does not think his understanding has to be made explicit or defended.

"BORN OF THE VIRGIN MARY"

There are many other examples of brief statements of belief in Mary's virginity. Aristides of Athens (ca. 145) confesses that the Son of God descended from heaven through the Holy Spirit and was born of a virgin (*Apology* 15:1).[168] The Old Roman Creed (expanded in the second half of the second century) speaks of Jesus "born of the Holy Spirit and the virgin Mary." No new and strange doctrines could be incorporated into such a creed; but what do the brief statements mean?

Scholars have noticed the uncertainty under which the majority of early writers labored as to the identity and role of the Holy Spirit referred to by the evangelists. One current view was that what had become incarnate in the virgin, as narrated by Matthew and Luke, was divine Spirit.[169] Kelly discusses the "all but unanimous exegetical tradition" of Luke 1:35, which equates the holy spirit and the power of the Most High not with the Holy Spirit but with the Christ, preexisting as spirit or Word, and incarnating himself in Mary's womb. It is probable that the Old Roman Creed reflects this idea: that Jesus Christ, the historic Son of God, was the product of the union of divine spirit with human nature in the womb of Mary.[170]

In the light of our discussion of the New Testament narratives and the pre-gospel and Jewish traditions, some of the statements above, usually understood as taking for granted a virginal conception, may be open to different interpretations. That is, simple references to Jesus born of the virgin Mary cannot be assumed to be always examples of belief in the biologically virginal conception of Jesus, conception without a male parent. It is possible that these point to his conception by Mary who *was* a virgin before the conception[171] and who continued to be known as "the virgin," this description gradually becoming part of her name. This might have been a very early way of implying her innocence, her lack of guilt, or simply a way of identifying her as Luke does in 1:27. On the other hand, these references, appearing in the brief, creedlike summaries, may have been formulated by those who believed in the doctrine of virginal conception, but whose intent was to stress the reality of Jesus' birth and his humanity.[172]

JUSTIN MARTYR

In the work of Justin Martyr (ca. 110–166), a Gentile native of Palestine, we find for the first time the following five explicit statements. (1) The virgin Mary conceived without sexual intercourse. "For if she had intercourse with anyone whatever, she was no longer a virgin." The Power of God "caused her while yet a virgin to conceive." She conceived "not by intercourse but by power" (*Apol.* 1:33). Jesus was "begotten by the Father by an act of will" (*Dial.* 61) and was "not the seed of a human race" (*Dial.* 68). The Word was produced "without sexual union" (*Apol.* 1:21), "born of God in a peculiar manner, different from ordinary generation" (*Apol.* 1:22).[173] The virginal conception is in keeping with the creative function of the Word of God, who made Eve from Adam's rib and in the beginning created all living beings apart from parentage (*Dial.* 84). For Justin the conception of Jesus was unlike the conceptions in Greek myths, which are diabolical counterfeits of the prophecies about Christ (*Dial.* 69; *Apol.* 1:33, 54), but are useful as analogies (*Apol.* 1:21, 22). According to von Campenhausen, the virginal conception was for Justin "an established and undoubted piece of genuine Christian tradition."[174]

(2) Mary was of Davidic descent (*Dial.* 43). (3) Isaiah 7 predicted the unique virginal conception (*Apol.* 1:33; *Dial.* 43:5–8; 66–67; 77–78; 84).[175] The virginal conception is regarded as a particularly obvious instance of fulfilled prediction.[176] (4) Some Jews, while regarding Jesus as the Messiah, consider him to be "a man of men." Justin apparently accepts them as Christians but does not agree with them, claiming they have a false trust in human dogmas (*Dial.* 48). Justin himself is able to separate the question of the divine sonship of Jesus from that of the manner of his birth: "Moreover, the Son of God called Jesus, even if only a man by ordinary generation, yet on account of his wisdom is worthy to be called the Son of God; for all writers call God the Father of men and gods" (*Apol.* 1:22). (5) Mary's conception of Jesus is to be contrasted with Eve's conception of disobedience and death (*Dial.* 100; cf. Tertullian, *The Flesh of Christ* 16).

While Justin may preserve some Palestinian noncanonical material,[177] even in his dialogue with Trypho the Jew[178] he does not allude to or directly combat the tradition of the illegitimacy of Jesus. In *Dial.* 78 he retells the Matthean narrative, adding that Joseph supposed Mary to be pregnant by intercourse with a man, that is, from fornication. But he was commanded in a vision not to put her away. "The angel who appeared to him told him that what was in her womb is of the Holy Spirit." Joseph was afraid and did not put her away. Trypho is never represented as adducing any concrete facts in opposition to Justin's story or as offering an alternative Jewish story of the actual circumstances of the conception of Jesus.[179] In *Dial.* 121:3, Justin admits that Christ's first advent was "without honor and comeliness, and very contemptible," but this meets the general objection that the Messiah would not have come into the world without fitting honor and glory.

Is it possible, however, that those Jewish Christians to whom Justin refers in *Dial.* 48[180] hold that Jesus was Messiah even though illegitimately conceived? He says only that they maintain that he was born "a man from men" (*anthrōpon . . . ex anthrōpon genomenon*). But if Justin knew of some who held that the Messiah was conceived illegitimately, we would expect him here (or in *Dial.* 78) to mention and refute this opinion. Later Origen speaks of the Ebionites divided into two classes, one that accepted and one that denied the virginal conception; the latter, he says, regarded Joseph as Jesus' father (*In Evang. Matt.* 16:10ff; cf. *Against Celsus* 5:61: "the twofold sect of Ebionites, who either acknowledge with us that Jesus was born of a virgin, or deny this, and maintain that he was begotten like other human beings"). He links no Jewish Christian beliefs with the story told by Celsus's "Jew."[181] Some Gnostics also held that Jesus was the son of Joseph and Mary (Cerinthus, the Carpocratians, the author of the *Acts of Thomas* 2 ["the son of Joseph the carpenter"]; cf. *Gospel of Philip* 73:8).[182]

What gospels were used by those Jewish Christians who held that Jesus' conception was natural? The problem of Jewish Christian gospels has been called one of the most difficult that the apocryphal literature presents; help in solving it will come not from new hypotheses but from new discoveries. Three have to be distinguished: the *Gospel of the Nazaraeans*, the *Gospel of the Ebionites*, and the *Gospel of the Hebrews*. The first two have a relationship to canonical Matthew, and all three are probably to be dated in the first half of the second century C.E. In the present state of research it is not possible to fit them into place in the history of Jewish Christianity or in the history of its theology.[183] We cannot be sure how the Matthean Infancy Narrative was read in these circles, nor do we know the full shape and origin of their other traditions concerning the conception.

IRENAEUS

Irenaeus (ca. 120–202) gives us extensive information about Gnostic and Jewish Christian teachings on the origins of Jesus, teachings that he regarded as heretical. His own belief is articulated in opposition to the two extremes; that of belief in the natural origin of Jesus, and that of belief in his supernatural origin, free from the pollution of inherently evil flesh (*Against Heresies* 1.22–31). Some, he says, believe that the Word and Christ never came into this world; that the Saviour, too, never became incarnate, nor suffered, but that he descended like a dove upon the dispensational Jesus; and that, as soon as he had declared the unknown Father, he did again ascend into the Pleroma. Some, however, make the assertion that this dispensational Jesus did become incarnate, and suffered, whom they represent as having passed through Mary just as water through a tube; but others allege him to be the Son of the Demiurge, upon whom the dispensational Jesus descended; while others, again, say that Jesus was born from Joseph and Mary, and that the Christ from above descended upon him, being without flesh, and impassible. But according to the opinion of no one of the heretics was the Word of God made flesh. For if anyone examines the systems of them all, he will find that the Word of God is brought in by all of them as not having become incarnate and as impassible, as is also the Christ from above. Others consider him to have been manifested as a transfigured man; but they maintain him to have been neither born nor to have become incarnate; while others [hold] that he did not assume a human form at all, but that, as a dove, he did descend upon that Jesus who was born from Mary (3.11.3).

In support of his own view, Irenaeus appeals to the authority of Scripture, reading Isa 7:14 as being about a generation "which could have been accomplished in no other way than by God the Lord of all . . . God giving this sign, but man not working it out," reading Dan 2:34, the "stone cut out without hands," as meaning that Joseph took no part in the conception of Jesus, and so forth (3.21.6–8).[184] With Irenaeus, the virginal conception becomes theologically significant, an essential part of Christian doctrine,[185] and we see most clearly the relationship between this belief and the denial of death. The Son of God became son of man "since he had a generation as to his human nature from Mary, who was descended from mankind and who was herself a human being" (3.19.3); his divine sonship is based on the fact that God, not man, was his father (3.21.8). Jesus' ability and excellent character are regarded as consequences of the virginal conception (1.30.12). The union of divine and human is the necessary means of human redemption.[186] A parallelism and moral antithesis are found between the virginal conception and the creation and fall (3.21.10). The virginal conception is seen as "a new generation" by which humanity escapes from "the generation subject to death" and receives adoption from God (4.33.4).[187]

Those who assert Jesus was a mere man, begotten by Joseph, "are in a state of death" (3.19.1).

TERTULLIAN

Tertullian (ca. 150–240) argues for the virginal conception in a syllogistic fashion.

Christ cannot lie. He said he was the son of man. Therefore he had a human parent. But God was his father. Therefore Mary, his mother, was the human parent. But if so, she was a virgin. Otherwise he had two fathers, a divine and a human one, the thought of which is ridiculous, like the stories of Castor and Hercules.[188] Moreover, the prophecy of Isaiah is alone fulfilled by the exclusion of a human father and the acceptance of the virginity of Mary . . . (*Against Marcion* 4:10)

He defends the real humanity of Christ by an appeal to the virginal conception. In *On the Flesh of Christ* 1, he writes, "Let us examine our Lord's bodily substance, for about his spiritual nature all are agreed. It is his flesh that is in question." Tertullian's belief is that the part played by God in the generation of Jesus was such as to utterly *exclude* human fatherhood, and that God, though not in a sexual sense, substituted for a human begetter.[189]

Tertullian may allude once to the story of Jesus' illegitimacy (*De Spec.* 30:6),[190] but he dismisses it with scorn. In Tertullian's writings we see some use of apocryphal materials,[191] and it is to an examination of some of these that we turn now.

b. New Testament Apocrypha

Among the motives for the composition of the apocryphal infancy narratives and other materials was the clearly strong desire to maintain and even show or prove that Mary was and remained a biological virgin.[192] The following four selections show how Christology developed in a docetic direction when the Matthean and Lucan accounts (blended with independent traditions and sometimes with elements from the Johannine prologue) were interpreted as accounts of a conception without sexual intercourse.

PROTEVANGELIUM OF JAMES

The attempt to demonstrate Mary's virginity "palpably" by means of a special narrative could be quite crude. The *Prote-*

vangelium of James, making use of the canonical narratives and traditions that may go back as far as 150 C.E., was written by a non-Jew ignorant of Palestinian geography and Jewish customs.[193] It claims to have been written by James, the Lord's brother, but cannot have originated in Jewish Christian circles. In it, the annunciation to Mary in Luke is rewritten to insist that this was no normal conception. When she is told by the angel of the Lord that she will conceive of the Lord's "Word," Mary doubts in herself and says, "Shall I conceive of the Lord, the living God, [and bear] as every woman bears?" The angel answers, "Not so, Mary; for a power of the Lord shall overshadow you . . ." (11:2–3). Both Mary and Joseph drink "the water of the conviction of the Lord,"[194] and both pass the test (chap. 16). A midwife witnesses with Joseph the miraculous birth of Jesus, and she testifies to Salome that "a virgin has brought forth, a thing which her nature does not allow." Salome insists "As the Lord my God lives, unless I put [forward] my finger and test her condition, I will not believe that a virgin has brought forth" (cf. John 20:25). When Salome puts forth her finger, however, her hand is consumed by fire; she is healed by touching the child (chaps. 19–20). In manuscripts judged by Cullmann as later, the midwife tells Mary to get ready for Salome's test, "for there is no small contention concerning you" (20:1). Mary, "the unsullied image of ascetic perfection,"[195] remains a virgin all her life; the aged widower Joseph never has sexual relations with her, and Jesus' brothers are said to be stepbrothers from Joseph's first marriage.

In the *Protevangelium of James,* are four motifs found also in the first century C.E. work *2 Enoch* 23, the story of the conception of Melchizedek.[196] These motifs are: (1) direct accusation by the husband of his wife's impurity, and insistence by the wife on her purity (*Protevangelium of James* 13:2–3); (2) ignorance on the part of the pregnant woman regarding her pregnancy (*Protevangelium of James* 13:3: Joseph asks Mary "Whence is this in your womb?" She replies, "As the Lord my God lives, I do not know whence it has come to me" [cf. 12:2: "Mary forgot the mysteries which the (arch)angel Gabriel had told her"];[197] cf. *Gospel of Bartholomew* 3:61: Jesus was contained in the body of the Virgin "without the Virgin knowing that she carried [him]"[198]); (3) conception by the

"Word" of God (*Protevangelium of James* 11:2; cf. *Gospel of Bartholomew* 2:20); (4) the sudden appearance of the child (*Protevangelium of James* 19:2).[199]

The combination of these four motifs indicates that the two works have a similar milieu, and their authors were in some sense in dialogue with each other. In my opinion, 2 *Enoch* 23, a Jewish work,[200] should not be regarded as an influence on the New Testament Infancy Narratives, nor an imitation of them, but rather as an influence on the New Testament apocryphal tradition. It provided a context in which some interpreted the New Testament narratives, against their original intent. That is, the story of the brief appearance on earth of the superhuman figure Melchizedek[201] led some like the author of the *Protevangelium of James* to read the Matthean and Lucan narratives as being about the miraculous conception of Jesus. The Christian author of the *Protevangelium of James* may be attempting to show that Jewish claims concerning the fatherless conception of Melchizedek were not unique. Once the conception of Jesus was regarded as miraculous, it had to be a *virginal* conception, since the Christian tradition was clear that Mary was only betrothed to Joseph, and virginity was mentioned by Matthew and Luke.

SIBYLLINE ORACLES

The author of late second century additions to the Jewish-Hellenistic *Sibylline Oracles* 8:456–73 rewrites the Lucan annunciation story with a Johannine slant. The Logos in the last times "changed his abode, and coming as a child from the womb of the virgin Mary he arose, a new light. From heaven he came, and put on mortal form." Gabriel addresses the maiden: "In thine immaculate bosom, virgin, do thou receive God." Grace is breathed into her by God, and she reacts with trembling, turmoil, laughter, shame, and courage. "The Word flew into her body, made flesh in time and brought forth to life in her womb, was moulded to mortal form and became a boy by virgin birth-pangs." This, the author comments, "a great wonder to mortals, is no great wonder to God the Father and to God the Son" (87:458–76).[202]

ASCENSION OF ISAIAH

The Christian-Gnostic author of *Ascension of Isaiah* 11, part of "the Vision of Isaiah" which may have originated in the mid–second century C.E.,[203] also rewrites the New Testament gospels to make certain beliefs clear. Both Joseph and Mary are said to be of Davidic descent (v 2). It is explicitly said that Joseph "did not put Mary away, but kept her" (v 4; contrast the story told by Celsus's "Jew"). Joseph did not reveal the matter to anyone (v 4), and after the birth both Mary and Joseph were told by a voice, "Tell this vision to no one" (v 11). The author underlines the belief that Joseph and Mary did not have sexual relations and that Mary was "a holy virgin" although she was pregnant (v 5). The birth is described as miraculous, the "small child" appearing when Mary and Joseph were alone (emphasized twice), to the amazement of Mary and apparently at first unknown to Joseph (vv 7–10; cf. motif [4] above, in *Protevangelium of James* and *Gospel of Bartholemew*). Even though the parents did not tell, "the report concerning the child was noised abroad in Bethlehem. Some said, 'The virgin Mary has given birth before she was married two months' [an implicit accusation of illegitimacy?], and many said, 'She has not given birth: the midwife has not gone up (to her) and we have heard no cries of pain.' And they were all in the dark concerning him, and they all knew of him, but no one knew whence he was" (vv 12–14). Isaiah is made to declare that "this was hidden from all the heavens and all the princes and every god of this world" (cf. Ignatius, *Eph.* 19:1). He is also said to have seen that in Nazareth Jesus "sucked the breast like a baby, as was customary, so that he would not be recognized" (v 17). The docetic character of this passage is evident.

ODES OF SOLOMON

The *Odes of Solomon,* called "the earliest Christian hymn-book,"[204] (first or second century) presents a unique understanding of the conception of Jesus in Ode 19:4–10 (Charlesworth translation):

The Holy Spirit opened Her bosom,
And mixed the milk of the two breasts of the Father.
Then She gave the mixture to the generation without their knowing,
And those who have received [it] are in the perfection of the right hand.
The womb of the Virgin took [it],
And she received conception and gave birth.
So the Virgin became a mother with great mercies.
And she laboured and bore the Son but without pain,
Because it did not occur without purpose.
And she did not require a midwife,
Because He caused her to give life.
She brought forth like a strong man with desire,
And she bore according to the manifestation,
And acquired with great power.

There does not seem to be any clear dependence in Ode 19 on the New Testament Infancy Narratives.[205] The feminine Holy Spirit appears also in Ode 36:5 ("For according to the greatness of the Most High, so She made me"). The "milk" may symbolize the Word of God.[206] How the conception of Jesus is imagined is not clear, but it is clear that his birth is painless and not normal. Cf. Ode 28:17 ("I did not perish, because I was not their brother, / Nor was my birth like theirs"); 48:1 ("I am from another race"); 32:2 ("the Word of truth who is self-originate"; lit.: "He who is from Himself"). Mary's "bringing forth like a strong man, with desire" apparently makes her "the only human parent, father-mother, of the Son of God."[207] Mary's role is one of decisive obedience (vv 5b–6, 10).

D. CONCLUSION

We have no evidence from the late first and the second centuries C.E. to indicate that Jewish or Gentile Christians ever entertained the possibility that Jesus was illegitimately conceived, ever regarded the tradition of Jesus' illegitimate conception as a Christian tradition, or ever read the New Testament Infancy Narratives as being about an illegitimate pregnancy. Outside the New Testament Infancy Narratives, the claim that he was illegitimately conceived appears to be solely a Jewish claim, put in the mouths of Jewish figures in Christian writings or found in

Jewish writings themselves. The early Christians whose writings we have consider Jesus the son of Joseph, or a supernatural being who was not conceived or born at all, or virginally conceived. I readily admit that the fact that we cannot prove that any early Christians read the Infancy Narratives of Matthew and Luke in the way I have proposed their authors intended is a major objection against my interpretation. Could these authors have failed so completely in their efforts to communicate the tradition to their early readers? Could the early Christians have failed so completely to understand an important aspect of these narratives? How could such failure be explained?

I can only add the following comments to the hypotheses with which we began this chapter. (1) My first point has to do with silence. We have only a fraction of the literature of the earliest Christians from this time. To claim that some early Christians (whose writings we do not have, or who did not write) might have understood the tradition and the narratives as I propose is an argument from silence, but silence that is understandable and even expected concerning such a tradition. The insistence of some Jewish Christians and others that Jesus was the natural son of Joseph may depend on a historical tradition in favor of human fatherhood, coming down in Palestine from the original Jews who believed in Jesus. Their stance, and that of the Gnostics who developed docetic christologies, are not entirely secondary views, directed against the doctrine of the virginal conception; they are, rather, evidence of how little that doctrine was taken as a matter of course up to the middle of the second century.[208] These views also may not be secondary to and directed against the illegitimacy tradition. It is another argument from silence to claim that this tradition was known to and rejected by some of those writers who do not mention a virginal conception, or who mention Jesus' conception in a confused manner or not at all, or who propose Joseph as the biological father of Jesus. The silence possibly indicates only ignorance of that tradition.

(2) We must ask whether the illegitimacy tradition has ever had a proper Christian hearing. The tradition was seen by the post–New Testament Christians whose writings we have (by Tertullian, Origen, the authors of the *Protevangelium of James* and of the *Ascension of Isaiah* 11, and others) as a lie, as slander and slur

against Jesus and his mother. Many modern authors who discuss this tradition speak of it as repulsive, repugnant, absurd, as an unthinkable alternative to virginal conception. Machen, for example, remarks, "If, when the miracle is rejected, a factual basis is sought for the story of the virgin birth, that factual basis must in the nature of the case be something of a repulsive (and thoroughly improbable) kind."[209] Such language betrays a strong, even vehement, reaction against the tradition; it can effectively deny a hearing to the charge and may mirror the reaction of early Christians. That reaction is appropriate, if the tradition is slander and an attempt to discredit. But it is inappropriate if the tradition is historical, with its own theological dimensions. One of the causes of the strong reaction is the desire to defend Mary from the accusation of immorality; the alternative of illegitimacy is regarded almost without fail as necessarily involving sin on her part. Many modern scholars, as we have seen, overlook the possibility of rape, and it is not surprising that the early Christians did too.[210] H. A. Hanke quotes L. N. Bell on "the awful alternative" of illegitimate conception: "If He was not virgin-born, then His mother was a promiscuous and dishonest woman and He was an illegitimate son. If He was not virgin-born, then He himself was deluded and the entire structure of His Person and Work is undermined and we become of all men most miserable."[211] "Undoubtedly," says Brown, "some sophisticated Christians could live with the alternative of illegitimacy; they would see this as the ultimate stage in Jesus' emptying himself and taking on the form of a servant (Philip 2:7), and would insist, quite rightly, that an irregular begetting involves no sin by Jesus himself." But "for many less sophisticated believers, illegitimacy would be an offense that would challenge the plausibility of the Christian mystery."[212] It is time to examine that "offense" in the context of the deepest strengths of Christianity.

Epilogue

What has been presented here is a series of interlocking arguments, suggestions, hypotheses, possibilities, probabilities, and open questions. I think of them as falling into place, into a new pattern, like the fragile glass pieces of a kaleidoscope that has been given a hard twist. It remains to be seen which of the pieces have a fragile strength, whether the pattern can be improved, and what it might mean for us today.

I have argued that the New Testament Infancy Narratives incorporate the tradition of Jesus' illegitimate conception, a tradition that is most likely historical. It was minimally theologized in the earliest period, regarded as a begetting through the Holy Spirit. Subsequently, in the gospels of Matthew and Luke, the focus of the tradition was altered by their two distinctive theological and Christological interpretations. The process of gradual Christian erasure of the tradition began here in the gospels, as the evangelists attempted to minimize the potential damage of the tradition and maximize its power. The tradition became a subtext, difficult to read. Polemicized before and after the writing of Matthew and Luke, the tradition survived outside the Christian communities. In early Christian circles, alternative traditions were found instead: Gnostic understandings of Jesus' nonhuman origin or the claim that Joseph was his natural father or belief in a virginal conception. During the second century, this belief became the dominant Christian doctrine of Jesus' origin. The Christian erasure of the illegitimacy tradition was nearly complete.

The reasons for the erasure and replacement of the illegitimacy tradition are surely complex. But at base it seems to me that it could not be passed down within a patriarchal form of Christianity. Within this patriarchal structure and mindset, the illegitimate conception of Jesus was a scandal so deep, an origin so "unfitting," that it simply had to be repressed.

How does this discussion of the tradition of the illegitimacy of Jesus appear in the light of the teaching of the Roman Catholic church on the virginal conception? It is not clear that such a reading of the Infancy Narratives as I have given is totally incompatible with church doctrine. Richard P. McBrien argues that belief in the virginal conception of Jesus is to be found in both New Testament Infancy Narratives, but that the "scales seem to tip" in favor of the theory that this belief is the result of a theologoumenon ("a non-normative, non-doctrinal theological interpretation that cannot be verified on the basis of historical evidence"). Nowhere, he says, did the church define the "how" of Jesus' conception. "Clearly, his origin is in God, and the Holy Spirit is directly operative in his conception. But whether the Holy Spirit's involvement positively excluded the cooperation of Joseph is not *explicitly* defined."[1] Through the belief in the virginal conception, "the Church clearly taught that Jesus is from God, that he is unique, that in Christ the human race truly has a new beginning, that the salvation he brings transcends this world, and that God works through human instruments, often weak and humble instruments at that, to advance the course of saving history. If in denying the historicity of the virginal conception, one is also denying such principles as these, then one has indeed moved outside the boundaries of the Christian, and certainly the Catholic, tradition."[2] There is no denial of these principles in this present work. What is denied is that the theologoumenon is present in the New Testament.

Not all scholars, however, agree with McBrien. R. E. Brown thinks that "in Roman Catholic theology, according to the usual criteria, the virginal conception would be classified as a doctrine infallibly taught by the ordinary magisterium."[3] A resolution of this issue is obviously beyond the scope of this book. I agree with the comment of Vincent Taylor concerning the doctrine: "What is needed more than anything else is a yet fuller disclosure of the unfettered mind of the Christian church; and for this we must wait." The church, he noted sixty-six years ago, has already expressed herself [*sic*]. "But has the church expressed her *unfettered* mind? Has she said her final word? Has she, indeed, ever been in a position to do these things?" It is in relation to the church's full voice that he hoped the doctrine would find its place.[4]

Texts acquire new meanings as they live on in different communities and situations. The doctrine of a virginal conception became at some point a meaning of the New Testament Infancy Narratives, a meaning out of which we today may still be able to create. Feminist scholars Mary Daly and Rosemary Radford Ruether have discovered new and positive significance in fragments of these narratives, seen through the lens of later Mariology, and shattered by their feminist consciousnesses. The New Testament Mary is alternately seen as victim and as free woman.

Daly reads the New Testament Infancy Narratives as being about a virginal conception *which is a rape*. The catholic Mary "is portrayed/betrayed as Total Rape Victim—a pale derivative symbol disguising the conquered Goddess," who is the creative divine life and integrity in concrete, existing women, and who is able to create parthenogenetically, on her own. The theme of the rape of the Goddess, almost universal in patriarchal myth, is "refined—disguised almost beyond recognition" in christianity.[5] Patriarchal myths such as this are like distorting lenses through which, however, we can still see into the sacred background. In order to use them as viewers, we must break their codes; "that is, we must see their lie in order to see their truth."[6] Once unmasked, Mary as the image of the Goddess can function to free the power of women's Self.

My own proposal is different. I agree that the doctrine of the virginal conception is a distortion and a mask, but I think behind it lies the illegitimacy tradition. Unmasked, that tradition presents us with fuller human realities and therefore with deeper theological potential. It presents us not with a Goddess, but with a woman in need of a Goddess, with a woman we look at, not up at. On the one hand, Catholic attitudes toward Mary can be expected to change once they no longer have to bear the burden of the repressed feminine dimension of the divine. On the other hand, as reinterpretation of the image of God brings to light the ways in which the symbol of Mary has usurped the functions of the divine, the way is clearer for reimaging God with female imagery.[7]

What, then, of the perennially attractive image of the Virgin Mother? As distortions of that image are corrected, it may serve to empower the creativity of women. A virgin: a woman never subdued. A mother: conceiving and giving birth and nurturing in power. To the extent that Mary can be called virgin—imagined as undefeated, integral, and creative, one who is not identified or destroyed by her relationship with men—she can function as a link or conduit to the Goddess and a memory for our re-membering of the Goddess. This is so whether, speaking historically, she was victim or free spirit or something in between—a question I see no way of answering. We will see if the doctrine of virginal conception can be reworked and nuanced in its connotations for all of us, affirmed in a new, metaphorical key. Can Jesus be believed as "born of the Virgin Mary," born of her who was a virgin, and who in some significant and deep way, by the action of God/ess,[8] retains or discovers her inviolate Self? When the (unintended) aspect of independence in the Virgin symbol is freed from the patriarchal setting, then "Virgin Mother" can be heard to say something about female autonomy within the context of sexual and parental and creative relationships.[9] This approach would not completely deny that the church has been correct in affirming a virginal conception, but it would initiate a new stage in the complex historical development of this belief.[10]

According to Ruether, in traditional Mariology the Virgin Mary represents a break with carnal sexuality and reproduction, a flight from the mortal body, and the denial of death.[11] She represents as well the primordial goodness of creation, nature before its alienation from the Spirit. Hidden in this theology is the repressed power of femaleness and nature as it exists beneath and beyond present male dualisms; the theology, however, is unacceptable in its sexism, scapegoating female sexuality for sin and death.

What is needed is an alternative Mariology, grounded in the Lucan Magnificat's identification of Mary as liberated Israel, and in the analogy Luke makes between her pregnancy and liberation. For Ruether, Mary's pregnancy does not follow from the proper role of women. Indeed, it puts her under danger as someone who has been making her own choices about her body and sexuality without regard for her future husband. She may be accused of being a prostitute or a "loose woman" and "put away." In Luke, the decision to have the redemptive child is between her and God. . . . Luke goes out of his way to stress that Mary's motherhood is a free choice.[12]

Ruether's alternative Mariology simply ignores many significant aspects of the belief in a virginal conception, which she assumes is present in the Infancy Narratives, without putting any other understanding of the conception in its place. The reading I have offered of the narratives as incorporating the tradition of the illegitimacy of Jesus supports and makes more precise the claim that Mary represents the oppressed who have been liberated; she becomes a symbol "whose power is a power of access to reality."[13] In this case there is a subversion of the patriarchal family structures: the child conceived illegitimately is seen to have value—transcendent value—in and of himself, not in his attachment and that of his mother to a biological or legal father.[14] Mary is a woman who has access to the sacred outside the patriarchal family and its control. The illegitimate conception turns out to be grace not disgrace, order within disorder. On the basis of belief in the Holy Spirit who empowers the conception of Jesus and his resurrection, and who creates and elects all,[15] a community is believed possible.

What I have tried to do in this book is to break the silence of the "silent night." But in the end I find myself silenced by some profundity I can only sense and not articulate. It has to do with birth, of course, and death. It has to do with the reality of one depending on the reality of the other. And with the reality of both grounding a hope in life through death.

Notes

Preface

For standard transliterations and abbreviations, see the *Journal of Biblical Literature* 95 (1976) 339–46.

1. See J. Plaskow, "Christian Feminism and Anti-Judaism," *Cross Currents* 28 (1978) 306–09; "Blaming the Jews for Inventing Patriarchy," *Lilith* 7 (1980) 11–12; "Feminists and Faith," ibid., 14–17; "Anti-Semitism: the Unacknowledged Racism," *Women's Spirit Bonding* (ed. J. Kalven and M. I. Buckley; NY: Pilgrim, 1984) 89–96; B. Brooten, "Jüdinnen zur Zeit Jesu: Ein Pläydoyer für Differenzierung," *Frauen in der Männerkirche* (ed. B. Brooten and N. Greinacher; Munich: Kaiser, 1982) 141–48; E. Schüssler Fiorenza, *In Memory of Her* (NY: Crossroad, 1983) 105–07, 141–42, 151–52; R. Kraemer, review of *In Memory of Her, RSR* 11 (1985) 6–9.
2. P. S. Minear, "The Interpreter and the Birth Narratives," *SBU* 13 (1950) 5–6.
3. Schüssler Fiorenza, *Memory*, xx.

1. Introduction

1. Saul Friedländer, *When Memory Comes* (NY: Avon, 1980) 151.
2. Especially the following: R. E. Brown, *The Virginal Conception and Bodily Resurrection of Jesus* (NY: Paulist, 1973); *The Birth of the Messiah* (Garden City: Doubleday, 1977); R. E. Brown, K. P. Donfried, J. A. Fitzmyer, J. Reumann, *Mary in the New Testament* (Philadelphia: Fortress, 1978), "A Collaborative Assessment by Protestant and Roman Catholic Scholars;" J. A. Fitzmyer, *The Gospel According to Luke I–IX* (AB28; Garden City: Doubleday, 1981); R. E. Brown, "Gospel Infancy Narrative Research from 1976 to 1986: Part I (Matthew);" "Part II (Luke)," *CBQ* 48 (1986) 468–83; 660–80.
3. The unfortunate term, Old Testament, is used in this study without any prejorative meaning, to refer to the Hebrew Bible and the LXX together.
4. Contrast T. Boslooper, *The Virgin Birth* (Philadelphia: Westminster, 1962) 131, and Brown, *Virginal Conception*, 66. Boslooper speaks of "the naive set of alternatives" (either virginal conception [the supernaturalists' position] or illegitimate conception [the naturalists' position]) that he argues was broken up by historical criticism. He thinks that Joseph was the biological father of Jesus, and that the myth of a virginal conception underlines the sanctity of marriage. But this makes no sense of Matthew 1. Brown argues more cogently that those who deny the virginal conception cannot escape the task of explaining how the rumor of illegitimacy and irregularity of birth arose (which he sees behind the Matthean narrative) and how they would answer the rumor without accepting "a very unpleasant alternative," illegitimacy. Both Boslooper and Brown, however, are discussing historical alternatives, not—as I am at this point—alternative readings of the evangelists' intent.

See also M. Miguens, *The Virgin Birth* (Westminster, MD: Christian Classics, 1975) 58–59, and the critical review by S. B. Marrow, *CBQ* 38 (1976) 577.

5. T. F. Glasson, "The Power of Anti-Tradition," *Epworth Review* 4 (1977) 86.
6. R. R. Ruether, "The Collision of History and Doctrine: the Brothers of Jesus and the Virginity of Mary," *Continuum* 7 (1969/70) 93–105.
7. See S. Brown, "Mary in the New Testament and the Problem of Hermeneutics," *Clergy Review* 65 (1980) 117–121.
8. Contrast the nineteenth-century views of authors of imaginative lives of Jesus, who held that he was born out of wedlock (Venturini, Noack, de Régla and others; see A. Schweitzer, *The Quest of the Historical Jesus* [London: A. & C. Black, 1954] 177–79, 326; J. G. Machen, *The Virgin Birth of Christ* [London: Clarke, 1958], n. 35, p. 11; cf. 273–79; Boslooper, *Virgin Birth,* 87–88), and nineteenth-century views concerning interpolation and pagan influence, outlined by P. W. Schmeidel, "Mary," and H. Usener, "Nativity," in *Encyclopaedia Biblica* (ed. T. K. Cheyne; London: Black, 1902) 3.2952–69, 3340–52. R. E. Witt ("The Myth of God's Mother Incarnate," *Studia Biblica* 3 [Sixth International Congress on Biblical Studies; ed. E. A. Livingstone; Sheffield: JSOT, 1978] 449) remarks that just as "parthenogenesis" was the great stumbling block to the authors of *The Myth of God Incarnate,* "so it would be to the *avant-garde* of the Women's Liberation Movement. The possibility of pregnancy through the agency of what Origen termed 'Divine Wisdom' would be loudly repudiated in that quarter. Instead, the Nativity story would be interpreted, in the manner of the Platonist Celsus and of our own latter-day William Blake, as the truth about an unmarried girl whose virginity had been lost. A mythical explanation would not avail." The brief comments of R. Ruether (*Sexism and God-Talk* [Beacon: Boston, 1983] 3) and D. Soelle (*The Strength of the Weak* [Philadelphia: Westminster, 1984] 43) are the only ones I know of that come close to fitting this description; both, I assume, are speaking historically and not about the NT texts.
9. C. Ozick, "Notes Toward Finding the Right Question," *Lilith* 6 (1979) 25.
10. See Tillie Olsen, *Silences* (NY: Dell, 1983).
11. S. Handelman (*The Slayers of Moses* [Albany: State University of NY, 1982] 207) remarks on the work of G. Scholem: only one who submits to the continuity of tradition of interpretive history gains the freedom and legitimacy to creatively interpret. For Scholem, there is no singular authority in the tradition, but rather many centers, many contradictory voices.
12. See especially E. Fox-Genovese, "For Feminist Interpretation," *USQR* 35 (1979/80) 5–14; B. Brooten, "Feminist Perspectives on New Testament Exegesis," *Conflicting Ways of Interpreting the Bible; Concilium* 138 (1980) (ed. H. Küng and J. Moltmann; NY: Seabury, 1980) 55–61; M. A. Tolbert, "Defining the Problem: The Bible and Feminist Hermeneutics," *Semeia* 28 (1983) 113–26; Schüssler Fiorenza, *Memory,* xiii–95; *Bread Not Stone. The Challenge of Feminist Biblical Interpretation* (Boston: Beacon, 1984); "Claiming the Center: A Critical Feminist Theology of Liberation," *Women's Spirit Bonding* (ed. J. Kalven and M. I. Buckley; NY: Pilgrim, 1984) 293–309; essays by Schüssler Fiorenza, Setel, Brooten, Osiek and Fuchs in *Feminist Perspectives on Biblical Scholarship* (ed. A. Y. Collins; Chico: Scholars, 1985); articles in *Feminist Interpretation of the Bible* (ed. L. M. Russell; Philadelphia: Westminster, 1985). See also *The New Feminist Criticism* (ed. E. Showalter; NY: Pantheon, 1985).
13. Hilda Smith, "Feminism and the Methodology of Women's History," *Liberating Women's History* (ed. B. A. Carroll; Urbana: University of Illinois, 1976) 370.

14. J. Culler, *On Deconstruction* (Ithaca: Cornell University, 1982) 56.
15. J. Fetterley, *The Resisting Reader. A Feminist Approach to American Fiction* (Bloomington: Indiana University, 1978) viii.
16. A. Kolodny, "A Map for Rereading," *New Feminist Criticism*, 59.
17. This is the goal of some feminist theologians, as articulated by P. Wilson-Kastner, "Christianity and New Feminist Religions," *Christian Century*, Sept. 1981, 866.
18. Tolbert ("Defining the Problem," 118) notes that the criteria themselves raise additional problems; the "public" who determine what is reasonable and who form a "consensus view" are special interest groups with different canons of validity. Interpretations called subjective may be ones which deviate from the view of the evaluating group.
19. H. Bloom, *A Map of Misreading* (NY: Oxford University, 1975); cf. S. Rawidowicz, "On Interpretation," *Studies in Jewish Thought* (ed. N. Glatzer; Philadelphia: Jewish Publication Society of America, 1974) 45–80.
20. K. Stendahl, *Meanings* (Philadelphia: Fortress, 1984) 2, 7.
21. Contrast the initial approach advocated by Gadamer: open and accepting and in the expectation that the text has something important to say. This approach is potentially conservative, suggesting how the tradition can be appreciated but not how it can be changed (S. McFague, *Metaphorical Theology* [Philadelphia: Fortress, 1982] 56–57).
22. E. Pagels, "Women, the Bible and Human Nature," *NY Times Book Review*, April 7, 1985, p. 3.
23. See E. Fuchs, "The Literary Characterization of Mothers and Sexual Politics in the Hebrew Bible," *Feminist Perspectives on Biblical Scholarship*, 117.
24. R. E. Brown, "Liberals, Ultraconservatives, and the Misinterpretation of Catholic Biblical Exegesis," *Cross Currents* 39 (1984) 315, 316, 318, 325–26. Brown charges that both (ultra)liberals and conservatives falsify what Catholic centrist scholars write, "by fitting it into preconceptions derived from elsewhere" (325). Implicit is the claim that the primary center of reflection for a centrist is some sort of pure exegesis. "Often liberal ideas have been shaped by theologians whose primary source of reflection is not exegesis but philosophy or sociology, or by theologians who have consciously or unconsciously chosen a radical, rather than a centrist, exegesis." He criticizes Küng and Schillebeecks for having read biblical studies "with a bias favoring the most radical conclusions" (326).
25. Schüssler Fiorenza, "Claiming the Center," 294. She rightly rejects the classification of a critical feminist theology of liberation as reformist in distinction to radical or revolutionary.
26. Contrast V. Taylor, *The Historical Evidence for the Virgin Birth* (Oxford: Clarendon, 1920), 122.
27. E. Schweizer, *The Holy Spirit* (Philadelphia: Fortress, 1980) 54–55.
28. See K. Rahner, *Mary, Mother of the Lord* (NY: Herder and Herder, 1963) 67–69: apart from the function of being the mother of God, Mary "is nothing." Cf. M. Daly, *Gyn/ecology* (Boston: Beacon, 1978) 83, 88.
29. A. Plummer, *An Exegetical Commentary on the Gospel according to St. Matthew* (London: Scribners, 1909) 7.
30. A. Paul, *L'Evangile de L'Enfance selon s. Matthieu* (Paris: Cerf, 1968) 75.
31. See Jean-Luc Godard's film, "Hail Mary." I do not understand the remark of Vincent Canby that this film has to do with "the ultimate expression of feminism" ("Halftime Report From the Festival," *New York Times* Oct. 6, 1985, p. 19).

32. Virgil Elizondo attempts to show that the appearance of the Virgin of Guadalupe counters sexual oppression. His remarks are worth quoting at some length. "In this case *virginity is in opposition to the scandal and shame of violated womanhood.* She was pure and unsoiled because she had not been touched by the raping hands of the conquistador. In her, Mexican womanhood is restored to its original dignity. Equally is the Mexican male liberated for no longer will he have to suffer the castrating effects of seeing his beloved women violated and not being able to do anything about it. What has been prostituted and abused by the conquistador is now virginized by God. In this case, virginity is the complete rehabilitation of abused personhood . . . [The Virgin Mother of Tepeyac] counters the insulting and dehumanizing effects of the rape and abuse of oppressed women and the destructive shame it equally casts upon its men. Even if poor women are forced into prostitution by the structures of oppression, they are kept virginally pure by the all-protecting Virgin Mother" ("Mary and the Poor: A Model of Evangelising Ecumenism," *Mary in the Churches; Concilium* 168 [ed. H. Küng and J. Moltmann; NY: Seabury, 1983] 62–63).

33. J. C. Engelsman, *The Feminine Dimension of the Divine* (Philadelphia: Westminster, 1979) 35. She relates the guilt feeling to the wish for mother-incest.

34. "A father, Stephen said, battling against hopelessness, is a necessary evil . . . Boccaccio's Calandrino was the first and last man who felt himself with child. Fatherhood, in the sense of conscious begetting, is unknown to man. It is a mystical estate, an apostolic succession, from only begetter to only begotten. On that mystery and not on the madonna which the cunning Italian intellect flung to the mob of Europe the church is founded and founded irremovably because founded, like the world, macro-and micro-cosm, upon the void. Upon incertitude, upon unlikelihood. Amor matris, subjective and objective genitive, may be the only true thing in life. Paternity may be a legal fiction. Who is the father of any son that any son should love him or he any son?
    What the hell are you driving at?
    I know. Shut up. Blast you! I have reasons."
James Joyce, *Ulysses* (NY: Vintage, 1966) 207.

35. K. Thomas, "The Virgin in History," *NY Review of Books,* Nov 11, 1976. Michael P. Carroll argues from a strictly Freudian viewpoint that "the father-ineffective family intensifies Oedipal desires in both sons and daughters, and so promotes Marian devotion." One of his hypotheses is that "Identifying strongly with the Virgin Mary allows women to experience vicariously the fulfillment of their desire for sexual contact with, and a baby from, their fathers" (*The Cult of the Virgin Mary. Psychological Origins* [Princeton: Princeton University Press, 1986] 61, 59).

36. See Nor Hall, *The Moon and the Virgin* (NY: Harper and Row, 1980) 11, 100. *Virgo intacta* is not a state particularly pleasing to the great virgin goddesses. "These goddesses are not saying that they will not give themselves sexually— but rather that they will not be taken or possessed by another being" (100).

37. K. Barth, *CD* I/2, # 15, 3, pp. 206, 209, 212, quoted by W. Pannenberg, *Jesus-God and Man* (Philadelphia: Westminster, 1968) 144.

38. N. Chodorow, *The Reproduction of Mothering* (Berkeley: University of California, 1978) 203.

39. M. Daly, *Pure Lust* (Boston: Beacon, 1984) 114. Parthenogenesis is no real comparison to virginal conception, since the latter is miraculous, and not a phenomenon of nature, and also because in the idea of the virginal con-

ception, Mary "does nothing, whereas in parthenogenesis the female accomplishes everything herself" (*Gyn/ecology*, 83).

40. E. Cady Stanton and the Revising Committee, *The Woman's Bible* (reprint Seattle: Coalition Task Force on Women and Religion, 1974) 113.

41. Anon., *Woman's Bible*, 114.

42. Victor Turner and Edith Turner, speaking of "appearances" of the virgin in Europe from 1830–1933 to poor and despised peasants, argue that "the improverished masses, the damned of the earth but blessed of heaven," can easily identify with such a figure ("Postindustrial Marian Pilgrimage," *Mother Worship* [ed. J. J. Preston; Chapel Hill: University of North Carolina, 1982] 151). "The regular connection between Mary, the laity, the poor, and the colonized, in the rapid development of pilgrimages from visions and apparitions of the corporeal type, and from related miracles, points to the hidden, nonhierarchical domain of the church, with its stress on the power of the weak, on communitas and liminal phenomena, on the rare and unprecedented, as against the regular, ordained, and normative" (p. 155). Mary is a figure of tremendous complexity and of various cultural expressions.

43. E. Schüssler Fiorenza, "Feminist Spirituality Christian Identity, and Catholic Vision," *Womanspirit Rising* (ed. C. Christ and J. Plaskow; San Francisco: Harper and Row, 1979) 138–39.

44. Ruether, *Sexism and God-Talk*, 155; M. Daly, *Beyond God the Father* (Boston: Beacon, 1973; reprinted with Original Reintroduction, 1985) 82–92 ("prophetic dimensions of the image of Mary"); *Pure Lust*, 92–121.

45. E. Schüssler Fiorenza, "Feminist Theology as a Critical Theology of Liberation," *TS* 36 (1975) 605, 621, 623.

46. E. A. Johnson, "The Marian Tradition and the Reality of Women," *Horizons* 12 (1985) 124; cf. Hunter College Women's Collective, *Women's Realities. Women's Choices* (NY: Oxford University, 1983) 31.

47. Ena Campbell, "The Virgin of Guadalupe," *Mother Worship*, 21.

48. De Beauvoir, *Second Sex* (NY: Knopf, 1952) 193. In most crèche scenes, Joseph stands, protectively.

49. M. Warner, *Alone of All Her Sex* (NY: Knopf, 1976) 336, 334.

50. *Aspects of the Feminine* from *The Collected Works of C. G. Jung*, vols. 6, 7, 9i, 9ii, 10, 17; Bollingen Series XX (Princeton: Princeton University, 1982) 20.

51. Mary Gordon, "Coming to Terms with Mary," *Commonweal* 109 (Jan. 15, 1982) 11–12.

52. See Brown, *Virginal Conception*, 21: he says that in a certain sense the problem of the virginal conception of Jesus "is not one of the most relevant problems of theology or exegesis. The solution to it will not help the wretched in the inner city or even the wretched in the suburbs; should it be resolved, there will remain questions of war and peace and even of priestly celibacy."

53. De Beauvoir, *Second Sex*, 203.

54. G. Wainwright, *The Ecumenical Moment* (Grand Rapids: Eerdmans, 1983) 170.

55. John McKenzie, "The Mother of Jesus in the New Testament," *Mary in the Churches*, 9–10.

56. Brown, *Virginal Conception*, 67.

57. See Schüssler Fiorenza, *Memory*, 28.

58. James M. Freeman, "Introduction: the Crosscultural Study of Mother Worship," *Mother Worship*, xxiv.

59. See P. Trible, *Texts of Terror* (Philadelphia: Fortress, 1984) 86; Tolbert, "Defining the Problem," 122–23; K. Sakenfeld, "Feminist Uses of Biblical Ma-

terials," *Feminist Interpretation*, 55–64; C. Osiek, "The Feminist and the Bible: Hermeneutical Alternatives," *Feminist Perspectives*, 93–105.

60. Janice Capel Anderson ("Matthew: Gender and Reading," *Semeia* 28 [1983] 3–6) discusses this as part of a third direction pursued in feminist literary criticism, but not yet fully explored in feminist biblical criticism.

61. E. Showalter, "Women and the Literary Curriculum," *College English* 32 (1971) 856. Carolyn G. Heilbrun ("Bringing the Spirit Back to English Studies, *New Feminist Criticism*, 23) says sarcastically, "There is no male or female viewpoint; there is only the human viewpoint, which happens always to have been male".

62. Fetterley, *Resisting Reader*, xxii, xii.

63. A. Kolodny, "Reply to Commentaries," *New Literary History* 11 (1980) 588. Kolodny analyzes short stories by Charlotte Perkins Gilman and Susan Keating Glaspell which have been underrated and misunderstood by male readers inadequately trained to decipher their specific systems of meaning or to understand their contexts in a female tradition. The stories themselves insist that men are different kinds of readers and, where women are concerned, often inadequate readers ("A Map for Rereading," *New Feminist Criticism*, 55, 57).

64. E. Showalter, "Toward a Feminist Poetics," *New Feminist Criticism*, 128. She shows how the opening scene of Thomas Hardy's *The Mayor of Casterbridge* is distorted by the fantasies of the critic Irving Howe (129–30).

65. See *The Authority of Experience. Essays in Feminist Criticism* (ed. A. Diamond and L. R. Edwards; Amherst: University of Massachusetts, 1977).

66. Culler, *On Deconstruction*, 58, 54–55; cf. M. Marini, "Feminism and Literary Criticism," *Women in Culture and Politics* (ed. J. Friedlander et al.; Bloomington: Indiana University, 1986) 148–51, 157–61.

67. C. Ozick, "Literature and the Politics of Sex: A Dissent," *Art and Ardor* (NY: Knopf, 1983) 284–89. Classical feminism, she insists, was conceived of as the end of false barriers and boundaries. She holds that women do not have a separate psychology and a separate body of ideas by virtue of being women; insofar as some women have separate bodies of experience, to that degree has their feminism not yet asserted itself. Rather, I think, to that degree feminism has *begun* to assert itself, and society with its barriers falls short of the egalitarian vision. Cf. Schüssler Fiorenza, *Memory*, 86; "Claiming the Center," 306.

68. Jean Baker Miller, *Toward a New Psychology of Women* (Boston: Beacon, 1976) 1.

69. C. Gilligan, *In a Different Voice* (Cambridge: Harvard University, 1982).

70. E. Showalter, "Introduction. The Feminist Critical Revolution," *New Feminist Criticism*, 10.

71. S. Gilbert and S. Gubar (*The Madwoman in the Attic. The Woman Writer and the Nineteenth Century Literary Imagination* [New Haven: Yale University, 1979] 73) suggest that women's writings are in some sense "palimpsestic," in that their "surface designs conceal or obscure deeper, less accessible (and less socially acceptable) levels of meaning." They speak of an art designed "both to express and to camouflage" (81). There is no evidence that the NT Infancy Narratives are "women's writings." But whether a woman's theological tradition lies behind the narratives will be explored in chapter four.

72. Women's own silence is the silence of those denied the full resources of language, forced into silence, euphemism, and circumlocution. See E. Showalter, "Feminist Criticism in the Wilderness," *New Feminist Criticism*, 255, 266.

She speaks of reading a woman's text as "a double-voiced discourse, containing a 'dominant' and a 'muted' story." Two alternative oscillating texts have to be kept simultaneously in view. Meaning is found in what has previously been empty space.

73. Schüssler Fiorenza, *Memory*, 41. "Rather than reject the argument from silence as a valid historical argument, we must learn to read the silences of androcentric texts in such a way that they can provide 'clues' to the egalitarian reality of the early Christian movement."

74. See A. Kolodny on her responses to Gilman's story, "The Yellow Wallpaper" ("Reply to Commentaries," 589).

75. S. B. Thistlethwaite, "Every Two Minutes: Battered Women and Feminist Interpretation," *Feminist Interpretation*, 96. For contemporary discussions of rape, see such works as Susan Brownmiller, *Against Our Will* (NY: Simon and Schuster, 1975); S. Griffin, *Rape: The Power of Consciousness* (NY: Harper and Row, 1979); E. A. Stanko, *Intimate Intrusions. Women's Experience of Male Violence* (London: Routledge and Kegan Paul, 1984); T. Beneke, *Men on Rape* (NY: St. Martin's, 1982). On illegitimacy, see Diana Dewar, *Orphans of the Living: a Study of Bastardy* (London: Hutchinson, 1968); *The Double Jeopardy, the Triple Crisis: Illegitimacy Today* (NY: National Council on Illegitimacy, 1969); E. Crellin, M. L. Kellmer Pringle, P. West, *Born Illegitimate: Social and Educational Implications* (London: NFER, 1971); H. D. Krause, *Illegitimacy. Law and Social Policy* (NY: Bobbs-Merrill, 1971); Jenny Teichman, *Illegitimacy: an Examination of Bastardy* (Ithaca: Cornell University, 1982).

2. Matthew's Account of Jesus' Origin

1. Inclusion of women in an ancient Jewish genealogy is not unprecedented, but it is rare; exceptions occur only in the case of irregularity of descent or where there is something noteworthy about the woman's name (Str-B 1.15; cf. *Mary in the NT*, 78.)

2. M. D. Johnson, *The Purpose of the Biblical Genealogies* (Cambridge: Cambridge University, 1969) 154–59; Brown, *Birth*, 70–74.

3. K. Stendahl ("Quis et Unde? An Analysis of Mt 1–2," *Judentum, Urchristentum, Kirche* [ed. W. Eltester; Berlin: Töpelmann, 1964] 101) thinks that God's intervention in the conception of Jesus led to slander, and that Matthew is presenting an apologetic argument about how Jesus was engrafted onto the Davidic pedigree. G. Kittel ("*Thamar, Rachab, Routh, hē tou Ouriou*," *TDNT* 3 [1965] 2; cf. E. Stauffer, "Jeschu ben Miriam: Kontroversgeschichtliche Anmerkungen zu Mk 6:3," *Neotestamentica et Semitica* [ed. E. E. Ellis and M. Wilcox; Edinburgh: Clark, 1969] 124) argues that the four women have no relationship to the fifth, Mary, since the only basis of comparison would be illegitimate conception. "But this would imply acceptance of the Jewish charge that Jesus was born illegitimately as the son of Panthera. It would be quite grotesque for the Evangelist to try to justify the Virgin Birth by reference to admitted harlots or adulteresses." In any case, he thinks that the Jewish charge had not yet been launched in the days of Matthew (contrast Stauffer and E. D. Freed, "The Women in Matthew's Genealogy," *JSNT* 29 [1987] 3–19).

4. See W. D. Davies, *The Setting of the Sermon on the Mount* (Cambridge: Cambridge University, 1964) 66.

5. G. Mussies, "Parallels to Matthew's Version of the Pedigree of Jesus," *NovT* 28 (1986) 38.

6. Brown, *Birth*, 74.
7. *Mary in the NT*, 81.
8. Trible, *Texts of Terror.*
9. G. Von Rad, *Genesis* (Philadelphia: Westminster, 1961) 353.
10. LXX: *idou en gastri echei ek porneias.*
11. Burning was prescribed for exceptional cases of forbidden intercourse (Lev 20:15 [if a man takes a wife and her mother also, he and they are to be burned]; 21:9 [if the daughter of a priest becomes a harlot, she is to be burned because she has profaned her father]). Some later rabbinic tradition considered Tamar the daughter of a priest, Shem = Melchizedek. On this penalty, compare R. deVaux, *Ancient Israel* (NY: McGraw-Hill, 1965), 1.36; M. C. Astour, "Tamar the Hierodule," *JBL* 85 (1966) 194; A. Phillips, "Another Look at Adultery," *JSOT* 20 (1981) 15.
12. See *T. Jud.* 13:4: Judah says, "I lay with Tamar who was espoused to my sons."
13. B. S. Childs, *Introduction to the Old Testament as Scripture* (Philadelphia: Fortress, 1979) 157. In a way, Judah performed the levirate duty for his son without intending to, because of Tamar's initiative. But Lev 18:15 (cf. Ezek 22:11) forbids sexual intercourse between a man and his daughter-in-law (see *T. Jud.* 14:6: "I wrought a great sin, and I uncovered the covering of my son's shame"; cf. *Jub.* 41:23).
14. He again considered her his daughter-in-law (Von Rad, *Genesis*, 356).
15. Johnson, *Purpose*, 154, 271.
16. E.g., *T. Jud.* 10:6; *b. Sota* 10b; *b. Hor.* 10b; *y. Sota* 1:4 (16d, 5a); *Gen. R.* 85.
17. *Leg. All.* 3.74; *Quod Deus* 137.
18. *De Cong.* 124; cf. *Fug.* 149–156; *Virt.* 220–222.
19. *Quod Deus* 137; cf. *Mut.* 134.
20. Judah Goldin, "The Youngest Son or Where Does Genesis 38 Belong?" *JBL* 96 (1977) 30.
21. Some of the traditions in the Palestinian Targums may be pre-Christian. See M. McNamara, "Targums," *IDBSup* 856–61; cf. G. Vermes ("Jewish Literature and NT Exegesis: Reflections on Methodology," *JJS* 33 [1982] 364).
22. R. Bloch, "Juda Engendra Pharès et Zara, de Thamar," *Mélanges bibliques rédigés en l'honneur de André Robert* (Paris: Bloud & Gay, 1957) 385. In the next breath, Judah announces that this happened because he did not give Tamar his son Shelah.
23. See *b. Sota* 10b: Judah knew Tamar was more righteous than he because "a bath kol issued forth and proclaimed, 'From me came forth secrets.'" Cf. the medieval Midrash Ha-Gadol I, p. 655, cited by Bloch, "Juda," 387: "When Judah said, 'She is righteous,' the Holy Spirit manifested itself and said, 'Tamar is not a prostitute and Judah did not want to give himself over to fornication with her; the thing happened because of me, in order that the King Messiah be raised up from Judah.'"
24. G. W. Coates, "Redactional Unity in Genesis 37–50," *JBL* 93 (1974) 15–17.
25. R. Alter, *The Art of Biblical Narrative* (NY: Basic Books, 1981) 21. On the themes the two stories have in common, see pp. 3–10.
26. E. A. Speiser, *Genesis* (AB1; Garden City: Doubleday, 1964) 292.
27. Origen, *In Matt.* 1:5. Elsewhere he speaks of the OT *Raab.* See J. D. Quinn, "Is Rachab in Mt 1,5 Rahab of Jericho?" *Bib* 62 (1982) 225–28. Quinn answers this question by saying it is an exegetical possibility which is pres-

ently indemonstrable; he finds it more probable that Rachab is an unknown woman.

28. R. E. Brown, "Rachab in Mt 1,5 Probably Is Rahab of Jericho," *Bib* 63 (1982) 79–80. Cf. Y Zakowitch, "Rahab als Mutter des Boas in der Jesus-Genealogie (Matth. I.5)," *NovT* 17 (1975) 1–5.

29. Consorting with them is regarded as foolish, dangerous and wrong, but Prov 6:26 suggests that it is cheaper and less dangerous to resort to a prostitute than to commit adultery. Philo (*Spec. Leg.* 3.51) insists that "the commonwealth of Moses' institution does not admit a harlot." She is "a pest, a scourge, a plague-spot to the public, let her be stoned to death" (cf. *De Ios.* 43, but contrast 1.81 where the repentant harlot may retain her civic rights and marry anyone except a priest, and presumably not merely escape death but remain unpunished). The OT does not suggest the death penalty.

30. T. Drorah Setel, "Prophets and Pornography: Female Sexual Imagery in Hosea," *Feminist Interpretation,* 89–90.

31. Her words here are the same as those in Deut 4:39b, but are not a confession of monotheism. See M. A. Beek, "Rahab in the Light of Jewish Exegesis," *Von Kanaan bis Kerala* (ed. W. C. Delsman, et al.; Kevelaer: Butzon and Bercker, 1982) 37–44.

32. See A. T. Hanson, "Rahab the Harlot in Early Christian Tradition," *JSNT* 1 (1978) 54.

33. P. Trible, *God and the Rhetoric of Sexuality* (Philadelphia: Fortress, 1978) 166.

34. E. Fuchs ("Literary Characterization," n. 4, p. 117) criticizes Trible for attempting to highlight suppressed evidence for what appears to be woman's point of view in the Hebrew Bible, while ignoring the patriarchal determinants of this point of view. In my opinion, what survives as a woman's (partial) point of view survives only because it is integrated into, and distorted by the androcentric perspectives.

35. B. A. Levine, "In Praise of the Israelite *Mišpāhâ:* Legal Themes in the Book of Ruth," *The Quest for the Kingdom of God* (ed. H. B. Huffmon, et al.; Winona Lake, IN: Eisenbrauns, 1983) 106.

36. Trible's translation. The noun *margĕlōtāyw* in 3:4,7,8,14, usually translated "feet" probably functions here as a euphemism for the genitals. "Just how much of the lower part of his body she is to uncover remains tantalizingly uncertain in the text. That sexual overtones are present is, however, patently certain" (Trible, *God,* 182); E. F. Campbell, Jr. (*Ruth* [AB7; Garden City: Doubleday, 1975] 131) argues that the passage can be read to mean that Ruth seduced Boaz.

37. Josephus comments primly that "it was wise to guard against scandal of that kind, and the moreso when nothing had passed" (*Ant.* 5.331).

38. See E. Fuchs, "Who Is Hiding the Truth?" *Feminist Perspectives* 137–44, esp. 141–42 on Tamar, Ruth, Rahab.

39. Levine, "In Praise," 97,104–06; cf. C. M. Carmichael, "A Ceremonial Crux: Removing a Man's Sandal as a Female Gesture of Contempt," *JBL* 96 (1977), n. 45, p. 334.

40. Trible, *God,* 193. According to Josephus (*Ant.* 5.335), the boy was born a year after the marriage, lest readers might think that the child was conceived at the threshing floor.

41. Campbell, *Ruth,* 28–29. "It is equally correct to say as well that God is the primary actor in the drama . . . God is present and active in the Ruth story especially in the way in which the people behave toward one another. God it is who brings about *shalom* in the context of this town, among these peo-

ple, through the caring responsibility of human beings for one another"
(p. 29). On the causative role of God as the one who blesses and curses in
hidden ways, see R. M. Hals, *The Theology of the Book of Ruth* (Philadelphia:
Fortress, 1969) 3–19. Cf. W. S. Prinsloo, "The Theology of the Book of
Ruth," *VT* 30 (1980) 330–41.

42. D. R. G. Beattie, *Jewish Exegesis of the Book of Ruth* (Supp. Series 2; Sheffield:
JSOT, 1977) 30, 72–73, 108, 128, 158, 167–68, 178–80, 186, 203. Cf. Carmichael, "Ceremonial Crux," 332–33: "The original recipients of the story
of Ruth would have fully understood the meaning of the language and
gestures at the threshing floor."

43. H. W. Hertzberg (*1 and 2 Samuel* [Philadelphia: Westminster, 1964] 309)
blames her for bathing in a place where she could be seen, "not of course
that this possible element of feminine flirtation is any excuse for David's
conduct." J. P. Fokkelmann (*Narrative Art and Poetry in the Books of Samuel*
[Assen: Van Gorcum, 1981] 51) recognizes that David's position on the roof
"carries the connotation of his being in the position of a despot who is able
to survey and choose as he pleases."

44. D. M. Gunn, *The Story of King David* (Sheffield: JSOT, 1978) 100.

45. For another interpretation, see Hertzberg (*1 and 2 Samuel*, 310): "We learn
nothing of Bathsheba's feelings; her consciousness of the danger into which
adultery was leading her (Deut 22.22) must have been outweighed by her
realization of the honour of having attracted the king. In any case, all this
is unimportant for the biblical narrator," who lays the blame squarely on
David's shoulders.

46. L. M. Epstein (*Sex Laws and Customs in Judaism* [NY: Bloch, 1948] n. 98, p.
213) thinks that Uriah's refusal to sleep with Bathsheba is really a refusal
to sleep with a defiled wife. See also D. Marcus, "David the Deceiver and
David the Dupe," *Prooftexts* 6 (1986) 165–66.

47. This son is born in wedlock, but some hold he is more truly the son of
Uriah, under the outlook of the rabbinic theory of retribution (C. T. Davis,
"The Fulfillment of Creation," *JAAR* 41 [1973] n. 41, p. 529). Solomon is
considered illegitimate by Matthew, according to Kittel ("*Thamar*," n. 5, p.
1).

48. J. A. Wharton, "A Plausible Tale. Story and Theology in II Samuel 9–20,
I Kings 1–2," *Int* 35 (1981) 342.

49. G. W. Coates, "Parable, Fable and Anecdote. Storytelling in the Succession
Narrative," *Int* 35 (1981) 377. Coates does not mention David's lack of pity
for Bathsheba. But since *lqh* can be used not only for taking something
from someone (in this case, Bathsheba from Uriah) but also for "taking"
sexually, seducing or capturing (e.g., Gen 34:2; Deut 22:13–14, 30), the
stress on this verb in the narrative also underlines David's treatment of
Bathsheba.

50. Presumably Absalom, but in 16:21–22 Absalom took David's concubines,
not his wives.

51. Hertzberg remarks that the theory that Jedidiah (beloved of Yahweh) is in
fact the name of the dead child is not as abtruse but equally as impossible
as the theory that Solomon is the child conceived in adultery (*1 and 2
Samuel*, n. a, p. 317).

52. Contrast R. N. Whybray (*The Succession Narrative* [Naperville: Allenson,
1968] 40) who regards her as "a good-natured, rather stupid woman who
was a natural prey both to more passionate and to cleverer men." Marcus

("David the Deceiver," 167) remarks that she deviously disposes of Solomon's rival.

53. See W. Brueggemann, "The Triumphalist Tendency in Exegetical History," *JAAR* 38 (1970) 367–80, esp. 372; "On Trust and Freedom," *Int* 26 (1972) 3–19, esp. 18. (These comments apply whether or not one accepts the Succession Narrative or Court History as representative of an early wisdom outlook.) Halls discusses the similarity of theological viewpoint between Ruth and the Court History (*Theology of the Book of Ruth,* 21–34).

54. See K. Koch, "Gibt es ein Vergeltungsdogma im Alten Testament?" *ZTK* 52 (1955) 1–42.

55. Von Rad, *Theology,* 1.314–15. The death of the child and the subsequent history of offenses by David's sons are linked to David's sin.

56. E.g., *T. Jud.* 15:2–6; CD 5:1–5.

57. See Josephus *Ant.* 7.131: when she became pregnant, she asked David "to contrive some way of concealing her sin," since she was deserving of death as an adulteress.

58. Rahab and Ruth are also included, but not Tamar.

59. S. Niditch, "The Wronged Woman Righted," *HTR* 72 (1979) 143–49. Most of the following points are drawn from her analysis.

60. Alter, *Art,* 146. Whether that flash of awareness which some claim to detect in the Bible is sometimes suppressed evidence for what appears to be woman's point of view, or one more literary strategy to promote patriarchal ideology, is one of the most important points to be debated by feminist critics.

61. There is no protest against the unjust lot of women, but rather an endorsement of social constraints.

62. As Neusner remarks, the very essence of the anomaly is woman's sexuality, scarcely mentioned but always just beneath the surface, and treated in a way wholly different from man's (*Method and Meaning in Ancient Judaism* [Brown Judaic Series 10; Missoula: Scholars, 1979] 98). For the following, see pp. 84, 87, 2, 97.

63. The verb *egennēthē* can mean either "was begotten" or "was born" when used of a pregnant woman. The former translation is preferred here for three reasons: (1) elsewhere in the genealogy the verb *gennan* means "to beget." (2) In 1:20, the related form *to gennēthen,* refers to the fetus begotten in Mary. (3) There is no indication in the rest of Matthew's narrative that he wants to focus on the mother bearing the child, rather than on the father begetting it, in order to contrast Mary's acceptance of the will of God with the willfulness of some of Joseph's forefathers (against A. Globe, "Some Doctrinal Variants in Matthew 1 and Luke 1, and the Authority of the Neutral Text," *CBQ* 42 [1980] 66).

64. See ibid., for the variants.

65. According to some critics, all thirty-nine instances of the verb *gennan* refer to legal, not physical descent. See Taylor, *Historical Evidence,* 89; cf. R. V. G. Tasker, *St. Matthew* (London: Tyndale, 1961) 62; D. Hill, *The Gospel of Matthew* (London: Oliphants, 1972) 76. Granted that the primary intention of the compilers of this genealogy was not strictly biological, still these begettings do involve the passing of physical life from father to son. With the use of Joseph's genealogy for Jesus, all of the begettings come to be understood (like the fatherhood of Joseph) in a legal sense with reference to Jesus, who is heir to the promises made to Abraham and to David.

66. Globe thinks the presence of 1:18, 20 in the translation shows that a virgin birth is still envisaged ("Doctrinal Variants," 64, 66).
67. Davis ("Fulfillment," n. 46, p. 531) insists that the passive in v 16 is clearly intended as a circumlocution for the divine agent. "In place of Joseph's generation as father, God himself appears."
68. The attribution of the number to gematria on the three consonants of David's name (*dwd* = 4+6+4), spelled traditionally, is the best explanation of the meaning of the number fourteen for Matthew.
69. J. Jeremias, *Jerusalem at the Time of Jesus* (Philadelphia: Fortress, 1969) 293–94; E. Lohmeyer, *Das Evangelium des Matthäus* (ed. W. Schmauch; Göttingen: Vandenhoeck & Ruprecht, 1962) 3; P. Winter, "Jewish Folklore in the Matthean Birth Story," *HibJ* 53 (1954/5), n. 2, p. 39; M. D. Goulder, *Midrash and Lection in Matthew* (London: SCPK, 1974) 229, 35. H. Hendrickx refers casually to the genealogy's "faulty mathematics" (*The Infancy Narratives* [London: Chapman, 1984] 23).
70. D. E. Nineham, "The Genealogy in St. Matthew's Gospel and Its Significance for the Study of the Gospels," *BJRL* 58 (1976) 428.
71. K. Stendahl, "Matthew," *PCB*, 770–71; cf. H. B. Green, *The Gospel According to Matthew* (Oxford: Oxford University, 1975) 54.
72. H. C. Waetjen, "The Genealogy as the Key to the Gospel of Matthew," *JBL* 95 (1976) 210–13. Cf. Davis, "Fulfillment," n. 13, p. 522: Matthew's reader stands in the final age; the Christ will initiate the fourth period.
73. Paul, *L'Evangile de l'Enfance*, 28, 35.
74. Brown, *Birth*, 83.
75. R. H. Gundry, *The Use of the Old Testament in St. Matthew's Gospel* (Leiden: Brill, 1967) 19.
76. B. M. Nolan, *The Royal Son of God* (Fribourg: Éditions Universitaires, 1979) 223.
77. M. J. Lagrange, *Evangile selon Saint Matthieu* (Paris: Gabalda, 1948) 8; R. T. Hood, "The Genealogies of Jesus," *Early Christian Origins* (ed. A. Wikgren; Chicago: Quadrangle, 1961) 10; Brown, *Birth*, 83–84.
78. Waetjen, "Genealogy," 209.
79. W. B. Tatum contends that since the Babylonian deportation was such a decisive turning point in the history of Israel, and involved the dethronement of Jechoniah as King of Judah, Matthew may have counted Jechoniah twice (" 'The Origin of Jesus Messiah' [Matt 1:1, 18a]. Matthew's Use of the Infancy Traditions," *JBL* 96 [1977], n. 20, p. 529). But the monarchy of David was also a decisive turning point, and David has not been counted twice; his double mention is left unexplained.
80. E. Auerbach, *Mimesis* (Princeton: Princeton University, 1953) 9, commenting on the Abraham narrative and on general biblical style. Davis ("Fulfillment," 524, 531) makes the application of Auerbach's comments to Matthew in 1, but in a very different way.
81. Danby translation.
82. Probably Joshua ben Hananiah, who lived in the latter part of the first century C.E.
83. See Johnson, *Purpose*, 147–48 for the list of other scholars who hold this position, and for the list of those (including Goldstein and Dalman) who think there is no reference here to Jesus.
84. J. Klausner, *Jesus of Nazareth* (NY: Macmillan, 1927) 232, 35–36.
85. R. T. Herford, *Christianity in Talmud and Midrash* (London: Williams and Norgate, 1903; republished by Gregg International Publishers, 1972) 45.

86. Johnson, *Purpose,* 148. The phrase, "book of the genealogy" (*biblos geneseōs*) in Matt 1:1 may be a translation of the late Hebrew and Rabbinic *spr ywḥsyn* (p. 146).
87. Stendahl, "Quis et Unde?" 102. In 1:18 *genesis* retains its genealogical sense (cf. 1:1 *biblos geneseōs*): "origin" rather than "birth" is the translation preferred by Stendahl, Tatum and others, since the birth of Jesus is not described by Matthew.
88. Brown, *Birth,* 53.
89. But see Epstein, *Sex Laws,* 197, 200; S. T. Lachs, "Studies in the Semitic Background to the Gospel of Matthew," *JQR* 67 (1977) 195–96; the latter points out that the man did not have responsibility for the support of the woman during this period, was not liable for funeral expenses should she die, and could not inherit from her. He was more properly called her betrothed (*'rwś*) rather than her husband (see, however, Gen 29:21; Deut 22:23–24; 2 Sam 3:14).
90. See Jeremias, *Jerusalem,* 364–68; Brown, *Birth,* 123; *m. Ketub.* 4:4–5; *t. Ketub.* 4. 1–4; *b. Ketub.* 46b–49a; *m. Ned.* 10:5; *m. Sanh.* 7:9; *b. Sanh.* 66b; *m. Qidd.* 1:1.
91. *M. Ketub.* 1:5; *m. Yebam.* 4:10 (cf. *b. Ketub.* 9b; 12a; *t. Ketub.* 1.4). See Ze'ev Falk, *Introduction to Jewish Law of the Second Commonwealth* (Leiden: Brill, 1978), 2. 284.
92. His charge would be grounded in the claim that he had found "an open opening" (i.e., the hymen had already been ruptured before his first intercourse with her), or that she did not bleed, according to *b. Ketub.* 9b; cf. Deut 22:14 ("the tokens of virginity").
93. The logic here seems to be that the quicker a girl is made a non-virgin, the safer she is, as the soldiers prefer virgins. Philo (*Spec. Leg.* 3.74) assumes the betrothed girl is a virgin.
94. Contrast Luke 1:26; 2:4, 39.
95. Brown, *Birth,* 124.
96. We are not told by whom it was discovered, or how (by the cessation of her menstrual periods, or by her pregnancy becoming obvious); we therefore have no way of knowing how far along in her pregnancy Mary was thought to be.
97. The Greek verb *sunelthein* has a wide range of meaning: cohabitation, sexual relations, and the formation of a family. It is used in the second sense by Josephus (*Ant.* 7.8.1 #168; 9.5 ##213–14) and Philo (*De Virt.* 22 ##111–12).
98. See Cant 8:2 LXX; Josephus, *Ant.* 1.302.
99. Contrast X. Leon-Dufour, "L'Annonce à Joseph," *Etudes d'Evangile* (Paris: Seuil, 1965) 73–74, who translates in a non-causal way the *gar* in v 20 followed by *de* at the beginning of the next verse.
100. Or: "of a holy spirit."
101. See, for example, R. H. Gundry, *Matthew. A Commentary on His Literary and Theological Art* (Grand Rapids: Eerdmans, 1982) 22: the angel repeats what Joseph already believed.
102. Or: "of a spirit which is holy."
103. Brown, *Birth,* 124; G. M. Soares Prabhu, *The Formula Quotations in the Infancy Narratives of Matthew* (Rome: Biblical Institute, 1976) 230–31; contrast L. Cantwell, "The Parentage of Jesus Mt 1:18–21," *NovT* 24 (1982) 306.
104. C. T. Davis ("Tradition and Redaction in Matthew 1:18–2:23," *JBL* 90 [1971] 413–14, 421) thinks the formulation in 1:20 carries a different

meaning from, and contrasts with that in 1:18; in v 20 the original reference was to a spirit which is holy as opposed to one which is unholy; but the redactor shows in v 18 that he understands the clause as a reference to the Holy Spirit of the Christian tradition.

105. The verb, to seduce, deceive, is found in Exod 22:15 (*yĕpatteh;* LXX *apatēsę̄*); see below.

106. Brown, *Birth*, 127; *Mary in the NT*, n. 174, p. 84; J. A. Fitzmyer, "The Matthean Divorce Texts and Some New Palestinian Evidence," *To Advance the Gospel* (NY: Crossroad, 1981) 90.

107. See Philo, *Spec. Leg.* 79–82; Josephus, *Ant.* 4.8.23 ## 246–48.

108. A. Tosato points out, with regard to the present case, that Deut 22:23–24 should not be taken in isolation, as this would lead to a misunderstanding of the norm's significance. ("Joseph, Being a Just Man [Matt. 1:19]," *CBQ* 41 [1979] n. 4, p. 548). Especially, it should not be isolated from the case of rape in vv 25–27; most commentators presume that Matthew indicates a situation in which Mary is suspected to have consented to sexual intercourse with another (e.g., Davis, "Fulfillment," 531). On the structure and redactional unity of Deut 22:13–29, see G. J. Wenham and J. G. McConville, "Drafting Techniques in Some Deuteronomic Laws," *VT* 30 (1980) 248–52.

109. A. M. Dubarle, "La Conception Virginale et la Citation d'Is., VII, 14 dans l'Evangile de Matthieu," *RB* 85 (1978) 362–67. He recognizes as I do that we cannot claim certainty in interpreting such a terse pericope; we can only explore possibilities.

110. Dubarle refers to the sometimes barbarous custom of betrothal by penetration (see *m. Ketub.* 4:4; *m. Qidd.* 1:1; *m. Nid.* 5:4).

111. Even if the pregnancy occurred during her betrothal to Joseph, Dubarle speculates that this might have been Joseph's motivation as implied in Matthew 1.

112. As the story progresses, it was not necessary to give any male the chance to step forward or to force him to step forward, because, according to Dubarle, the angel revealed that Jesus was conceived by the Holy Spirit without the intervention of a human father. I give a different interpretation of the angel's words, but think the time-frame of the pregnancy that Dubarle has proposed is possible.

113. LXX: *ho boēthēsōn ouk ēn autę̄.* The term *môšía'* appears in 2 Kings 13:5; Isa 19:20; Ob 21; Ne 9:27; etc.; with the negative, as here, in 1 Sam 11:3; 2 Sam 22:42; Ps 18:42; Deut 28:29, 31; Isa 47:15, etc. God is the *môšía'* (saviour) in Isa 45:15, 21; 63:8; 2 Sam 22:3; Ps 106:21, etc.

114. Tosato, "Joseph," 548–49.

115. *Eleos kai sungnōmē.* I prefer the translation "fellow-feeling" to Colson's translation (LCL 7.521), "forgiveness"—for what? The point Philo is making is that the raped woman should be treated with sensitivity, and her experience understood empathetically.

116. See R. LeDéaut, *Targum du Pentateuque* (Paris: Cerf, 1980), 4. 185. *Targum Neofiti I* has no such addition; see A. Díez Macho, *Neofiti I* (Madrid: Consejo Superior de Investigaciones Científicas, 1978), 5. 524.

117. I. W. Slotki comments ([London: Soncino, 1936] 297): "And a wife who willingly played the harlot is forbidden to her husband." (Cf. Josephus, *Ant.* 4.8.23 #245: there must be no marriage with a prostitute, "since by reason of the abuse of her body God could not accept her nutpial sacrifices" [see #206]; elsewhere he says that a priest is forbidden to marry a prostitute [3.12.2 #276]).

118. See H. Danby, *The Mishnah* (Oxford: Oxford University, 1933), n. 11, p. 250.
119. M. McNamara, "Targums," 858.
120. Tosato, "Joseph," 549.
121. See also L. Finkelstein, "The Book of Jubilees and the Rabbinic Halaka," *HTR* 16 (1923) 55–57; M. A. Friedman, "The Ransom Clause of the Jewish Marriage Contract," *Gratz College Anniversary Volume* (ed. I. D. Passow and S. T. Lachs; Philadelphia: Gratz College, 1971) 68.
122. See Deut 22:30; Lev 20:11; 20:12, 14; 18:15.
123. Tosato, "Joseph," n. 7, p. 549. See J. A. Fitzmyer, *The Genesis Apocryphon of Qumran Cave 1* (Rome: Pontifical Biblical Institute, 1966) 6, 115, 125; cf. Josephus, *Ant.* 1.8.1 #163–64; *J.W.* 5.9, 4 #381. Tosato also claims that confirmation of the antiquity and importance of the strict halakah is found in *m. Ned.* 11:12; but it is not clear that this law applies to laymen as well as priests. Danby assumes the husband is a priest; cf. *m. Ketub.* 2:9 (Danby, *Mishnah*, n. 6, p. 280).
124. We have no evidence illustrating the divorce of a betrothed virgin who was raped.
125. See S. R. Driver, *Deuteronomy* (ICC; 3rd ed.; T&T Clark, 1901; reprinted 1965) 271.
126. This concerns the divorce of a wife after the marriage is completed.
127. See G. J. Wenham, "Matthew and Divorce," *JSNT* 22 (1984) 96 on the essence of the bill of divorce: "You are free to marry any man" (*m. Git.* 9:3).
128. Ze'ev W. Falk, *Introduction to the Jewish Law of the Second Commonwealth* (Leiden: Brill, 1978), 1. 154, 287–88, 308–14.
129. 11QTemple 57:17–19 and CD 4:12b–5:14a show that there were at least some Jews in Palestine of the first century C.E. who proscribed divorce: the Qumran sectarians (so Fitzmyer, "Matthean Divorce Texts," 93–97; J. R. Mueller, "The Temple Scroll and Gospel Divorce Texts," *RevQ* 10 (1980/ 81) 251). But obviously Matthew's Joseph does not belong to this group.
130. Brown holds that there did exist in the first century a "less severe legal system," in which the command to purge the evil could have been met by the requirement to divorce an adulterous wife. (*Birth,* 127). But the existence at that time of such a legal system and requirement of denunciation or divorce have both been regarded as purely speculative by Myles M. Bourke. He holds that divorce may have been chosen at times rather than denunciation, and that pardon may also have been given (review of Brown's *Birth of the Messiah, CBQ* 40 [1978] 121).
131. Even though Mary is not explicitly threatened with death in Matthew 1, the threat of death is part of the situation Matthew describes.
132. What was expected to happen to the guilty wife ("a sagging thigh, a distended belly") was related in some way to pregnancy; the outcome of the ordeal would probably be miscarriage or sterility (A. Phillips, "Another Look at Adultery," *JSOT* 20 [1981] 8).
133. D. Hill, "A Note on Matthew 1. 19," *Exp Tim* 76 (1964/65) 133–34.
134. J. Milgrom, "The Case of the Suspected Adulteress, Numbers 5:11–31," *The Creation of Sacred Literature* (Berkeley: University of CA, 1981) 73. He thinks the death penalty was not put into effect in such cases because the adulteress was not apprehended by man.
135. See W. C. Trenchard, *Ben Sira's View of Women* (Chico: Scholars, 1982) 104–05. In general, Wisdom literature discourages adultery, warning mainly of damage to a man's reputation and general unpleasantness that would follow

detection; the penalty seems to have been a matter of the husband's discretion (H. McKeating, "Sanctions against Adultery in Ancient Israelite Society," *JSOT* 11 [1979] 61).

136. For a debate concerning the early formulation of the laws about adultery, the inclusion of women under those laws, and the roles of private (family) vs public (sacral/criminal) law, see McKeating, "Sanctions," and Phillips, "Another Look."

137. It is debated whether public humiliation was a prelude to death or a substitute for it.

138. It is notoriously difficult, if not impossible, to untangle the story or stories in Hos 1–3, but in the allegory of Israel's covenantal history in chapter 2, divorce (v 2) and punishment (vv 3–13) precede re-betrothal (vv 14–23).

139. See A. Büchler, "Die Strafe der Ehebrecher in der nachexilischen Zeit," *MGWJ* 55 (1911) 196–219; Epstein, *Sex Laws*, 199.

140. The literature on this question as it relates to the trial and execution of Jesus is immense, and to my mind the issue is an open one.

141. *Y. Sanh.* 1.18a, 34; 7.24b, 41.

142. *Hypothetica* 7.1. #357.

143. Epstein, *Sex Laws* 202, 209. Strict requirements almost impossible to fulfill put an end to the practice of capital punishment for adultery (p. 211; cf. Hauck, *"moicheuō,"* *TDNT* 4 [1967] 731; Ze'ev Falk, *Introduction*, 1. 293, on the requirement concerning two witnesses).

144. See B. Lindars, *The Gospel of John* (Grand Rapids: Eerdmans, 1972) 309; R. E. Brown, *The Gospel according to John* (AB29; Garden City: Doubleday, 1966), 1. 336–38; D. Daube, "Biblical Landmarks in the Struggle for Women's Rights," *The Judicial Review* 23 (1978) 177–97, for different opinions about the meaning of the story.

145. B. F. Westcott, *The Gospel According to St. John* (London: Murray, 1903) on 8:11.

146. See Epstein, *Sex Laws*, 213; A. Isaksson, *Marriage and Ministry in the New Temple* (Lund: Gleerup, 1965) 40–43, on *m. Soṭah* 5:1; *m. Yebam.* 2:8.

147. See Bourke, review of Brown, *Birth*, 121. In the OT period, Bourke points out, the husband could pardon his adulterous wife. Bourke refers to R. deVaux, who cites Hos 2:5, 11–12; Ezek 16:37–38; 23:29 to show that the husband could pardon her, but he could also divorce her, and their punishment entailed disgrace (*Ancient Israel*, 1.37). In biblical and rabbinic law, no provision is made for the husband's pardon of his wife, since adultery is seen as more than an injury to her husband (Epstein, *Sex Laws*, 199, 201).

148. Tosato ("Joseph," 550–51) speaks of a woman in this case as a suspected adulteress or presumed guilty.

149. Bourke, review of Brown's *Birth*, 121–22.

150. He refers to *m. Soṭah* 1:3; 3:6; 4:2, all instances, however, of the elimination of the trial by bitter waters. This is not, as we have seen, and as he recognizes, the procedure outlined in Deut 22:23–27 for the case of the betrothed virgin, and according to the Mishnah itself the betrothed virgin is not to be submitted to this test (*m. Soṭah* 4:1).

151. E.g., *m. Soṭah* 6:3; *m. Ned.* 11:12; *m. Yebam.* 2:8; *m. Soṭah* 5:1. Tosato, "Joseph," nn. 10, 12, p. 550.

152. Only one document from pre-Christian times, the Genesis Apocryphon, seems to support this theory. See above, p. 49.

153. Tosato ("Joseph," n. 14, p. 551) suggests that the husband might have "a desire to share in what could have been a drama suffered in silence because of a sense of shame." He would in this case simply pay the *Kĕtūbbâ,* the

sum of money the husband had pledged to pay to the bride in the event of his death or of his divorcing her.

154. Translation by Trenchard, *Ben Sira's View*, 95. Vv 18–21 deal with the adulterer, but in quite different and less severe terms.

155. A. Büchler, "Ben Sira's Conception of Sin and Atonement," *JQR* 13 (1922/23) 466; W. Frankenberg, "Über Abfassungs -Ort und -Zeit, sowie Art und Inhalt von prov. I–IX," *ZAW* 15 (1895) 121.

156. Jeremias, *Jerusalem*, 340; see also C. Tschernowitz, "The Inheritance of Illegitimate Children According to Jewish Law," *Jewish Studies in Memory of Israel Abrahams* (ed. G. A. Kohut; NY: Jewish Institute of Religion, 1927) 407: the offspring of an adulterous wife or of one who had committed incest within the degrees of kinship, forbidden in Leviticus.

157. See above, p. 39. Also A. Büchler, "Family Purity and Family Impurity in Jerusalem Before the Year 70 C.E.," *Studies in Jewish History* (ed. I. Brodie and J. Rabbinowitz; London: Oxford University, 1956) 77 (this text shows the term *mamzēr* was current and well understood before 70).

158. *B. Nid.* 10a Bar.; *b. Ned.* 20a–b (the view of R. Eliezer); *t. Ketub.* 4.9, 264 and par.; *y. Ketub.* 4.8, 28d.69; *b. B. Mes.* 104a (the view of Hillel and others of his time). On this last text, see A. Büchler, "The Jewish Betrothal and the Position of a Woman Betrothed to a Priest in the First and Second Centuries," *Studies in Jewish History*, n. 1, p. 139, and 77–78. The implication here is that a child conceived illegitimately during the period of betrothal (in the way that betrothal was understood in Palestine) was a *mamzēr*. See also the LXX translation of *mamzēr* in Deut 23:2 by *ek pornēs* (which Buchler thinks means all forbidden intercourse ["Family Purity," 77]) and see Heb 12:8, where *nothos* is used in contrast to *huios*.

159. See Jeremias, *Jerusalem*, 341–42, 337 and references there.

160. Tschernowitz, "Inheritance," 402–03. Adoption was not known as a *legal institution* in Jewish law of the period (Ben-Zion Scheveschewsky, "Adoption, Later Jewish Law," *EncJud* 1.300–301).

161. See S. Feigin, "Some Cases of Adoption in Israel," *JBL* 50 (1931) 186–200; contrast E. A. Speiser, " 'People' and 'Nation' of Israel," *JBL* 79 (1960) 161–62. In Greece and Rome illegitimate children received no share in their father's estate.

162. Danby, *Mishnah*, n. 6, p. 220.

163. Tschernowitz, "Inheritance," 404–05. He points out that it is difficult to suppose that the *mamzēr* is included in *m. Yebam.* 2:5, since one would suppose this would be stated explicitly, and since 2:5 would then be in contradiction to 2:4. He refers also to the unanswered question in *t. Yebam.* 3.3; *b. Yoma* 66b.

164. Contrast the following analysis with those of J. D. M. Derrett, "Virgin Birth in the Gospels," *MAN* 6 (1971) 289–93; Dubarle, "La Conception," 362–80; Cantwell, "Parentage of Jesus," 304–15.

165. S. Benko, *Protestants, Catholics and Mary* (Valley Forge: Judson, 1968) 14.

166. See Nolan, *Royal Son*, 124, n. 1, p. 125; Waetjen, "Genealogy," 225. Contrast Brown, *Birth*, 125–27; Soares Prabhu, *Formula Quotations*, 248; B. Przybylski, *Righteousness in Matthew and His World of Thought* (Cambridge: Cambridge University, 1980), 121; n. 185, p. 156.

167. H. Schlier, "*deiknumi, ktl*" *TDNT* 2 (1964) 31. The rare word *deigmatizō* used in v 19 has the connotation of making a public display, and is associated in secular Greek with the shame heaped upon convicted adulteresses. Cf. *paradeigmatizō* in LXX Num 25:4; Jer 13:22.

168. It need not be argued either that a suspected adulteress had to be divorced,

or that Joseph was allowed and wished to divorce her. Other possibilities are that Joseph suspected Mary had been raped, and he thought himself obligated to divorce her or wished to divorce her.

169. Lohmeyer, *Matthäus* n. 3, p. 14; Brown, *Birth*, 128. Brown is thinking, however, of the elimination of the trial by bitter waters (Num 5:11–31), if this was still in effect in NT times, and he thinks of Joseph as deciding not to publicly accuse Mary of adultery.

170. Tosato, "Joseph," 551. Cf. F. R. McCurley, *Ancient Myths and Biblical Faith* (Philadelphia: Fortress, 1983) 105: Mary's virginity was confirmed by Joseph in a dream by the angel.

171. Including: there is no prior betrothal.

172. So Wenham, "Matthew and Divorce," 95–107; A. L. Descamps, "Les Textes évangéliques sur le Marriage (suite)," *RTL* 11 (1980) 5–50; E. Lövestam, "Die synoptisken Jesus-orden om skilsmässa och omgifte," *SEÅ* 43 (1978) 65–73, summarized in *NTA* 23 (1979) 153.

173. Fitzmyer argues that it is not impossible that it means prostitution or harlotry, but probable that in Matt 5:32; 19:9 it means illicit marital unions within the degrees of kinship proscribed by Lev 18:6–18 ("Matthean Divorce Texts," 88–89); see also J. Jensen, "Does Porneia Mean Fornication? A Critique of B. Malina," *NovT* 20 (1978) 161–84; A. Stock, "Matthean Divorce Texts," *BTB* 8 (1978) 24–33; Mueller, "Temple Scroll," 247–56.

174. Isaksson (*Marriage and Ministry*, 135–41) thinks it is unlikely that Joseph would be said to have done something or decided to do something which clearly conflicted with the teaching of Jesus later in this Gospel. He argues that *porneia* means premarital unchastity or premarital fornication. Cf. Nolan, *Royal Son*, 125–26.

175. B. Gerhardsson, "The Hermeneutic Program in Matthew 22:37–40," *Jews, Greeks and Christians* (ed. R. Hamerton-Kelly and R. Scroggs; Leiden: Brill, 1976) 129–50.

176. Contrast Davis ("Fulfillment," 531–35), who thinks Joseph is caught between the clear demands of the Law and the demands of the angel; obedience places him outside the Law in the common eye, causes him to bear the stigma of a "lawless man." Joseph becomes the model of a *new* righteousness, a response to the presence of Christ. Cf. E. Schweizer, *Good News According to Matthew* (Atlanta: John Knox, 1975) 35: Joseph gives up his "previous moral principles" in light of God's promises.

177. In Genesis, both fathers and mothers name children. In Luke 1:62, Mary is told to name Jesus.

178. Cf. F. W. Beare, *The Gospel According to Matthew* (San Francisco: Harper and Row, 1981) 66: this is not precisely an adoption, but an acknowledgment of a child born in wedlock. In the interpretation offered here, Joseph *does* adopt another man's son.

179. Rather than with its actual root, *šw'* (to help).

180. Or: "Yahweh, save" (see F. W. Albright and C. S. Mann, *Matthew* [AB26; Garden City: Doubleday, 1971] 2). Or: "Yahweh is salvation" (M. Noth, *Die Israelitischen Personennamen* [Stuttgart: Kohlhammer, 1978] 106–07).

181. See Philo, *Mut.* 12.121; G. Strecker, *Der Weg der Gerechtigkeit* (2nd ed.; Göttingen: Vandenhoeck, 1966) 54.

182. W. C. Van Unnik, "Dominus Vobiscum," *NT Essays* (ed. A. J. B. Higgins; Manchester: Manchester University, 1959) n. 59, p. 302; Fitzmyer, *Luke*, 1. 345. Cf. Luke 1:77; 2:11.

183. The explanation of the name is reminiscent of Ps 130:8. Some argue that

this allusion has been modified in Matt 1:21 through the presence of another allusion, to Judges 13:5; see Gundry, *Use of the OT*, 92; Soares Prabhu, *Formula Quotations*, 293. Winter ("Folklore," 39), without reference to Ps 130:8, thinks that the motif from Judges 13:5 has been applied to Jesus via its application to Moses; see Josephus, *Ant.* 2.9.3 #215. On the other hand, W. L. Knox (*Sources of the Synoptic Gospels* [Cambridge: Cambridge University, 1957], 2. n. 1, p. 126) insists that the phrase in Matt. 1:21 is merely "an unconscious assimilation of the story to biblical language"; cf. Stendahl ("Quis," 103): "the Spirit or Angel neither quotes nor exegizes."

184. He is not stressing, in my opinion, Mary's virginity, as many critics think (among them, Vögtle, Schweizer, Brown, Soares Prabhu, Nolan).

185. Davis, "Tradition and Redaction," 413; cf. A. M. McNeile, *The Gospel according to St. Matthew* (London: Macmillan, 1955) 7; Nolan, *Royal Son*, 32.

186. C. K. Barrett, *The Holy Spirit in the Gospel Tradition* London: SPCK, 1966) 17; J. Schaberg, *The Father, the Son and the Holy Spirit. The Triadic Phrase in Matt 28:19b* (Chico: Scholars, 1982) 23–24.

187. G. Delling, *"parthenos,"* TDNT 5 (1967) n. 53, p. 834; Brown, *Birth*, 523, 138, 140; Goulder, *Midrash and Lection*, 234; J. D. Kingsbury, *Matthew: Structure, Christology, Kingdom* (Philadelphia: Fortress, 1975) 43.

188. Cf. Str-B. 1.124; Barrett, *Holy Spirit*, 8, 18. He remarks, however, "Whether the activity of the Spirit excludes the possibility of procreation by Joseph is a question to which no one is able to give an answer, unless he has excluded all possibility of miracle on *a priori* grounds" (p. 24).

189. C. F. D. Moule writes that "It seems to be intended, literally and exclusively, that it was from no man, but from the very Spirit of God that the semen came" (*The Holy Spirit* [Grand Rapids: Eerdmans, 1978] 55). But Moule shows more interest in the biology of the event than Matthew or Luke do.

190. R. H. Fuller, "The Virgin Birth: Historical Fact or Kerygmatic Truth?" *BR* 1 (1957) 5.

191. Delling, *"parthenos,"* 835.

192. Moule, *Holy Spirit*, 19–20. Nolan (*Royal Son*, 24) argues that there is "no close OT analogue to the life-imparting Holy Spirit of the Gospel of Origins."

193. W. D. Davies, *The Setting of the Sermon on the Mount* (Cambridge: Cambridge University, 1964) 82, cf. 67–72. But the coming of Christ is continuous with Judaism when seen as the fulfillment of Davidic and Mosaic hope (p. 83).

194. See Hill, *Matthew*, 76; A. Vögtle, "Die Genealogie Mt 1,2–16 und die mattaische Kindheitsgeschichte," *BZ* 8 (1964) 45–58, 239–62; 9 (1965) 32–49. He who comes at the end of the OT inaugurates a new humanity; by the work of the Holy Spirit something new is called into being by God.

195. See above, n. 86.

196. See Davies, *Setting*, 70; H. Gese, "Natus ex Virgine," *Probleme biblischer Theologie* (ed. H. W. Wolff; Munich: Kaiser, 1971) 73.

197. Compare Kingsbury, *Matthew*, 43; Brown, *Birth*, 137; Nolan, *Royal Son*, 222; Soares Prabhu, *Formula Quotations*, 252; Waetjen, "Genealogy," 224; Moody, "Virgin Birth," 789; G. Vermes, *Jesus the Jew* (NY: Macmillan, 1973) n. 108, p. 265.

198. But this seems to be the position of E. Schillebeeckx, *Jesus: an Experiment in Christology* (NY: Seabury, 1979) 554.

199. Lagrange, *Matthieu*, 10.

200. And Luke's statements in 1:34–35.

201. Philo's allegorical statements about the patriarchs (who represent certain virtues) being begotten by God or by "virgin mothers" (who also represent virtues) are not evidence of a Hellenistic Jewish notion of virginal conception, and not an influence (direct or indirect) on the NT narratives. See R. Bultmann, *History of the Synoptic Tradition* (NY: Harper and Row, 1968) 291, 304; P. Grelot, "La Naissance d'Isaac et celle de Jésus," *NRT* 94 (1974) 569; Gese, "Natus," n. 2, p. 72; Boslooper, *Virgin Birth*, 219–20; Brown, *Birth*, 524. Contrast M. Dibelius, "Jungfrauensohn und Krippenkind," *Botschaft und Geschichte* (Tübingen: Mohr, 1953; orig., 1932), 1. 1–78; Paul, *L'Evangile de l'Enfance*, 76–76. Philo's stress on virginity is linked to his dualistic anthropology and his open hostility toward women, traits which—like allegory—do not appear in the NT Infancy Narratives.

202. The only exception may be the story of the conception of Melchizedek in *2 Enoch* 23 (Vaillant edition, *Le Livre des Secrets d'Hénoch* [Paris: Institute d'études slaves, 1952]; F. I. Anderson, "2 Enoch," *OT Pseudepigrapha* [ed. J. H. Charlesworth; Garden City: Doubleday, 1983] chapters 71–73). This occurs "by the Word of God" and apparently without human paternity. It is not, however, a *virginal* conception, and in my opinion the author is primarily depicting the appearance on earth of a superhuman, perhaps angelic, being, not the conception of a real human being. I hope to show at a later time that *2 Enoch* 23 is neither an influence on the NT Infancy Narratives, nor influenced by them. Rather, it influenced the way some read the NT narratives, as being about a miraculous conception. See further, in chapter 4.

203. See *Mary in the NT*, 289.

204. Brown, *Virginal Conception*, 62. On this scholarly consensus, see G. H. Box, "The Gospel Narratives of the Nativity and the Alleged Influence of Heathen Ideas," *ZNW* 6 (1905) 80–101; *The Virgin Birth of Jesus* (London: Pitman, 1916); Boslooper, *Virgin Birth*, 135–86; H. Rahner, *Greek Myths and Christian Mystery* (NY: Harper & Row, 1963) 130–31; Davies, *Setting*, 63–65; Brown, *Virginal Conception*, 61–63; *Birth*, 522–23; *Mary in the NT*, 93, 121, 291.

205. The virginal conception, a unique and unparalleled belief, is unlike other early Christian beliefs. The belief in the resurrection of Jesus Christ, for example, can be seen as prepared for in the OT and intertestamental Judaism, whereas the belief in a virginal conception cannot.

206. R. Alter, "How Convention Helps Us Read," *Prooftexts* 3 (1983) 121. See H. W. Wolff, *Anthropology of the OT* (Philadelphia: Fortress, 1981) 93, 98, 177. McCurley remarks, "Perhaps nowhere in the bible is the trend toward demythologization more strongly pronounced" than in regard to the motif of fertility (*Ancient Myths*, 186). He thinks, however, that the NT comes dangerously close to mythology in the discussion of the conception of Jesus.

207. Cf. *b. Nid.* 31a; *Gen.R.* 809; *b. Sota* 17a; Philo, *De Dec.* 22 #107; 23 #120.

208. R. A. Culpepper, "The Pivot of John's Prologue," *NTS* 27 (1980) 19; cf. R. H. Fuller, "The Conception/Birth of Jesus as a Christological Moment," *JSNT* 1 (1978) 44.

209. Deut 32:18; Philo, *De Vita Mosis* 1.50 #279.

210. *1QapGen* 5:27.

211. Ps 2:7; cf. 110:3 LXX.

212. Jer 1:5; cf. Isa 49:1, 5.

213. 1QSa 2:11–12.

214. Gal 4:29; John 3:3–8; John 1:12–13; 1 John 2:29; 3:9; 4:7; 5:1–4; 5:18.

215. The participation of both man and woman is ruled out in v 13. Divine begetting is a supernatural action performed by God alone.

216. Gese ("Natus," 80) speaks of a peculiar interpenetration (*Ineinander*) of divine and human fatherhood for the enthroned Davidic king. The authors of *Mary in the NT* recognize that there is no background in the OT for Matthew to conclude that since Jesus was God's son, he had no human father (p. 93).

217. Contrast Box, *Virgin Birth*, 19.

218. See S. McFague, *Metaphorical Theology* (Philadelphia: Fortress, 1982) 38–42.

219. Stendahl ("Quis," 103–04) argues that it is, that no christological argument or insight is deduced from God's "intervention" through the Spirit of Jesus' conception. Stendahl questions whether Matthew has thought of this intervention as an absolutely unique event. "Does he not see it as a glorious heightening of the divine intervention of old?"

220. See A. Milavec, "Matthew's Integration of Sexual and Divine Begetting," *BTB* 8 (1978) 108–16. I disagree, however, with Milavec's exegesis of Matt 1:18–25, in which he argues (if I understand him correctly) that Joseph was the biological father of Jesus, and in which he presents no clear explanation of Joseph's dilemma. So also W. E. Phipps, *Was Jesus Married?* (NY: Harper and Row, 1970) 39–46.

221. If Matthew (and/or the pre-gospel tradition) has been indirectly influenced by the widespread stereotypical pagan pattern Talbert identifies for the life of an "immortal," it is a pattern that has been broken. The pattern is: supernatural conception / virtuous life / exaltation to heaven (see C. H. Talbert, "The Concept of Immortals in Mediterranean Antiquity," *JBL* 94 [1975] 419–436). Matthew's Jesus does not wait until the end of his earthly career to receive his status of Son of God (see 14:33; 16:16) or his power (9:6; 10:1; 21:27). And Matthew does not think of him as God or equal to God, although the category of immortal is closer to Matthew's thought about Jesus than that of divine man. Talbert holds that Matthew's portrait of Jesus is indebted to Jewish portraits of Moses as an immortal. "If the Christian converts in Matthew's church came from such circles [those which depicted Moses as an immortal], the First Gospel's portrayal of Jesus is meaningful." I think that the imitation of this pattern does not explain the presence in the pre-gospel tradition or in Matthew and Luke of an association of the Holy Spirit with the conception/begetting of Jesus, or the stress on Mary's virginity. But perception in terms of the pattern and in terms of pagan "parallels" of supernatural begetting may help explain how the gospels were *later* understood to be about a virginal conception, with divine paternity *replacing* the human.

222. Matthew's Gospel, however is without a theology of the divine begetting of Christians, and without a developed theology of divine life contrasted to human life, or of Spirit and flesh as radically different modes of existence.

223. Deut 22:26: "But to the young woman you shall do nothing."

224. The less rigorous halakah; the provisions for legal paternity.

225. The pattern of command—citation—obedience to command appears also at Matt 21:1–7.

226. The Hebrew participial/adjectival construction could mean that the woman would become pregnant, or was already pregnant.

227. See G. Rice, "The Interpretation of Isa 7:15–17," *JBL* 96 (1977) 363–69; R. Bartelmus, "Jes 7:1–17 und das Stilprinzip des Kontrastes," *ZAW* 96 (1984) 50–66 for interpretations of this difficult passage.

228. The term 'almâ normally refers to a young girl who has reached puberty and is marriageable. No stress is placed on biological virginity, although most girls in this situation would have been virgins.

229. On the problem of identification, see G. Rice, "A Neglected Interpretation of the Immanuel Prophecy," ZAW 90 (1978) 220–27; W. Berg, "Die Identität der 'jungen Frau' in Jes 7, 14.16," BN 13 (1980) 7–13; Delling, "parthenos," 832; O. Kaiser, Isaiah 1–12 (Philadelphia: Westminster, 1972) 103; G. Föhrer, Das Buch Jesaja (Zürich/Stuttgart: Zwingli, 1960), 1. 102–03; R. H. Fuller, The Foundations of NT Christology (NY: Scribners, 1965) 24; S. Mowinckel, He That Cometh (NY: Abingdon, 1954) 112–14; H. M. Wolf, "A Solution to the Immanuel Prophecy in Isaiah 7:14–8:22," JBL 91 (1972) 449–56.

230. R. G. Bratcher, "A Study of Isaiah 7:14," BT 9 (1958) 110–11; contrast H. R. Weber, Immanuel, 12; B. Lindars, NT Apologetic (Philadelphia: Westminster, 1961) 215, on the identification of the child as Hezekiah. Isa 11:1 was understood messianically in targum and Talmud (see, e.g., b. Sanh. 93b).

231. See C. H. Dodd, "NT Translation Problems I," BT 27 (1976) 301–05; Brown, Birth, n. 45, p. 148. Contrast C. D. Isbell, "Does the Gospel of Matthew Proclaim Mary's Virginity?" BAR 3 (1977) 18–19, 52.

232. S. Sandmel, Judaism and Christian Beginnings (NY: Oxford University, 1978), n. 3, p. 462; cf. Fitzmyer, "Virginal Conception," n. 33, p. 551. Contrast H. F. Wickings, "The Nativity Stories and Docetism," NTS 23 (1976) 459.

233. Brown, Birth, n. 49, p. 149; 523–24. Contrast Delling, "parthenos," 833; Paul, L'Evangile de l'Enfance 74.

234. Reflection on Isa 7:14 LXX "might have caused a Christian to compose a story about Jesus' mother being a virgin, but it could scarcely have led him to compose a narrative wherein Joseph was the main figure." At most, argues Brown, reflection on Isa 7:14 colored the expression of an already existing Christian belief in the virginal conception of Jesus (Birth, 100. 149). The phrase en gastri echousa in v 18b parallels en gastri hexei in v 23; but it is unlikely that the Matthean narrative has been colored by the quotation, since the first phrase is a standard OT idiom for pregnancy (H. Boers, "Language Usage and the Production of Matt 1:18–23," Orientation by Disorientation [ed. R. A. Spencer; Pittsburgh: Pickwick, 1980] 224). The formulaic introduction to his fulfillment citations was composed by Matthew (Strecker, Weg, 50).

235. K. Stendahl, The School of St. Matthew (2nd ed.; Lund: Gleerup, 1967) 98.

236. Lindars (NT Apologetic, 215) suggests the text was first used by Christians in its Hebrew form to support the Davidic origins of Jesus. But we have no evidence of this use; and the Isaian text itself is not clearly about a Davidic child (see J. Lust, "The Immanuel Figure: a Charismatic Judge-Leader," ETL 47 [1971] 464, 466–67; Gese, "Natus ex virgine," 83–87). Luke does not allude to Isa 7:14.

237. Davis, "Tradition and Redaction," 412. But note that Matthew does not call Mary a parthenos in the narrative (contrast Luke 1:27 [twice]).

238. Dodd ("NT Problems," 304) argues that Matthew has defined the word in advance with his phrase in v 18, "before they came together." All this phrase says, however, is that the marriage has not been completed; the story makes clear that Joseph is not the father of the child.

239. In Isa 7:13 Ahaz is addressed as "house of David."

240. Cf. Dibelius, "Jungfrauensohn," 42–43; Tatum, "Origin," 531; van Unnik,

"Dominus Vobiscum," 287 Brown, *Birth*, 149, 97. To the above explanation of Matthew's choice, contrast Waetjen, "Genealogy," 228–29; Goulder, *Midrash and Lection*, 234.

241. Plummer, *Matthew*, 8. In fact, it has been noted that by those who see a virginal conception here that Matthew strangely seems to presuppose rather than announce it. My argument is that Matthew presupposes the illegitimacy tradition.

242. Matthew may be alluding to Isa 11:1 (among other passages) in his fulfillment citation in 2:23. His final citation in the first major section of his Gospel (according to Kingsbury's schema; *Matthew*, 50), is Isa 9:1–2 at Matt 4:15–16.

243. Brown, *Birth*, 150.

244. Delling, *"parthenos,"* 832.

245. J. T. Willis, "The Meaning of Isaiah 7:14 and Its Application in Matthew 1:23," *Restoration Quarterly* 21 (1978) 1, 4; M. E. W. Thompson, "Isaiah's Sign of Immanuel," *ExpTim* 95 (1983) 71; J. Lindblom, *A Study on the Immanuel Section in Isaiah* (Lund: Gleerup, 1958) 16.

246. Dubarle, "La Conception," 367.

247. Also, no text vindicates a woman who has willingly become pregnant by someone other than her husband.

248. J. P. Mackey, *Jesus the Man and the Myth* (NY: Paulist, 1979) 271–72. If I understand him correctly, Mackey holds that historically Jesus was conceived illegitimately, but the NT Infancy Narratives present this as a (biologically) virginal conception (pp. 276–79).

249. J. A. Sanders, "Isaiah in Luke," *Int* 36 (1982) 145.

250. By the mid–second century, Justin Martyr makes the first explicit affirmation that Isa 7:14 announces a virginal conception (*Apol.* 33; *Dial.* 43:5–8; 66–67; 77–78; 84).

251. This biblical structure of birth announcements will be treated in the next chapter.

252. See M. M. Bourke, "The Literary Genius of Matthew 1–2," *CBQ* 22 (1960) 160–75; Brown, *Birth*, 107–117, 157, 231.

253. Vermes, *Jesus the Jew*, 221.

254. Contrast *Mary in the NT*, 290: the authors think that traditional and redactional elements even in their Matthean form can be read so as to suggest nothing unusual about the conception of Jesus. "However, it is clear that any such understanding is made impossible by the Matthean narrative in its totality."

255. See D. Patrick, *The Rendering of God in the Old Testament* (Philadelphia: Fortress, 1081) 83–84, on God's "intervention through recognizable means." Cf. the essays in *God's Activity in the World: the Contemporary Debate* (ed. O. C. Thomas; Chico: Scholars, 1983).

256. O. A. Piper ("The Virgin Birth," *Int* 18 [1964] 145) thinks Joseph is placed in the foreground in this narrative for reasons that have to do with the humbling of his "male pride."

257. Anderson, "Matthew: Gender and Reading," 10.

258. B. Reicke, "Christ's Birth and Childhood," *From Faith to Faith* (ed. D. Y. Hadidian; Pittsburgh: Pickwick, 1979) 153–54: Joseph is central to Matthew's narrative because Christian knowledge of Jewish scripture is central here; attention is concentrated on the fulfillment of scripture as experienced by Joseph.

259. Contrast D. O. Via, "Narrative World and Ethical Response: the Marvelous

and Righteousness in Matt 1–2," *Semeia* 10–13 (1978) 127, 137. Because Via thinks the narrative is about the virginal conception of Jesus, he argues that Joseph's natural interpretation of everyday reality is overturned. "What appears as an immoral act on Mary's part is *rather* an act of God for the salvation of his people."

260. E. Schweizer, *Das Evangelium nach Matthäus* (Göttingen: Vandenhoeck & Ruprecht, 1973) 129; *Matthäus und seine Gemeinde* (Stuttgart: Katholisches Bibelwerk, 1974) 48; Davies, *Setting*, 256–315.

261. So Plummer, McNeile, Box, Taylor, Stendahl, Stauffer, Gundry, Soares Prabhu, Fitzmyer, and others. Contrast Davies, Vögtle, Strecker, Hahn, Hill, Nolan, and others. I would not hold that Matthew's narrative is to be understood in a narrowly apologetic sense; the dichotomy between christology/theology and apologetic here (see Box, *Virgin Birth*, 17–18) is a false one. Further, among some Matthew's own work probably increased skepticism and slander.

262. Winter ("Jewish Folklore," 36) holds that Matthew 1 contains "no teaching matter." My point is that the narrative itself is a teaching about the Law.

263. Matthew omits Mark's references to Jesus' relatives who think he is insane (Mark 3:21) and who do not honor him (Mark 6:4; cf. Matt 13:57), and to Jesus as "the son of Mary" (Mark 6:3; cf. Matt 13:55), probably a slur charging him with being illegitimate, a charge Matthew has already dealt with in his Infancy Narrative. On these texts, see below, chapter 4.

264. Fuchs, "Literary Characteristics," 128–29.

265. Schüssler Fiorenza, *Bread*, 138.

266. Fitzmyer, *Luke*, 1. 306. This is more evident in Luke, since Luke probably composed his first two chapters with the hindsight not only of the pre-Lucan gospel tradition but also of the Lucan Gospel proper and Acts. Contrast C. H. Talbert, "Prophecies of Future Greatness," *The Divine Helmsman* (ed. J. L. Crenshaw and S. Sandmel; NY: Ktav, 1980) 130, and see W. Kurz, "Luke 3:23–38 and Greco-Roman Biblical Genealogies," *Luke-Acts. New Perspectives from the SBL Seminar* (ed. C. H. Talbert; NY: Crossroad, 1984) 172–75. H. Conzelmann's theory that the Lucan Infancy Narrative is not by the same author as the rest of Luke-Acts, and that this narrative is not in accord with the theology of Luke (*The Theology of St. Luke* [NY: Harper and Row, 1960] 20, 23, 118, 172) has no critical following today.

267. When Matthew 1 is understood as being about a virginal conception, it is often noted that this belief seems to find no real echo or development in the rest of the Gospel. The same is true for Luke.

268. Anderson, "Matthew: Gender and Reading," 20–21. See also M. J. Selvidge, "Violence, Woman and the Future of the Matthean Community," *USQR* 39 (1984) 213–23.

269. See Fiorenza, *Memory*, 147; "Luke 2:41–52," *Int* 36 (1982) 403. On the economic causes of the breakup of the patriarchal family in NT times, see L. Schottroff, "Women as Followers of Jesus in NT Times," *The Bible as Liberation* (ed. N. K. Gottwald; Maryknoll: Orbis, 1983) 423.

3. Luke's Account

1. See Kenneth R. R. Gros Louis, "Different Ways of Looking at the Birth of Jesus," *Bible Review* 1 (1984) 33.

2. Cf. J. Schmid, *Das Evangelium nach Lukas* (3rd ed.; Regensburg: Pustet, 1955) 90; C. Perrot, "Les Récits d'Enfance dans la Haggada Antérieure au IIe Siècle de Notre Ère," *RSR* 55 (1967) 510–11; Fitzmyer, *Luke*, 1. 307.

3. Taylor, *Historical Evidence*, 116. Luke is said to witness to a very early stage in the spread of the virginal conception tradition; the tradition is stated but its problems (such as that of the Davidic descent) are scarcely felt. Luke's "is almost, but not quite, a simple narrative of what is implicitly accepted as fact" (pp. 84–85).

4. As Stendahl remarks, both Taylor (1920) and Machen (1930) take their point of departure in Luke, and treat Matthew as corroborating or supplementary material ("Quis et Unde," n. 2, p. 95).

5. See J. A. Fitzmyer, *A Christological Catechism. NT Answers* (NY: Paulist, 1982) 68; cf. *Mary in the NT*, 290. Against this tendency, see the opinion of C. D. Isbell, "Does the Gospel of Matthew Proclaim Mary's Virginity?" *BAR* 3 (1977) 19: "Matthew simply does not address the question of Mary's virginity except to say, as we have noted, that she was sexually celibate between the time of her marriage to Joseph and the time of the birth of her son. Rather, it is the Book of Luke which, employing precisely the traditional terminology one would expect in the description of a 'virgin' [in 1:34], provides the basis for the early Church doctrine of the virgin birth."

6. Q is usually posited as a Greek written source for about 230 verses common to Matthew and Luke, mostly sayings of Jesus not found in Mark.

7. Gundry, *Matthew*, 20, 5.

8. M. D. Goulder and M. L. Sanderson, "St. Luke's Genesis," *JTS* 8 (1957) 13; J. Drury, *Tradition and Design in Luke* (Atlanta: John Knox, 1976) 7, 46–48, 66, 59–60, 122–27.

9. The Gospel of Matthew has been often set by scholars in or around Syrian Antioch, and (like that of Luke) in the decade of the 80s. Fitzmyer proposes that Luke himself may have been a native of Antioch, although he ventures no guess about where this Gospel was actually written, and does not claim it was for the church at Antioch (*Luke*, 1. 42, 57). If he is right, the possibility may be strengthened that Matthew's work was known to Luke, or vice versa, or (more likely) that Antioch was the provenance of their common infancy tradition. But this is just speculation.

10. T. L. Brodie, "Greco-Roman Imitation of Texts as a Partial Guide to Luke's Use of Sources," *Luke-Acts. New Perspectives*, 36, 25.

11. According to this theory, Matthew and Luke both used the Gospel of Mark, Q and special material (M, L) available to each. See R. H. Fuller, *A Critical Introduction to the New Testament* (London: Duckworth, 1966) 69–78, for a clear explanation; cf. F. Neirynck, "The Synoptic Problem," *IDBSup*, 845–48.

12. C. H. Talbert speaks of "widespread loss of confidence" in the two source theory that has occurred in the last fifteen years. He does not assume it or any other source theory in his recent work, *Reading Luke. A Literary and Theological Commentary on the Third Gospel* (NY: Crossroad, 1982). Cf. E. P. Sanders, "NT Studies Today," *Colloquy on NT Studies: A Time for Reappraisal and Fresh Approaches* (Macon, GA: Mercer University, 1983) 11–28: source criticism is in disarray and the synoptic problem must be regarded as open.

13. J. A. Fitzmyer, "The Virginal Conception of Jesus in the New Testament," *TS* 34 (1973) 566–7.

14. Ibid., 571.

15. Brown, "Luke's Description of the Virginal Conception," *TS* 35 (1974) 360–63; *Birth*, 299–301; R. E. Brown, et al., *Mary in the NT*, 290.

16. See Fitzmyer, *Luke*, 1.338; and "Postscript (1980)" to his 1973 article, in Fitzmyer, *To Advance the Gospel* (NY: Crossroad, 1981) 61–2.

17. Fitzmyer, "Postscript (1980)," 61. The virginal conception is clearly asserted in Matthew, "perhaps less clearly" in Luke 1:31–35 (*Christological Catechism*, 68).
18. Or "climactic parallelism" (W. Grundmann, *Das Evangelium nach Lukas* [Berlin: Evangelische Verlag, 1974] 46).
19. Literally: "do not know." For the use of the verb "to know" for sexual relations, see Gen 4:1, 17, 25; Judges 11:39; 21:12, etc. and Matt 1:25.
20. B. S. Easton, (*The Gospel according to St. Luke* [Edinburgh: Clark, 1926] 12) opts for the sense of "husband" in Luke 1:27 and 34.
21. A. Plummer (*A Critical and Exegetical Commentary on the Gospel According to St. Luke* [ICC; 6th ed.; NY: Scribner's, 1903] n. 1, p. 24) argues against H. Lasserre's translation, "mon mari," a translation Lasserre linked to the very unlikely notion that the whole phrase marks a vow of conjugal virginity taken by Mary. Plummer insists that it is impossible that *andra*, without either article or possessive pronoun, could mean *my* husband (emphasis mine). Cf. A. George, *Marie dans le Nouveau Testament* (Paris: Desclée de Brouwer, 1981) 31, 52; he translates also "mon mari," but links it to a theory that Gabriel is announcing an immediate pregnancy (also unlikely; see below).
22. Fitzmyer, *Luke*, 1. 348–9.
23. See J. Carmignac, "The Meaning of *Parthenos* in Luke 1.27. A Reply to C. H. Dodd," *BT* 28 (1977) 329. The phrase in Luke 1:34 does not mean, says Carmignac (against Dodd), "I am still a virgin."
24. A. Feuillet, *Jésus et sa Mère*, (Paris, 1974) 113. This stress is unlikely.
25. See also I. H. Marshall, *The Gospel of Luke. A Commentary on the Greek Text* (Grand Rapids: Eerdmans, 1978) 69.
26. S. Schneiders, ("The Foot Washing [John 13:1–20]: An Experiment in Hermeneutics," *CBQ* 43 [1981] n. 27, p. 83) discusses the interaction between Jesus and Simon Peter in that passage, considering her exploration not a matter of "psychologizing" in the sense of trying to divine the intrapersonal states of the historical characters, but a matter of taking seriously the literary text.
27. B. Hubbard, "Commissioning Stories in Luke-Acts," *Semeia* 8 (1977) 120.
28. Grundmann, *Lukas*, 57.
29. Brown, *Birth*, 251, 289, 301–03, 307; Fitzmyer, *Luke*, 1.309, 311, 336–37; *Mary in the NT*, 115–17.
30. G. M. Soares Prabhu, " 'Rejoice Favored One!' Mary in the Annunciation-Story of Luke," *Biblebhashyam* 3 (1977) n. 15, p. 274.
31. Vermes, *Jesus the Jew*, 221.
32. The uncertain practice of celibacy at Qumran (related to the Levitical and eschatological ideals of that community) is no real parallel for a commitment to virginity in marriage. See *Mary in the NT*, n. 245, p. 115.
33. See Brown, *Birth*, 229–30, 303–07; Fitzmyer, *Luke*, 1.337, 348–49.
34. See Fitzmyer, "Virginal Conception," 567.
35. Fitzmyer (*Luke*, 1.349–50) finds this the best of the "psychological" interpretations (see below), but argues that it tends to obscure the future tense used by the angel. This is so if the conception is thought of as "then and there" but not if as in the future before the still distant home-taking.
36. See L. Legrand, *L'Annonce à Marie* (Paris: Cerf, 1981), 78, 96–98; cf. J. M. Creed, *The Gospel according to St. Luke* (London: Macmillan, 1930) 10; J. Gewiess, "Die Marienfrage, Lk 1, 34," *BZ* 5 (1961) 221–54.
37. Fitzmyer, "The Virginal Conception," 569.

38. J. F. Craghan, "The Gospel Witness to Mary's 'Ante Partum' Virginity," *Marian Studies* 21 (1970) 55.
39. See Soares Prabhu, " 'Rejoice,' " n. 15, pp. 274–75. He thinks, however, that "in the context of the story Mary is to be understood as expecting an immediate fulfillment of the angel's oracle—as does happen in other call narratives, where the charismatic leader is invested with his charismatic power from the moment he is called." But as we will see, the form here is a mixed one (annunciation of birth and commission narrative). Cf. Marshall, *Luke,* 69–70.
40. See C. T. Davis III, "The Literary Structure of Luke 1–2," *Art and Meaning. Rhetoric in Biblical Literature* (ed. D. J. A. Clines, D. M. Gunn, A. J. Hauser; Sheffield: JSOT Press, 1982) 221–22. Davis nevertheless insists that the question ("a common sense objection") is a literary necessity. Without it, he argues, the angel cannot "spring the ultimate surprise," divine paternity.
41. This is an assertion made by Drury (*Tradition and Design,* 59), who thinks the "plot" of the two Lucan annunciations is the same.
42. Plummer (*Luke,* 29) finds this more probable than that the time intended is at the visit to Elizabeth. But he notes that it is "a mark of the delicacy and dignity of the narrative that the time is not stated."
43. Cf. 2:1; 4:2; 5:35; 6:12; 9:36; 23:7.
44. B. Hospodar, "*Meta Spoudēs* in Lk 1, 39," *CBQ* 18 (1956) 14, 16. Hospodar thinks the phrase in Luke 1:39 should be translated, "in a serious mood of mind"; the idea is the grave pensiveness, rather than of excitement and eagerness.
45. See Harder, "*spoudazō, spoudē, spoudaios*," TDNT 7 (1971) 562–3. Other such examples include: Qoh 8:3; Job 4:5; 21:6; 22:10; Isa 21:3; Deut 16:3; Zeph 1:18.
46. E. Burrows, *The Gospel of the Infancy and Other Biblical Essays* (ed. E. F. Sutcliffe; London: Burns, Oates and Washbourne, 1940) n. 1, p. 5.
47. Legrand, *L'Annonce,* 83. Compare the different explanations of A. Loisy, *L'Evangile selon Luc* (Paris: Minerva, 1924; reprint Frankfurt: Minerva, 1971) 92, and Dibelius, "Jungfrauensohn," 5–6.
48. Legrand holds that the Lucan annunciation scene belongs to the annunciation-of-birth genre, but follows an apocalyptic pattern of thought. Luke sees the angelic annunciation as "the primordial revelation which unveils in and through the child to be born the fulfillment of God's promises and the eschatological manifestation of the power of God" (*L'Annonce,* 135. See also Hendrickx, *Infancy Narratives,* 55–56).
49. Easton, *Luke,* 10.
50. Box, *Virgin Birth,* 214.
51. Some ancient versions do read "his wife" or the equivalent in 2:5, but there is superior manuscript evidence for the reading "his betrothed."
52. See *Mary in the NT,* 146; Fitzmyer, *Luke,* 1.407.
53. Brown, *Birth,* n. 12, p. 521.
54. Plummer, *Luke* 53; cf. Marshall, *Luke,* 105. Luke does not state explicitly that Mary did not have sexual relations with Joseph after the annunciation.
55. Fitzmyer, *Luke,* 1.343. In *Mary in the NT,* 123, the authors see the possibility of influence from Deut 22:23 in the Matthean account, and they comment that this "may have been a factor in any pre-gospel tradition of a virginal conception of Jesus." I agree with those critics who find no clear allusion in Luke to Isa 7:14; Fitzmyer, *Luke,* 1.336; Brown, *Birth* 524; *Mary in the NT,* 124; contrast A. Vögtle, "Offene Fragen zur Lukanischen Geburts- und

Kindheitsgeschichte," *Das Evangelium und die Evangelien* (Düsseldorf: Patmos, 1971) 46; Stendahl, "Quis et Unde," n. 7, p. 96; H. Schürmann, *Das Lukasevangelium* (Freiburg: Herder, 1969), 1.62–63; Legrand, *L'Annonce*, 76.

56. The possibility of composition by the historical Mary should be excluded (see *Mary in the NT*, 139–40).

57. Hendrickx, *Infancy Narratives*, 84; cf. W. Stegemann, *The Gospel and the Poor* (Philadelphia: Fortress, 1984) 26; J. Miranda, *Marx and the Bible* (Maryknoll: Orbis, 1974) 17, 217. Soelle (*Strength*, 46) calls the Mary of the Magnificat a subversive, a sympathizer.

58. E. Schweizer (*The Good News according to Luke* [Atlanta: Knox, 1984] 35) speaks of the psalm's praise of "the equalizing work of God, which treats all alike."

59. P. Winter, "Magnificat and Benedictus—Maccabean Psalms?" *BJRL* 37 (1954) 328–47. Fitzmyer (*Luke*, 1.361) finds such an origin for vv 51–53 plausible, but argues that the full hymn echoes a Jewish Christian setting. Cf. J. H. Charlesworth, "A Prolegomenon to a New Study of the Jewish Background of the Hymns and Prayers in the New Testament," *JJS* 33 (1982) 276, 280.

60. L. T. Brodie, "A New Temple and a New Law," *JSNT* 5 (1979) 35. Brodie is thinking of Gen 3:15; Rev 12:1–6. But of what is Luke thinking?

61. F. W. Danker, "Greco-Roman Cultural Accomodation in the Christology of Luke-Acts," *SBL Seminar Papers 1983* (ed. K. H. Richards; Chico: Scholars, 1983) n. 19, p. 394.

62. See *Mary in the NT*, 139; S. Farris, *The Hymns of Luke's Infancy Narratives* (Sheffield: JSOT, 1985) 114–16. The aorists which appear in v 47 ("my spirit delighted in God my saviour") and vv 51–53 (all 6 verbs concerning God's great reversal of human conditions) have been differently explained. In v 47 (in parallelism with the present tense in v 46: "My soul extols the Lord") the aorist is considered a timeless aorist (BDF # 333.2) or ingressive aorist ("has begun to delight"; cf. BDF # 331). In vv 51–53 the aorists may reflect the original situation for which the hymn composed, a Maccabean victory; or they may be gnomic aorists (BDF #333), descriptive of Yahweh's tendency to reverse these conditions. Fitzmyer insists there is no evidence the Magnificat ever existed in a Semitic form, so these aorists are not to be interpreted as rendering Hebrew prophetic perfects (*Luke*, 1.359, 360–61, 366. Contrast Goulder and Sanderson, "St. Luke's Genesis," 25; Plummer, *Luke*, 33; Talbert, *Reading Luke*, 26; R. Buth, "Hebrew Poetic Tenses and the Magnificat," *JSNT* 21 [1984] 67–83).

63. Fitzmyer, *Luke*, 1.360–61.

64. See J. G. Davies, "The Ascription of the Magnificat to Mary," *JTS* 15 (1964) 307–08. On this question, see further, S. Benko, "The Magnificat: A History of the Controversy," *JBL* 86 (1967) 263–75.

65. Metzger, *Textual Commentary*, 130.

66. Brown, *Birth*, 335.

67. Vv 51–53 speaks of God punishing the oppressors, but no punishment is found in the narrative. The Magnificat reflects confidence in the ultimate victory of God, God's eschatological establishment of a just society.

68. Cf. Luke 1:38 and 1 Sam 1:11. In Luke 2:22–40 also Hannah is a model for Mary (see 1 Sam 1:21–28; 2:19–20). I do not think that the dependence in Luke 1–2 on 1 Samuel 1–3 is "material, verbal, literary; not formal, ideal" and that 1 Samuel 1–3 is only a literary archetype, meaning that the

correspondences between the characters as types is of little importance. So argues Burrows, *Gospel of the Infancy*, n. 1, p. 11.

69. P. Trible, *Texts of Terror*, 83, 50.
70. R. C. Tannehill, "The Magnificat as Poem," *JBL* 93 (1974) 267, 274–75, 270.
71. Ibid., 265.
72. As was the Benedictus, 1:68–79 and perhaps also the Nunc Dimittis, 2:29–32.
73. See above, p. 82.
74. Brown, *Birth* 336; Fitzmyer, *Luke*, 1.359.
75. Luke 1:47 may echo several LXX texts: Ps 25:5; 35:9; Hab 3:18; 1 Sam 2:1 ("I have rejoiced in your salvation").
76. On the structure of the canticle, and arguments that v 48 was inserted by Luke, see Fitzmyer, *Luke*, 1.360, 367; Easton, *Luke*, 15; Farris, *Hymns*, 21–26.
77. Note that this is the first reason, the second appearing in v 49.
78. This connection is why I think Schweizer is wrong to hold that only v 48b was composed by Luke (*Good News*, 33).
79. Fitzmyer, *Luke*, 1.367.
80. W. Grundmann, "*tapeinos ktl*," *TDNT* 8 (1972) 21.
81. Plummer, *Luke*, 32. Contrast his interpretation of *tapeinous* in v 52: the oppressed poor as opposed to tyranical rulers.
82. See Brown, *Birth*, n. 12, p. 448.
83. Luke's interest is in the fulfillment of the law. See B. Reicke, "Jesus, Simeon, and Anna (Luke 2:21–40)," *Saved by Hope* (ed. J. I. Cook; Grand Rapids: Eerdmans, 1978) 99.
84. See Brown, *Birth*, 511.
85. L. Schottroff ("Das Magnificat und die älteste Tradition über Jesus von Nazareth," *Evang Theol* 38 [1978] 298–313) holds that together with other texts such as Luke 6:20–21, the Magnificat represents the oldest apocalyptic tradition concerning Jesus, and reflects an understanding of *paraklesis* as the divine equalization of social destinies.
86. Contrast the Lucan beatitudes (Luke 6:20–21) with the Matthean (Matt 5:3–10). R. Karris speaks of the poor in this Gospel as "those who cannot demand justice for themselves, and trust in the justice of God, especially as revealed in the Christ event." *Luke: Artist and Theologian. Luke's Passion Account as Literature* (NY: Paulist, 1985) 32; cf. "The Poor and the Rich," *Perspectives in Luke-Acts*, 112–125; R. J. Cassidy, *Jesus, Politics and Society* (Maryknoll: Orbis, 1978) 20–33.
87. Drury, *Tradition*, 185–6; it describes the condition of David in 2 Kings 16:12, and of Israel in general in 1 Kings 9:16; 2 Kings 14:26, besides that of those we have mentioned.
88. Soares Prabhu, " 'Rejoice,' " 264; n. 12, p. 273. Cf. Legrand (*L'Annonce*, 70): "une jeune fille, non mariée, représentente ce qui est faible, sans importance."
89. Brown, *Birth*, 361; n. 52, p. 314; *Mary in the NT*, 121. J. Ratzinger thinks of Mary as one who surrendered herself into the barrenness made fruitful by God (*Daughter Zion* [San Francisco: Ignatius, 1983] 52).
90. See Von Rad, *Genesis*, 326. Sometimes the rape of a virgin is used as a symbol for military defeat.
91. Goulder and Sanderson argue that the word *tapeinōsis* echoes both Han-

nah's prayer and the story of Leah. "Which theme occurred to the evangelist first it is hard to be sure" ("St. Luke's Genesis," 20–21). I think that the allusion to Hannah is more primary than that to Leah.

92. Brown, *Birth*, 328, 350–55, 361, 363. He thinks that in using the terms *tapeinōsis* and *doulē* for Mary, Luke is associating her with all the memories of the poor ones evoked by those terms.

93. Against Brown, *Birth*, 530. As J. A. Sanders remarks, sanctity and purity in the dominant biblical theme—*errore hominum providentia divina*—"are gifts of God, imposed from without upon a scene of human frailty and sin" (review, *USQR* 33 [1978] 194–5).

94. Luke characterizes Mary, Elizabeth, and Anna as prophets (Schüssler Fiorenza, *Memory*, 299).

95. L. Schottroff, "Frauen in der Nachfolge Jesu in neutestamentlicher Zeit," *Traditionen der Befreiung* (Munich: Kaiser, 1980), 2.112. Cf. S. Benko, "A New Principle of Mariology: the Kenotic Motif," *Oikonomia* (ed. F. Christ; Hamburg-Bergstedt: Herbert Reich Evang. Verlag, 1967) 259–72.

96. Schüssler Fiorenza, *Memory*, 142.

97. See above, p. 83. Fitzmyer ("Postscript [1980]," 61) accepts the correction of his previous position (that Luke's annunciation scene can be read as concerning a pregnancy that occurs in the normal way) because he thinks the point about step parallelism is well taken, and also because when the scholars who were involved in the discussions which produced the book *Mary in the NT* examined Fitzmyer's interpretation, eleven of the twelve voted against it, *mainly* because of the step-parallelism. Fitzmyer concludes that "such a peer-vote in this matter should be given proper attention."

98. Delling (*"parthenos,"* 836): in the barren woman what is effected is the ability to conceive, but in Mary's case what is effected is conception itself. The conception of Jesus is "more spectacular" that that of John (Boslooper, *Virgin Birth*, 231).

99. Brown, "Luke's Description," 361. Whereas there are OT parallels to the conception of John, there are none to the conception of Jesus (n. 8, p. 360).

100. See *Mary in the NT*, 121. My contention, however, is that Mary is "helped" by God even more than Elizabeth is.

101. For a different translation and interpretation, see above.

102. Fitzmyer, *Luke*, 1.315; "Postscript (1980)," 61.

103. See C. G. Montefiore, *The Synoptic Gospels* (London: Macmillan, 1927), 2.369 for a different view.

104. Fitzmyer, *Luke*, 1.193.

105. P. Bird, "Images of Women in the Old Testament," *Religion and Sexism* (ed. R. Reuther; NY: Simon and Schuster, 1974) 62–63.

106. Brown, *Birth*, 156.

107. X. Léon-Dufour, "L'Annonce," 77, using the commission of Moses in Exod 3:2–12, and of Gideon in Judges 6:12–33.

108. R. Alter, "How Convention Helps Us Read," *Prooftexts* 3 (1983) 119. J. G. Williams, (*Women Recounted. Narrative Thinking and the God of Israel* [Sheffield: Almond, 1982] 40; n. 13, p. 135; pp. 52, 55) makes use of Alter's work, but prefers the terminology "typic scene"; he calls the annunciation a "promise scene."

109. Cf. the five motifs proposed by W. Richter (*Traditionsgeschichtliche Untersuchungen zum Richterbuch* [Bonn: Hanstein, 1963] 141); see also the threefold structure of the OT form identified by R. Neff, "The Annunciation in the Birth Narrative of Ishmael," *BR* 17 (1972) 52–53, followed by E. Conrad,

"The Annunciation of Birth and the Birth of the Messiah," *CBQ* 47 (1985) 656–63.
110. Or: will grant; *yittēn* is either a prediction (if imperfect) or a prayer (if jussive).
111. See also 1 Kings 13:1–6 (Josiah's birth predicted by a man of God); 1 Chron 22:7–10 (in the context of David's commissioning of Solomon to build the temple, David recounts an annunciation made to him by Yahweh). On Isa 7:14, see above, chapter 2.
112. The following is a complete list of the annunciation scenes in the OT: Gen 16:7–13; 17:1–21; 18:1–15; 25:19–25; Judges 13:3–23; 1 Samuel 1; 1 Kings 13:1–6; 2 Kings 4:8–17; Isa 7:10–17; 1 Chron 22:7–10. Ten in all.
113. As Alter points out, the annunciation to Rebekah in Gen 25:19–25 is also to a woman already pregnant. As a result, it is directed not to the fact of future birth, but to the fate of the sons who will be born ("Convention," 122).
114. Perrot, "Les Récits," 505.
115. Alter, "Convention," 121.
116. Trible, *Texts of Terror*, 17.
117. Schweizer, *Good News*, 25–26.
118. Williams, (*Women Recounted*, 55, 82) insists that the only difference in pattern between the gospel annunciation scences and the ancient Israelite model is that the woman is not barren but a young virgin. The young virgin is "an image in opposition to the barren wife." But, he says, "the opposites meet in that the outcome is the same in both cases: through a wonderful divine providence the religious hero is conceived in a womb brought to conception by no human father. For early Christianity this was one symbolic mode of expressing the transcendent meaning of its salvific revelation event: the reality of this son is not of human origins, but of God." Williams holds that the OT examples of once-barren women concern wombs which are not or cannot be brought to conception by human fathers. But the OT stories of conception by the once-barren are stories of dual (divine and human) paternity.
119. In 1:48 it is not a precise verbal allusion, but, as we have seen, an allusion to the content of the law in Deuteronomy, to the situation that law deals with.
120. Burrows (*Gospel of the Infancy*, n. 1, p. 53; cf. pp. 9, 29–30) thinks that "It is not sufficiently noticed that Mary is suffering spiritually at the Annunciation." According to him, there are three moments: (1) great trouble of mind and fear (1:29–30); (2) something like an apparent conflict of duties (revealed in Mary's question in 1:34); (3) an act of resignation (her response in 1:38). Burrows is right to recognize this nuance, although the tone of the Lucan narrative is predominantly joyous.
121. So P. Benoit, *Exégèse et Théologie* (Paris: Cerf. 1968) 3.193–96; Brown, *Birth*, 247, 251, 265, 273.
122. So Fitzmyer, "Postscript (1980), *Luke*, 1.309, 315, 317, 335. See the list of other scholars who hold this view in W. Wink, *John the Baptist in the Gospel Tradition* (Cambridge: Cambridge University, 1968) n. 1, p. 60. Wink (following R. Laurentin, *Structure et Théologie de Luc I-II* [Paris: Gabalda, 1957] 110–16) postulates mutual dependence between the two stories (70–79).
123. See Schweizer, *Good News*, 15–16.
124. See Fitzmyer, *Luke*, 1.335.
125. Parallelism is one of the stylistic techniques preferred by Luke; see C. H.

Talbert, *Literary Patterns, Theological Themes and the Genre of Luke-Acts* (Missoula: Scholars, 1974) 15–45, 103–43.

126. Alter, "Convention," 116.

127. In his layout of the structure of the Lucan Infancy Narrative, Fitzmyer (*Luke*, 1.313) presents as the first parallel between 1:5–25 and 1:26–38 the introduction of the parents: vv 5–10 (John's parents are introduced, expecting no child because barren); vv 26–27 (Jesus' parents are introduced, expecting no child because unmarried). Clearly Fitzmyer means "because only betrothed" instead of "unmarried." But while it is true that they are not literally expecting a child at the moment of the annunciation, the fact that they are betrothed means that they would reasonably expect to have a child in the future.

128. Contrast M. Chevallier, *L'Esprit et le Messie dans le Bas-Judaïsme et le Nouveau Testament* (Paris: Presses Universitaires de France, 1958) 87: "Au 'Comment?' de Marie, l'ange répond: 'Par le Saint-Esprit.'"

129. Goulder and Sanderson, "St. Luke's Genesis," n.2, p. 19. Laurentin (*Structure*, 32–33) argues that the response to Zechariah is a reprimand, that to Mary a revelation.

130. Davis, "Literary Structure," 220.

131. Also, both passages occur in contexts of comparison and contrast between Jesus and John the Baptist (hinted at in John 3:5, developed in 3:22–36).

132. C. K. Barrett, *The Gospel According to St. John* (London: SPCK, 1962) 173–76.

133. See Brown, *John* 1. 130, 141.

134. Barrett (*John*, 175) on John 3:6: "There are two contrasting orders of existence and hence two contrasting orders of generation . . . each produces results corresponding to itself. Flesh is flesh and not spirit; yet it remains true that flesh—and in particular fleshly generation—supplies a parable by which begetting from the Spirit may be apprehended."

135. Luke, however, does not use the language of divine begetting.

136. In Acts 14:19, Jews hostile to Paul come from Antioch and Iconium.

137. E. Haenchen, *The Acts of the Apostles* (Philadelphia: Westminster, 1971) 246.

138. See S. Ringe, "Luke 9:28–36: the Beginning of an Exodus," *Semeia* 28 (1983) 92–94.

139. Fitzmyer, *Luke*, 1.351.

140. In Exod 25:20, winged cherubim overshadow [*suskiazō*] the mercy seat or top of the Ark; cf. 1 Chr 28:18 [*skiazō*].

141. See S. Terrien, *The Elusive Presence* (NY: Harper & Row, 1978) 416; n. 13, p. 441.

142. MT: "A rich man's wealth is his strong city, and like a high wall protecting him." D. Daube (*NT and Rabbinic Judaism* [London: Athlone, 1956] n. 1, p. 20) notes that *episkiazō* may be intended as a cover.

143. This passage deals with God's eschatological purification of the remnant in Jerusalem (they will be called "holy" v 3), purification with "the spirit of judgment, and the spirit of burning" (v 4). God's glory is a defence (v 5), "for a shadow from the heat, and as a shelter and a hiding from inclemency (of weather) and from rain." Note the presence here of the terms holy, spirit, shadow.

144. Cf. Isa 32:2 Symmachus (kings and princes are like the shadow [*skia*] of a Great Rock). The synonym *skepē* (covering, shelter, shadow) is used for divine protection in Ps 16 (17):8; 35 (36):7; 62 (63):7; 90 (91):1; 120 (121):5; Isa 49:2; 25:4–5.

145. The Old Syriac is missing at this point, but S. Brock thinks it likely that it read *naggen 'al* there ("Passover, Annunciation and Epiclesis: Some Remarks on the Term *Aggen* in the Syriac Versions of Luke 1:35," *Nov T* 24 [1982], n. 1, p. 222).

146. Ibid., 224, 232; cf. Brock, "An Early Interpretation of *pāsah:* '*aggēn* in the Palestinian Targum," *Interpreting the Hebrew Bible* (ed. J. A. Emerton and S. C. Reif; Cambridge: Cambridge University, 1982) 32–33.

147. So Brock, "Passover," 225. He argues that to translate "protect" is to make too much of the Hebrew cognate *māgēn*, "shield."

148. See Gese, "Natus," n. 26, p. 82.

149. Aramaic version: "under the *telal* (cover, shadow) of the Shekinah of his glory."

150. Against Daube, *NT and Rabbinic Judaism*, 27–36; J. M. Ford, "Mary's Virginitas Post Partum and Jewish Law," *Bib* 54 (1973) 272.

151. See above, p. 28.

152. Daube thinks this interpretation is opposed as dangerous in the Targum, which renders Ruth 3:9, "May your name be called over your handmaid, and may you take me to wife." He regards this rendering as "homey," not exceptionally refined, and avoidance of (a) the literal Hebrew and of (b) an "elevated" Aramaic translation which he thinks may have existed ("spread the shadow of your wing" or "overshadow") and of (c) the Lucan interpretation, which he thinks the public had no difficulty in detecting (as sexual).

153. Brown, *Birth*, 290. Contrast Dibelius, "Jungfrauensohn," 19–22; Davis, "Literary Structure," 222–23; n. 9, p. 229.

154. McCurley, *Ancient Myths*, 96.

155. Laurentin, *Structure*, 64–71; independently, S. Lyonnet, "*Chaire kecharitōmenē*," *Bib* 20 (1939) 131–141; cf. Soares Prabhu, " 'Rejoice,' " 268; J. McHugh, *The Mother of Jesus in the New Testament* (Garden City, NY: Doubleday, 1975) 37–52; L. Sabourin, "Recent Views on Luke's Infancy Narratives," *Religious Studies Bulletin* 1 (1981) 23–24.

156. A. Mintz, "The Rhetoric of Lamentations and the Representation of Catastrophe," *Prooftexts* 2 (1982) 3.

157. Brown, *Birth*, 321. The authors of *Mary in the NT* remark that they cannot deny the possibility of the Lyonnet thesis, but the arguments against it mean that nothing certain or probable can be built on it (p. 132). Marshall (*Luke*, 65) holds that a typological identification of Mary with the daughter of Zion is nowhere explicit, and "it would tend to distract attention from the coming Messiah to the mother." Cf. R. Schnackenburg, "Das Magnificat, seine Spiritualität und Theologie," *Geist und Leben* 38 (1965) 354–55.

158. They are not confined to the five suggested allusions to Zeph 3:14–17 discussed by Fitzmyer (*Luke*, 1.345).

159. There is no reason to regard vv 34–35 as later Lucan insertion or afterthought.

160. Fitzmyer discusses a portion of the text in his articles, "Qumran Aramaic and the New Testament," *NTS* 20 (1973/74) 392–93; "The Aramaic Language and the Study of the New Testament," *JBL* 99 (1980) 14–15. See Schaberg, *The Father, the Son and the Holy Spirit*, 240.

161. According to Plummer (*Luke* 25), both terms pneuma and hagion in Luke 1:35 have a special point, the former implicitly contrasted to the flesh.

162. This verb does appear in the Western reading of Luke 3:22, but this is a reading judged by many critics to be secondary.

163. Fitzmyer, *Luke*, 1.337. Talbert (*Reading Luke*, 18) speaks of Jesus in Luke as conceived of the Holy Spirit; Waetjen ("Genealogy," 222) says that v 35 discloses "the procedure of the begetting"; Brown (*Birth*, 432, cf. 313–14) remarks that for Luke divine sonship seems to have been brought about through the virginal conception. Cf. *Mary in the NT*, n. 268, p. 122: v 35 describes the product of divine begetting.

164. Danker, "Graeco-Roman Cultural Accomodation," 407; cf. W. B. Tatum, "The Epoch of Israel," *NTS* 13 (1966/67) 187: Jesus is conceived through the agency of God's Spirit.

165. The present participle, passive, neuter, is used, *to gennomenon*. But I do not think this must be considered a theological passive.

166. See Kurz, "Luke 3:23–38," 176.

167. Fitzmyer (*Luke*, 1.340) thinks that the affirmation of Mary's virginity "is never presented in any biological sense." This he says is implied by the figurative use of "come upon" and "overshadow." Nevertheless, he says, 1:35 is about Mary conceiving through divine intervention.

168. Goulder and Sanderson think it possible that the overshadowing by the Holy Spirit is intended by Luke to recall the brooding of the Spirit over the waters; but if so Luke "has given small linguistic hint of his intention" ("St. Luke's Genesis," n. 1, p. 20).

169. There are no Jewish genealogies contemporary with Luke's which extend back to God (see Johnson, *Purpose*, 237).

170. Mackey, *Jesus the Man and the Myth*, 276; cf. Schweizer, *Good News*, 29 ("Mary experiences what took place when the Spirit caused the world to arise out of chaos and life out of dried bones"); Talbert, *Reading Luke* 19, 46–47; H. Flender, *St. Luke Theologian of Redemptive History* (Philadelphia: Fortress, 1967) 136.

171. A parallel has been said to exist between the father-son relationship of God and Adam, and that of God and Jesus: both are said to be cases of God's creative fatherhood, not of sexual begetting. In addition, there is a legal fatherhood (in terms of inheritance and treatment as a son) of God for Adam and of Joseph for Jesus (Kurz, "Luke 3:23–38," 179). Kurz thinks that Luke does present a virginal conception in chapter 1, and reads the genealogy as harmonized with this notion. But see further, below. I accept the second parallel, of two legal fatherhoods, but the first, of creative fatherhood, only if this is interpreted as not necessarily involving the notion of Jesus' virginal conception.

172. Gen 2:7 (cf. 1 Cor 15:45) depicts life breathed into Adam by God; cf. Philo. *De Virt.* 203.

173. Kurz, "Luke 3:23–38," 171, 176–179; Johnson, *Purpose*, 234–38; Plummer, *Luke*, 105; Fitzmyer, *Luke*, 1.190.

174. Johnson asks, "If Jesus is shown to be Son of God by virtue of his descent from Adam, the son of God *par excellence*, does this not constitute a close parallel with the Hellenistic and Roman attempts to prove the 'divinity' of heroes and emperors by tracing their pedigree to a god?" He answers that question in the negative: although Luke may have been aware that such a genealogy would have a special significance to his readers among the Gentiles, the genealogy has a Jewish provenance (*Purpose*, 239).

175. Kurz, "Luke 3:23–38," 179.

176. Many have seen that in Luke 3–24 and in Acts, Jesus' status is not connected with a unique conception.

177. Brown (*Birth*, 312–13) considers Luke 1:35 simply the Lucan version of an

early Christian christological formula. I do not think, however, that the retrojection process is the sole explanation of the christology of the Infancy Narratives as we now have them. See Fuller, "The Conception/Birth," 37–52.

178. Fitzmyer, *Luke*, 1.340.

179. Ibid., 338. See also Craghan, "Gospel Witness," 65: "the overshadowing of the Spirit and the resulting divine filiation do not demand a Virgin Birth."

180. I do not know what Taylor is thinking of here. The association of *marital* sex and "impurity of soul" was not common in Judaism. And there is no evidence Luke was influenced by such a view of sex or marriage.

181. Taylor, *Historical Evidence*, 36. Cf. Chevallier, *L'Esprit*, n. 5, p. 87. Taylor argues that Luke received the tradition of a virginal conception after he had composed the annunciation narrative, and he inserted this tradition in vv 34–35. But these verses are part of the original Lucan composition.

182. In *Jub* 1:23–25 the notions of a holy spirit, cleansing, and divine paternity are linked.

183. Grundmann ("*dynamai, dynamis*," *TDNT* 2 [1964] 300) states that behind the Lucan story "stands the biblical concept of God and His verbal act," but (against Grundmann) I do not think for Luke this is an act of begetting.

184. Fitzmyer, "The Virginal Conception," 569; see his revision of this statement in *Luke*, 1.338.

185. Talbert, "Concept of Immortals"; "Prophecies of Future Greatness," 134–45. See above, n. 221. On the lack of firm documentation for the concept of "divine man" in Christian or pagan literature of the first century C.E., see H. C. Kee, "Divine Man," *IDBSup*, 242–43.

186. See Danker, "Cultural Accomodation," n. 36, pp. 408–09, 414. Danker finds Talbert's discussion of biography and literary patterns helpful, but contends that it needs to be freshly examined in the light of the larger context Danker himself explores.

187. Talbert, "Concept of the Immortals," 435. Hellenistic biographical tradition made its impact on Judaism also, before and alongside its impact on Christianity, so that Luke's readers of Jewish background shared some of the same literary expectations (Perrot, "Les Recits," 507). In addition, the fact that the genre of Luke is in some respects similar to that of Greco-Roman biographies of heroes and immortals does not take away from the fact that in other respects Luke is also strikingly close to biblical and post-biblical stories of "men of God" (Elijah, Elisha, Samuel, Moses); see Brodie, "Greco-Roman Imitation," n. 133, p. 45; D. Tiede, *Prophecy and History in Luke-Acts* (Philadelphia: Fortress, 1980) 8, 14–17.

188. W. G. Kümmel, *Introduction to the NT* (Nashville: Abingdon, 1975) 149–50. Fitzmyer regards Luke as a non-Jewish Semite, not a Greek (*Luke*, 1.41–45); Schweizer (*Good News*, 6) thinks Luke before his baptism may have been a proselyte, a Gentile who attended Jewish worship and kept the major commandments without being circumcized. E. E. Ellis ("Luke, Saint," *Encyclopedia Britannica;* 15th ed., 1974; vol. 11, p. 178) represents a minority opinion when he writes that Luke was not a Gentile but a Jewish Christian who followed a Greek life-style and was comparatively lax in ritual observances.

189. Fitzmyer, *Luke*, 1.58–59. H. Koester argues that Luke wrote as if he were speaking primarily to the pagan world, yet he was always mindful of his Christian readers. *Introduction to the New Testament* (Philadelphia: Fortress, 1982), 2. 310. In my opinion, Luke was addressing himself to the Christian

world at large, a world that was predominantly of Gentile descent by Luke's time. He was not writing mostly for Jewish Christians (against J. Jervell, *Luke and the People of God* [Minneapolis: Augsburg, 1972]).

190. Promising to act or to let it be according to the word (*rēma*) of another is a common LXX phrase (see Gen 30:35; Josh 2:21; Judges 11:10; etc.).

191. See S. Terrien, *Elusive Presence*, 414; B. J. Hubbard, "Commissioning Stories," 103–126; Soares Prabhu, " 'Rejoice,' " 260. J. P. Audet ("L'Annonce à Marie" *RB* 63 [1956] 346–74) shows how close the annunciation to Mary is to Gideon's call (Judges 6:11–24).

192. Hubbard, "Commissioning Stories," 105; cf. the five structural elements analyzed by Soares Prabhu, " 'Rejoice,' " 262; and T. Y. Mullins, "New Testament Commission Forms, Especially in Luke-Acts," *JBL* 95 (1976) 603.

193. Hubbard, "Commissioning Stories," 115–116.

194. Soares Prabhu, " 'Rejoice,' " 262–64.

195. On S. Muñoz Iglesias' treatment of the blended form, annunciation and commission ("El Evangelico de la Infancia en S. Lucas," 329–82), and Legrand's criticism of it, see *L'Annonce*, 98–101. Muñoz Iglesias's analysis includes v 35 only as part of 1:26–38 (apparition), but assigns it no specific function.

196. Mullins, "NT Commission Forms," 606–08.

197. *Mary in the NT*, 126.

198. Legrand allows that the Lucan scene can be called a commission of Mary in the former sense only.

199. D. M. Smith, "Luke 1:26–38," *Int* 29 (1975) 413.

200. J. Rohde, *Rediscovering the Teaching of the Evangelists* (Philadelphia: Westminster, 1968) 68–69 on H. J. Held's dissertation, "Matthew as Interpreter of the Miracle Stories."

201. Luke 7:50; 8:48, 50; 17:19.

202. Talbert, *Reading Luke*, 246; P. J. Achtemeier, "The Lucan Perspective on the Miracles of Jesus," *Perspectives on Luke-Acts*, 153–67.

203. Mullins finds 37 instances of the commission form in the NT, 27 in Luke-Acts. None besides Mary's annunciation-commission contains a verbal consent ("NT Commission Forms," 603–14).

204. Hubbard, "Commissioning Stories," 107–113, 122–23.

205. See Luke 9:59–62 for possible exceptions: "I will follow you, Lord, but first let me go and bury my father . . . say farewell to those at my home." But Jesus' response shows that these are not acceptable statements of consent. Luke 9:58 is a consent preceding the call, in advance of knowledge of its demands. Simon reacts to Jesus' command in Luke 5:5 with both a protest and consent: "Master, we toiled all night and took nothing, but at your word I will let down the nets."

206. Soares Prabhu, following A. Feuillet, has also noted that an explicit mention of the acceptance of the call by the person called is not normally part of the call narrative form. Unlike Feuillet, who insists this means Luke is not in the annunciation scene following a Hebrew Bible form (*Jésus et sa Mère* [Paris: Gabalda, 1974] 159), Soares Prabhu argues correctly that Luke is modifying the pattern in order to highlight Mary's reply (" 'Rejoice,' " n. 10, p. 273).

207. *Mary in the NT*, 175.

208. Ibid., 167–70; contrast Conzelmann, *Theology*, 35, 47–48. On Luke 11:27–28 see Schüssler Fiorenza, *Memory*, 146.

209. P. J. Bearsley ("Mary the Perfect Disciple," *TS* 41 [1980], n. 47, p. 476)

makes the suggestion that Luke may have based his understanding on a tradition about her which does not surface explicitly in the Gospel, but which is reflected in the incidents concerning her which Luke narrates. See further next chapter, on the pre-gospel tradition.

210. The parallel in the Mount of Olives story is seen also by R. H. Fuller, "A Note on Luke 1:28 and 38," *The NT Age* (ed. W. C. Weinrich; Macon GA: Mercer University, 1984) 202.

211. Soares Prabhu, " 'Rejoice,' " n. 24, p. 276.

212. See Plummer, *Luke*, 26; Easton, *Luke*, 11; Burrows, *Gospel of the Infancy*, 9, 29. Luke 1:38 is, says Burrows, a formula of resignation, an act of submission, not a prayer or a welcoming or giving permission.

213. Brown (*Birth*, 301, 344) argues that Elizabeth's praise of Mary's belief is another indication that Luke is writing about a miraculous virginal conception; no belief would really be required if Mary was to conceive as any other young girl would conceive. On the contrary, I hold that Mary is presented as believing in God's empowerment and protection of her and her child in an implied situation of danger and perhaps violence. She believes also, of course, in the promise of a glorious destiny for her son.

214. Soares Prabhu, " 'Rejoice,' " 265.

215. See V. Taylor, *The Passion Narrative of St. Luke* (ed. O. E. Evans; Cambridge: Cambridge University Press, 1972) 69. Taylor thinks that Luke 22:39–46 is not Luke's free composition. Others argue that Mark is Luke's primary source for the Mount of Olives pericope; see E. Linnemann, *Studien zur Passionsgeschichte* (FRLANT 102; Göttingen: Vandenhoeck & Ruprecht, 1970) 35–37. Luke 1:37 is echoed in 18:24–30.

216. See Taylor, *Passion Narrative*, 69; Drury, *Tradition and Design*, 54; Schweizer, *Good News*, 342–43; J. Neyrey, "The Absence of Jesus' Emotions," *Bib* 61 (1980) n. 1, p. 153. Contrast Metzger, *Textual Commentary*, 177; B. D. Ehrman and M. A. Plunkett, "The Angel and the Agony," *CBQ* 45 (1985) 401–16.

217. At the tomb itself, "two men" give the message of Jesus' resurrection to the women, although later the disciples walking to Emmaus remark that the women have had "a vision of angels."

218. In Acts, angels appear to liberate and/or commission in 5:19–20 (an angel opens the prison doors and frees the apostles, commissioning them to "Go and stand in the temple and speak to the people all the words of this Life"); 8:26 (an angel sends Philip to the desert road from Jerusalem to Gaza, where he encounters the Ethiopian eunuch); 10:3–6; cf. v 22; 11:13 (in a vision, an angel commissions Cornelius the centurion to send to Joppa for Peter); 12:6–11 (an angel liberates Peter from prison); Acts 27:23–24 (Paul says that an angel appeared to him to tell him that he must stand before Caesar and assure him that he and those with him will not perish at sea).

219. See, for example, the Pastoral Letter of US Bishops: "Behold Your Mother: Woman of Faith"; Nov 21, 1973, in *Catholic Mind* 72 (1974) ## 142, 60; Pope Paul VI, *Marialis Cultus*, ET: Devotion to the Blessed Virgin Mary; *The Pope Speaks* 19 (1974/75), ## 34–37, 73–75.

220. Contrast the valuing of a woman's own will in harmony with the will of others, in a Goddess-centered framework (C. Christ, "Why Women Need the Goddess," *Womanspirit Rising*, 184).

221. See W. Zimmerli, " 'Slavery in the OT," *IDBSup* 829–30; W. G. Rollins, "Slavery in the NT," Ibid., 830–31; H. W. Wolff, "Masters and Slaves," *Int* 27 (1973) 259, 66–71; K. Rengstorf, "*doulos, ktl,*" *TDNT* 2 (1964) 271.

222. See S. Pomeroy, *Goddesses, Whores, Wives and Slaves* (NY: Schocken, 1975) 139–40, 191–93, 195–97. In a poetic fragment in 1 Macc 2:11, profaned and despoiled Jerusalem is spoken of as reduced to the status of a *doulē*.

223. J. Vogt, "Ecce ancilla domini: eine Untersuchung zum sozialen Motiv des antiken Marienbildes," *VC* 23 (1969) 246; cited by Brown, *Birth*, n. 73, p. 364. Brown comments that it is no accident that some of the offense of the cross rubbed off on Mary. One of the objections against Christianity in the early dialogue between Christians and Jews was that God would never have had his Messiah enter the world without fitting honor and glory, "born of a woman who admitted that she was no more than a handmaid, a female slave."

224. Wolff, "Masters and Slaves," 272.

225. Cf. Luke 17:10; Acts 16:17. See D. L. Jones, "The Title 'Servant' in Luke-Acts," *Luke-Acts, New Perspectives*, 148–65.

226. R. Ruether, "Feminist Interpretation: A Method of Correlation," *Feminist Interpretation*, 120–21.

227. She is depicted as understanding Gabriel to be speaking of pregnancy in the imminent future; but the home-taking must be still in the relatively distant future.

228. On Luke's theme of the "ignorance of the faithful" (2:49–50; 18:34; 24; Acts 1:7), see Tiede, *Prophecy and History*, 32.

229. Even though, as argued above, the consent may be thought of as consent to the pregnancy, not to the act that causes it.

230. He is declared innocent by Pilate (23:4, 14–15, 22), Herod (23:15), one crucified with him (23:41), and the centurion (23:47).

231. C. K. Barrett, *Luke the Historian in Recent Study* (London: Epworth, 1961) 23.

232. E. Käsemann, "Ministry and Community in the NT," *Essays on NT Themes* (London: SCM, 1964) 92. He thinks that a *theologia gloriae* is in process of replacing the *theologia crucis;* but see Fitzmyer, *Luke*, 1.22–23; R. H. Fuller and P. Perkins, *Who Is the Christ?* (Philadelphia: Fortress, 1983) 92.

233. Conzelmann, *Theology*, 201.

234. Fitzmyer, *Luke*, 1.219–21; cf. W. G. Kümmel, "Current Theological Accusations Against Luke," *ANQ* 16 (1975) 138; R. Zehnle, "The Salvific Character of Jesus' Death in Lucan Soteriology," *TS* 30 (1969) 420–44.

235. Cf. Fitzmyer, *Luke*, 1.23.

236. See J. M. Ford, *My Enemy Is My Guest* (Maryknoll: Orbis, 1984) 20, 28, 36, for the theory that the Lucan Infancy Narrative, based on non-pacifist sources, presents the expectation that Jesus will be an aggressive, military, political messiah—an expectation contrary to the policy of the nonviolent Lucan Jesus. The new age inaugurated by Jesus is thus thrown into higher relief. See, however, F. W. Danker, *Jesus and the New Age* (St. Louis: Clayton, 1972) 16, on 1:51–53.

237. Its traditions were originally independent of the tradition behind chapter 1.

238. Fitzmyer translation. For different interpretations of these verses, see A. Feuillet, "L'épreuve prédite à Marie par la vieillard Siméon," *À la Rencontre de Dieu* (LePuy: Mappus, 1961) 243–63; Brown, *Birth*, 462–66.

239. Schüssler Fiorenza, "Luke 2:41–52," 401–03.

240. On the statistics concerning the 42 passages concerning women or the feminine in Luke, 23 found only in this Gospel, see L. Swidler, *Biblical Affirmations of Women* (Philadelphia: Westminster, 1979) 254–56, 259, 261, 280–

81. On Luke's use of sexually parallel stories and images, see pp. 165–72, 257–58, 271.
241. Schüssler Fiorenza, *Memory*, 146. The focus on Mary in Luke's annunciation scene does not coincide with an emphasis on the patriarchal institution of motherhood (cf. Fuchs, "Literary Characterization," 128).
242. B. Witherington III, "On the Road with Mary Magdalene, Joanna, Susanna, and Other Disciples—Luke 8:1–3," *ZNW* 70 (1979) 244; R. F. O'Toole, "Luke's Position on Politics and Society in Luke-Acts," *Political Issues in Luke-Acts* (ed. R. J. Cassidy and P. H. Scharper; Maryknoll: Orbis, 1983) 12–13.
243. Schüssler Fiorenza, *Bread*, 16.
244. See Schüssler Fiorenza, *Memory*, 49–52. Luke has little focus on the radical figure of Mary Magdalene. The Gospel reflects, I think, discussion of the position of women in church leadership, and a conservative, mediating stance.
245. Williams (*Woman Recounted*, 79, cf. 112) calls Mary a "dependent heroine"; like Esther, she never initiates any kind of action, and serves ends that finally focus more on masculine roles. Christian story and art have construed her importance in relation to God the Father and God the Son. But Williams recognizes that in Luke her passivity is associated with her complete dependence on God, which makes her independent of human males (p. 83–84, 103).
246. Contrast the Matthean Mary; H. P. West, Jr., "A Primitive Version of Luke in the Composition of Matthew," *NTS* 14 (1977/78) 80.
247. Joseph is in the background of this story, simply assumed to acquiesce.
248. Legrand, *L'Annonce*, 82.
249. See V. Saiving, "The Human Situation: a Feminine View," *JR* 40 (1960) 108–09; "the temptations of woman *as woman* are not the same as the temptations of man *as man*, and the specifically feminine forms of sin . . . have a quality which can never be encompassed by such terms as 'pride' and 'will-to-power.' They are better suggested by . . . underdevelopment or negation of the self." The relationship of feelings of worthlessness to self-sacrifice is noted by Daly (*Gyn/ecology*, 378).
250. He omits any reference to them exercising a ministry of proclamation, and in fact in 14:26; 18:29b gives the impression that the Jesus movement was a movement of itinerant charismatic men (Schüssler Fiorenza, *Memory*, 145). See her unpublished address to the General Meeting of the Catholic Biblical Association of America, San Francisco, Aug. 24, 1978, "The Role of Women according to Luke/Acts"; E. M. Tetlow, *Women and Ministry in the New Testament* (NY: Paulist, 1980) 101–09; Schottroff, "Women as Followers," 420.
251. Burrows, *Gospel of the Infancy*, 55.
252. See Fuchs, "Literary Characterization," 129, on how unthinkable it would be that an unmarried barren woman would be visited by God and miraculously released from her barrenness. "This would be unthinkable, since the child born out of wedlock would not be able to carry on his father's lineage and would be ostracized from the community as a 'mamzer' (Deut 23:3), while his mother would at best be branded as 'zona' ('whore')." Mary communicates directly with the divine; but as Fuchs notes ("Female Heroines," 153), there is a "Biblical policy" which "allows women characters to hold direct discourse with God (or his agent) only in a 'procreative' context."
253. Brown, *Birth*, 8.

4. The Pre-Gospel Tradition and Post-Gospel Traditions

1. A. Schweitzer, *Quest,* 293, 305.
2. If another source theory is accepted, with Matthew and/or Luke thought prior to Mark and available to him, it would have to be explained why Mark has no Infancy Narrative at all. It can be speculated that Mark understood the narratives as I am proposing, as theological treatments of the illegitimate conception of Jesus, and refused to hand down this tradition. Mark might then also be responsible for turning favorable statements about the mother and brothers of Jesus into criticisms of them (see below). But this speculation raises more questions than it can answer, and must be left aside here. What of the possibility that Matthew knew Luke's narrative, or vice versa? The supposition that Matt 1:18–25 was written with Luke 1 as its source has much less merit than the suggestion of that Luke wrote with Matthew's Infancy Narrative in view. But this fascinating puzzle also cannot be pursued here.
3. See Soares Prabhu, *Formula Quotations,* 2–3.
4. Stendahl, *Meanings,* 96.
5. See p. 79.
6. See Nolan, *Royal Son* 64.
7. Neuter, aorist participle. Literally, "what was begotten."
8. Neuter, present participle. Literally, "that which is begotten" or "born." The present participle has a future significance (Brown, *Birth,* 391).
9. This tradition may have passed through different stages on its ways to Matthew and to Luke.
10. It has been suggested that the dream format was chosen by Matthew because Joseph the patriarch, dreamer of dreams, is a model here, and there is patterning on tradition about the infancy of Moses (Brown, *Birth,* 154–63). The Matthean dream is straightforward, without symbols, and needs no interpretation.
11. Perez and Zerah, Boaz, Obed, and Solomon are "from" (*ek*) the women mentioned (vv 3, 5, 6); Jesus is "from" (*ek*) Mary (v 16), and "from" (*ek*) the Holy Spirit (v 18b).
12. See above, n. 104, p. 79; pp. 107, 111. The spirit of God is opposed to lust in *T. Benj.* 8:2–3.
13. Taylor, *Historical Evidence* 40–87.
14. But there is no certainty that traditions grow always from the simpler to the more complex. See W. H. Kelber, *The Oral and the Written Gospel* (Philadelphia: Fortress, 1983) 4–5, 8, 29; E. L. Abel, "The Psychology of Memory and Rumor Transmission and Their Bearing on Theories of Oral Transmission in Early Christianity," *JR* 51 (1971) 276.
15. This is a separate question from the question concerning the provenance and authorship of the tradition.
16. Step 1. is missing in Luke (since the plight has not yet occurred), as is 4g (perhaps because his predominantly Gentile audience would not understand the etymology). Steps 3, 5, and 6 are missing in Matthew (perhaps because the dream is itself a countering of Joseph's objection to the completion of the marriage).
17. W. Manson, *The Gospel of Luke* (NY: Harper and Brothers, 1930) 276: no single narrative of the birth story was in possesion of the field. See Brown, *Birth,* n. 4, p. 298. He deliberately uses the word "tradition" because he

does not want to commit himself to a fixed story that Matthew and Luke each drew upon. He thinks rather of "a tendency in popular reflection to construct an annunciation of the birth of the Davidic Messiah, perhaps a tendency already at work in Judaism and adapted to Jesus by Christians."

18. The etymology of the name might have meant that, hearing the cry of the raped woman, God saves.

19. Contrast Brown, "Luke's Description," n. 8, p. 361: the tradition may have consisted chiefly of (1) a Christological statement about Jesus as Son of God through the power of the Holy Spirit; (2) a translation of that statement into historical terms involving a virginal conception; (3) the tendency to dramatize the message in the literary form of an annunciation.

20. Kelber, *Oral and Written Gospel*, 27.

21. Fitzmyer, "Virginal Conception," 562.

22. Contrast Boslooper, *Virgin Birth*, 131. He faults those who do not consider Joseph's paternity as historical, for rather taking "Joseph's attitude in the Matthean narrative as historical." But actually both Matthew and Luke agree on this point: that Joseph was not Jesus' biological father.

23. Cf. *The Ascension of Isaiah* 11:2–16

24. See J. Z. Lauterbach, "Jesus in the Talmud," *Rabbinic Essays* (Cincinnati: HUC, 1951) 536.

25. Luke 3:23; 4:22; John 1:45; 6:42; cf. Matt 13:55; Luke 2:27, 41, 43, 48.

26. Contrast the story told of Demartus, born early at seven months, but publicly repudiated at first by his father. It is the public repudiation which forms the basis for his enemies' successful attempts to depose him (Herodotus 6:61–71).

27. The public knowledge of early birth, it is held by some, may have been a historical catalyst for the notion of virginal conception, a notion which insisted on the sinlessness of Jesus, extending even to his origins. See Brown, *Birth*, 526–28; *Mary in the NT*, 94–95, 290; J. K. Elliott, *Questioning Christian Origins* (London: SCM, 1982) 13. Some see an early birth as the minimal historical basis for Jesus' virginal conception, making his conception—like the empty tomb—a potentially scandalous fact, which Christian faith interpreted in a positive sense but Judaism interpreted differently, as illegitimacy. Jesus' sinlessness, however, is never explained in the NT by reference to his origin. (See 2 Cor 5:21; 1 Pet 2:22; Hebr 4:15; 1 John 3:5.) The authors of *Mary in the NT* hold that even if one does accept "this clearly tenuous explanation of the derivation of the idea of a virginal conception, it is easier to presume that both Evangelists derived their knowledge of it from an earlier theological interpretation of the facts surrounding Jesus' birth."

28. If there existed a fuller story of the circumstances of the conception, this was probably not passed down in Christian circles.

29. The objections raised by Vögtle ("Offene Fragen," 43–54), Brown (*Birth*, 525–26) and Fitzmyer (*Luke*, 1.308, 341–42) against the theory that family tradition lies behind the Infancy Narratives do not tell against the above analysis.

30. In connection with Lucan tradition, this is recognized by Box (*Virgin Birth*, 179–80), Taylor (*Historical Evidence*, 86–87), Reicke ("Christ's Birth," 158–59), Burrows (*Gospel*, 54) and others. Swidler (*Biblical Affirmations*, 261–62, 271, 281) suggests that Luke's special source, including Luke 1–2, is the work of a woman.

31. See Kelber, *Oral and Written Gospel*, 24–25. He speaks of "the oral conviction that truth is not to be known nor redemption to be had by concepts estranged from life" (70).
32. Schüssler Fiorenza, *Memory*, 61.
33. Schüssler Fiorenza, *Bread*, 111. Cf. Ruether, "Feminist Interpretation: A Method of Correlation," *Feminist Interpretation*, 113, 117, 122–24.
34. Brown (*Birth*, 526–27) accepts the possibility that family tradition (of a virginal conception) was an auxiliary to the positive explanation of the historical catalyst of an early birth. But he recognizes that this solution leaves unanswered many questions, for example, Mary's understanding of the conception. In the few ministry scenes in which she appears, there is no memory that she showed any understanding of Jesus' divine origins. Perhaps at first these were family members.
35. Perhaps at first these were family members.
36. Kelber, *Oral and Written Gospel*, 75.
37. Some argue that Matt 1:18–25 should be designated as "an agologetic safeguard" (W. Trilling, *Das Wahre Israel* [Munich: Kösel, 1964] 74) or a defense against misunderstanding and slander (Dibelius, "Jungfrauensohn"). Others disagree, and see in Joseph's role no apologetic considerations but a positive explication of the faith of the church (Waetjen, "Genealogy," 219; Strecker, *Weg*, 54). This question is rarely raised with regard to the Lucan narrative. If there were no rumor and/or slander, why not keep silent? I do not think that the desire to satisfy curiosity about the early life of Jesus and to imitate the biographies of heroes and immortals was motive enough for the creation of the NT Infancy Narratives.
38. V. P. Branick, "The Sinful Flesh of the Son of God (Rom 8:3)," *CBQ* 47 [1985] 261) thinks that one of the traditions Paul inherited was that Jesus "as son of Mary was a scandal to his kinsmen, so common did his origins and life seem."
39. Accepted as such by Green, *Matthew*, 54; C. K. Barrett, *The Gospel of John and Judaism* (Philadelphia: Fortress, 1975) 71; *John*, 288; R. Laurentin, "Pluralism about Mary," *The Way Supplement* 45 (1982) 80; Hoskyns and Davey, *Fourth Gospel*, 2. 392 (they find other allusions to a peculiarity concerning the birth of Jesus in 1:13, 14; 7:27, 28; 8:19); B. Witherington III, *Women in the Ministry of Jesus* (Cambridge: Cambridge University, 1984) n. 67, p. 184 (he thinks that John 9:29 also suggests there were questions about Jesus' origins); R. A. Whitacre, *Johannine Polemic* (Chico: Scholars, 1982) n. 82, p. 198. The trace of the charge in 8:41 is regarded as plausible but far from certain by Brown, *Birth*, 541; as possible by Bultmann, *John* n. 2, p. 316; Lindars, *John*, 328; *Mary in the NT*, 205.
40. On the Gospel of John as a two-level drama in which aspects of the Evangelist's concerns are presented as elements in the story of Jesus, see J. L. Martyn, *History and Theology in the Fourth Gospel* (Nashville: Abingdon, 1979) 18–21.
41. R. E. Brown, *The Community of the Beloved Disciple* (NY: Paulist, 1979) 77–78. He argues that these claimed the patronage of James the brother of the Lord, and insisted on the importance of physical Jewish descent.
42. The question, "Who are 'the Jews' in the Fourth Gospel?" has not yet received a satisfactory answer. See W. E. Sproston, " 'Is Not This Jesus, the Son of Joseph . . .?' (John 6:42)," *JSNT* 24 (1985), n. 21, p. 95.
43. Hoskyns and Davey, *Fourth Gospel* 2. 392. The debate as a whole, and at the level of the commpleted Gospel, seems to concern monotheism vs what is considered ditheism, and perhaps the role of the law (see T. B. Dozeman,

"Sperma Abraam in John 8 and Related Literature," *CBQ* 42 [1980] 342–58).

44. D. W. Wead (*The Literary Devices in John's Gospel* [Basel: Reinhardt, 1970] 61–62), classifies v 41 as irony, and sees the possibility of an ironic hint to the same effect in v 19 ("Where is your Father?"). Cited by Brown, *Birth*, 541.

45. Is it possible that "Jews who believed in Jesus" could hold that he was illegitimately conceived? An examination of the beliefs of Jewish Christians in the writings of Church Fathers shows that some believed Jesus to be the son of Joseph, and some believed in his virginal conception. We sometimes encounter phrases like, "a man born of men," leaving the father unnamed. This phrase seems to come from those who accepted the paternity of Joseph; if it indicates (also) that there were some Jewish Christians who, like Matthew and Luke, believed in Jesus as Messiah in spite of, or even in, his illegitimate conception, the Fathers were apparently unaware of this.

46. A. Terian, "The Immediate Context of John 9," *AAR Abstracts* 1983, 158.

47. For other speculations about the placement of this story, see Brown, *John*, 1. 336.

48. John 3:3–8. See E. Haenchen, *A Commentary on the Gospel of John* (Philadelphia: Fortress, 1984) 2. 31–32; R. Schnackenburg, *The Gospel according to St. John* (NY: Herder and Herder, 1968), 1.372–73.

49. I am not suggesting that the Johannine notions of begetting or birth from above, much less the theology of incarnation, were developed to meet the challenge of the charge of illegitimacy; I am suggesting only that they do meet this challenge.

50. Bultmann, *John*, 62–63; Sproston, " 'Is Not This Jesus,' " 80. The author of the Fourth Gospel himself may have regarded Jesus as the son of Joseph (1:45; 6:42).

51. Contrast 1:1, where the chief priests and scribes and the rest of the Jews say "we know that this man is the son of Joseph the carpenter and was born of Mary."

52. F. Scheidweiler, in Hennecke-Schneemelcher, *NT Apocrypha*, 1. 445. He thinks the *Acts of Pilate* represents a form of the story of Jesus' illegitimacy earlier than the one known to Celsus (see below).

53. According to J. D. Crossan ("Mark and the Relatives of Jesus," *NovT* 15 [1973] 102, 112) Mark removed the name of Joseph from the tradition behind 6:3 because Joseph held no place in the Jerusalem church. Mark, engaged in writing a manifesto against that church's jurisdictional and doctrinal hegemony, was therefore "positively uninterested" in Joseph. Cf. J. M. Robinson, *The Problem of History in Mark and Other Marcan Studies* (Philadelphia: Fortress, 1982) n. 1, p. 129: the omission of the father in 6:3 (cf. 3:31–35; 10:29–30) is intentional.

54. So the authors of *Mary in the NT*, 64; H. K. McArthur, "Son of Mary," *NTS* 15 (1973) 55–58. Fitzmyer ("Virginal Conception," 557) finds the phrase cryptic and possibly innocuous.

55. Luke omits the entire episode of Mark 6:1–6a; but the question quoted appears in Luke as in Mark and Matthew during Jesus' only visit during his ministry to his hometown, Nazareth. Luke, however, may be following a different source than Mark.

56. Stauffer, "Jeschu ben Mirjam," 119–128. See also Stauffer, *Jesus and His Story* (London: SCM, 1960) 23–25; J. Delorme, "A Propos des Evangiles de l'Enfance," *Ami du Clergé* (1961) 762; D. E. Nineham, *Saint Mark* (Bal-

timore: Penguin, 1963) 166; V. Taylor, *The Gospel According to St. Mark* (NY: St. Martin's, 1966) 299–300; M. Smith, *Jesus the Magician* (San Francisco: Harper & Row, 1978) 26–28; Laurentin, "Pluralism," 80; Witherington, *Women*, 88; n. 67, p. 184; 99.

57. Brown, *Birth*, 541.

58. See *Mary in the NT*, 72; contrast R. Pesch, *Das Markusevangelium* (Frieburg: Herder, 1976) 322–25; Ruether, "Collision"; Benko, *Protestants, Catholics, and Mary*, 20; Witherington, *Women* 89–92.

59. See H. K. McArthur, "Son of Mary," *NovT* 15 (1973) 39–47; J. Winandy, "Note complémentaire sur la conception virginale dans le Nouveau Testament," *NRT* 104 (1982) 425–31.

60. E. Stauffer, *Jerusalem und Rom* (Bern: Francke, 1957) 118. See *b. Yebam.* 4:13.

61. Stauffer, "Jeschu ben Mirjam," 125–26. He shows that in the extra-biblical history of the phrase, it is used almost exclusively in a polemical sense.

62. See "The Beginnings of Christianity According to the Samaritans," introduction, text, translation, and notes by J. Macdonald; commentary by A. J. B. Higgins, *NTS* 18 (1971/2) 54–80, on the Samaritan Chronicle II. Macdonald believes that criticism of Jesus' ancestry comes from a medieval source underlying this document. Compare the translation and analysis of S. Isser, "Jesus in the Samaritan Chronicles," *JJS* 32 (1981) 166–94.

63. The former are religious leaders of Judea, according to Macdonald; the latter, those of the same tribe, Judah, according to Higgins ("Beginnings," 55, 76).

64. McArthur, "Son of Mary," 52. But for what follows, contrast McArthur, 52–53.

65. If the phrase is understood as an insult, it is highly unlikely that it is Marcan redaction; it is difficult to believe Mark could record such a statement unless it had some basis in fact. Contrast Crossan's opinion mentioned above in n. 53, p. 269.

66. Cf. Smith, *Magician*, 28.

67. *Mary in the NT*, 53; see 51–59. The point of 3:31–35 is not to exclude the physical family from *ever* joining Jesus' eschatological family.

68. Robinson, *Problem*, n. 1, p. 129.

69. Luke softens Mark 3:31–35 by explaining why Jesus' mother and brothers are "outside" ("they could not reach him for the crowd" [Luke 8:19]); by explaining that they desire to see him (v 20); and by omitting the reference to those who sat around him inside, so that the saying is ambiguous, and can even be read as praise of his family: "My mother and my brothers are those who hear the word of God and do it" (v 21). Contrast Danker (*Jesus and the New age*, 105) who sees in Luke 8:19–21 a continued criticism of Mary, working out the theme of the sword piercing her (2:48–51) and the sword of Jesus' rejection of her.

70. The natural family must therefore be "hated"; see Luke 14:26; *Gospel of Thomas* logia 55; 101.

71. See S. Brown, "Mary in the New Testament," 119: the unfavorable implication for her is the result of Mark having joined two originally distinct units of tradition, identifying Jesus' relatives in 3:21 as his mother and brothers in 3:31.

72. See John 2:3–4a; Luke 2:48–50 with Mark 3:32–35.

73. Witherington, *Women*, 82–84.

74. Contrast Elliott, *Questioning*, 16–17. He notes that the derogatory refer-

ences to Jesus' family (Mark 3:21; Matt 12:46–50; John 7:5) seem very strange in the light of the birth narratives, which he interprets as being about a virginal conception. "They may, however, be explicable in so far as animosity against Jesus' family seems to reflect conditions when the pro-Pauline branch of the church sought to disparage the representatives of the Jerusalem church, which was headed by Jesus' brother, and in which Jesus' mother and the rest of his family were prominent (according to Acts 1:14). . . . The birth stories, on the other hand, were later compositions, written at a time when the need to separate Jesus from his historical milieu and his family was a less important factor. The old animosity fostered by Paul between the pro-Gentile branch of the church and the pro-Jewish faction headed by Jesus' disciples and family was irrelevant when the nativity stories took shape." Cf. the opinions of Crossan, above, n. 53. and Kelber, *Oral and Written Gospel*, 102–05.

75. D. Flusser, *Jesus* (NY: Herder and Herder, 1969) 20, 22. Cf. G. D. Kilpatrick, "Jesus, His Family and His Disciples," *JSNT* 15 (1982) 11: rejection as a condition of discipleship is more easily understood "if there is a rupture between Jesus and his family in the background." His explanation of the estrangement, based on evidence in Acts, is that the family members opposed Jesus because they insisted on strict observance of the Law.

76. Translation by Thomas O. Lambdin, in *The Nag Hammadi Library* (J. M. Robinson, director; San Francisco: Harper and Row, 1977).

77. "Spirit" is a feminine noun in Hebrew and Aramaic. *Gospel of Thomas* 101 seems to contrast Jesus' natural mother with his true mother, the Holy Spirit. See the *Gospel according to the Hebrews*, in Jerome, *Commentary on Isaiah* 11:2 (the Holy Spirit calls Jesus "my son . . . my firstborn son" at his baptism) and in Origen, *Homily on Jeremiah* 15:4 ("my mother, the Holy Spirit"). In the *Apocryphon of James* 6:19–20, Jesus speaks of himself as "the son of the Holy Spirit." Cf. *Odes of Solomon* 19:2–4; 36:1, 5.

78. See H. Koester, Introduction, in *Nag Hammadi Library*, 117; he thinks the Greek (or even Syriac or Aramaic) collection behind the fourth-century Coptic manuscript was composed possibly as early as the second half of the first century, in Syria, Palestine, or Mesopotamia. J. E. Ménard ("Thomas, Gospel of," *IDBSup*, 902) sees no reason to modify the usual dating of ca. 140 C.E.

79. Contrast M. W. Meyer. *The Secret Teachings of Jesus. Four Gnostic Gospels* (NY: Random House, 1984) 107; *Mary in the NT*, 265. Tertullian (writing ca. 197) mentions among the Jewish charges against Jesus that he was the son of a prostitute (quaestuariae filius; *De Spectaculis* 30:6).

80. John 8:41: "the Jews who had believed in him."

81. In Justin's *Dialogue with Trypho*, written about the middle of the second century, Trypho the Jew is not represented as putting forth any alternative story of the actual circumstances of Jesus' conception and birth.

82. This, according to Smith (*Jesus the Magician*, 59), is strong evidence for Celsus's use of independent tradition from a Jewish source. M. Goldstein (*Jesus in the Jewish Tradition* [NY: Macmillan, 1950] 36–37) doubts that Celsus really used Jewish sources for this story, or at least that he accurately reported on them. He argues that Celsus despised Judaism as well as Christianity. "How cunning, therefore, it would be for him to manufacture a fictitious spokesman of one religion, which he held in no high regard, wherewith to strike a blow at the other contemporary religion which he argued was unworthy." Even though the dialogue may be fictional, however,

and elements of it exaggerated, in my judgment there is much here from early Jewish tradition. M. Lods proposes that Celsus used a written Jewish source which in hostile fashion portrayed the life of Jesus from birth to baptism ("Etudes sur les sources juives de la polémique de Celsus contre les Chrétiens," *RHPR* 21 [1941] 1–33) but the evidence Lods draws upon cannot be used to certify the existence of an earlier single written source (E. V. Gallagher, *Divine Man or Magician? Celsus and Origen on Jesus* [SBLDS 64; Chico: Scholars, 1982] 51). R. L. Wilken says cautiously that it is possible that the story Celsus presents was circulating in the empire, perhaps in Jewish circles (*The Christians as the Romans Saw Them* [New Haven: Yale University, 1984] 110).

83. "The Jew" believed Jesus was begotten "by a certain Panthera, *phtheirantos tēn parthenon.*"

84. Machen, without any real examination of the "utterly unbelievable slanderous" story, assumes in an unscholarly way that it does not represent any independent tradition, but is based merely (by way of polemic) on the NT. The mere fact of such opposition "is of no importance whatever, for it is only what was to be expected." Unless the opponents were to become Christians, he reasons, they could hardly accept the virginal conception (*Virgin Birth*, 11). It is difficult to tell firmly whether Celsus was following canonical Matthew or parallel traditions.

85. The rejection theme also evokes the strange story of the women in Revelation 12, who flees to the wilderness—but only after she has given birth.

86. See Smith *Jesus the Magician*, 47, 182: Jesus is never referred to as "son of the virgin" in the Christian material from around 30–130 C.E.; to suppose the name Panthera appeared as a caricature of a title not yet in use is less plausible than to suppose the name was handed down by polemic tradition. See also Goldstein, *Jesus*, 35–36.

87. See Brown, *Birth*, n. 7, p. 535, for references to patristic writings in which it is so treated. These are probably attempts to integrate the name into Christian tradition.

88. E. Bammel ("Christian Origins in Jewish Tradition," *NTS* 13 [1966] 324) comments that only in Celsus's citations does Panthera figure as a Roman soldier. Later Jewish tradition takes it as self-evident that the lover of Mary was a Jew (he was, according to the Wagensell version of the Toledoth, a soldier, but a scion of the tribe of Judah [n. 4, p. 324]).

89. See A. Deissmann, "Der Name Panthera," *Orientalische Studien T. Nöldecke gewidmet* (ed. C. Bezold; Geissen: Töpelmann, 1906) 871–75. L. Patterson ("Origin of the Name Pantera," *JTS* 19 [1917/18] 79–80) thinks it is not impossible that the similarity between Panthera and *parthenos* prompted the choice of the genuine name Pantera.

90. See Goldstein, *Jesus*, 3–4.

91. See Gallagher, *Divine Man*, 54.

92. So H. von Campenhausen, *The Virgin Birth in the Theology of the Ancient Church* (London: SCM, 1964) n. 6, p. 58.

93. *Hom. Luc.* 6, on the last point following Ignatius, *Eph.* 19:1.

94. So N. R. M. de Lange, *Origen and the Jews* (Cambridge: Cambridge University, 1976) 99. (For other such mistakes, see n. 60, p. 152; Origen's knowledge of Hebrew was probably slight [n. 61, p. 154], and many of his mistakes may be due to reliance on transliterated texts.) He thinks that Origen seems to have inserted this argument simply to impress his Greek-speaking audience, and that it is possible that he compressed a longer ar-

gument, unwittingly here resting the burden of his evidence on the one weak link. Perhaps translating or paraphrasing Origen's full argument, Jerome quotes this same text of Deuteronomy as evidence for the use of *'almâ* (In Isa. III.7:14). In *Dial. Tim. et Aq.* 111, the Christian quotes Deut 22:25 to show that *neanis* and *parthenos* are synonymous.

95. Worms in *Hom. Luc.* 14.
96. P. Lapide (*Fils de Joseph?* [Paris: Desclée, 1975] 50) insists that it was not against Jesus, but against the christology of the primitive church that rabbinic polemic was later directed, while the whole Jewish people was the butt of patristic attacks. I do not wish to deny the importance and sadness of the two-way polemic, but to focus on something else in the texts. Schalom Ben-Chorin ("A Jewish View of the Mother of Jesus," *Mary in the Churches,* 12–16) writes of Mary as a young oriental Jewish mother, "obviously exposed to some extraordinary commotions the meaning of which is beyond the understanding of a barely adolescent mother." Joseph had his suspicions about her, Ben-Chorin says, but he does not develop this idea. Jesus' parables give the impression that for him the love of the father was decisive while the love of the mother played no part whatever. Ben-Chorin interprets this to mean Jesus wanted to idealize a fatherly love he longed for but never had. The editors note that this article is an extract from Ben-Chorin's book, *Mutter Miriam, Maria in jüdischer Sicht* (Deutscher Taschenbuchverlag, Munich, No. 1784), and apart from Schalom Asch's novel about Mary, which appeared over twenty years ago, Ben-Chorin's book is the only Jewish work which has tackled this subject. But now see D. Flusser's contribution in J. Pelikan, D. Flusser, J. Lang, *Mary. Images of the Mother of Jesus in Jewish and Christian Perspective* (Philadelphia: Fortress, forthcoming).
97. Lapide documents a new mood in Jewish writings on Jesus. The holocaust modified the image of Jesus in Jewish literature, rendered it more human, avoiding deification and defamation (*Fils de Joseph?*, 18). With regard to Jesus' origins, some contemporary manuals of Israelite history speak of Jesus as the son of a family of carpenters, or as belonging to the simple people, or as son of Joseph. When the virginal conception is mentioned, it is as belonging to the later legendary tissue of the NT, and the theory of the pagan origin of this myth is discussed (see pp. 57, 66, 68).
98. There are various spellings of the name (*pntyr'*, vocalized *Pantērâ*): Pantira, Pandera, Pantiri, Panteri; Brown, *Birth*, n. 8, p. 536.
99. Smith, *Jesus the Magician*, 46, 178; cf. M. Goguel, *The Origins of Christianity* (NY: Harper, 1960), 1, 73.
100. So Brown, *Birth*, 536; cf. Herford, *Christianity in Talmud and Midrash*, 40; Goguel, *Origins*, 1.73.
101. See above, p. 39.
102. Klausner, *Jesus* 36. Christians of the time of Simeon ben Azzai healed in the name of Jesus, and this would have been reason enough for Jews to avoid mentioning his name. It is also possible that the term *plwny* was later introduced into this passage when Christianity was more widespread and the name would no longer be mentioned " 'by reason of the anger of the Minim' (i.e., Jews rightly or wrongly suspected of a leaning towards the new Christian 'heresy')." But *plwny* seems to be the original reading (Lauterbach, "Jesus in the Talmud," 540; he can think of no reason why the rabbis of this period would seek to shield Jesus, and therefore doubts the reference is to him).

103. S. Krauss, "Jesus—in Jewish Legend," *The Jewish Encyclopedia* (NY: Funk and Wagnalls, 1904), 7. 170.
104. See Goldstein, *Jesus*, 68, for this and other reasons against the position that Jesus is referred to.
105. See *m. Sanh.* 7:4, which lists among those to be stoned "he that has connection with a girl that is betrothed" (cf. 7:9).
106. Goldstein (*Jesus*, 72) denies the attribution; Klausner (*Jesus of Nazareth*, 30) questions it, as does Herford (*Christianity*, 49). D. N. Freedman and M. P. O'Connor ("Bastard," *IDBSup*, 93) think that it possibly alludes to the story told by Celsus's informant; cf. G. Dalman, *Jesus Christ in the Talmud, Midrash, Zohar, and the Liturgy of the Synagogue* (Cambridge: 1900) 33.
107. *šwšbyny;* especially the bridegroom's friend or best man, or the bride's friend or agent (see Jastrow, *Dictionary*, 2, 1543). Herford translates "groomsman"; Goldstein translates "paranymph."
108. See Goldstein, *Jesus*, 71–72.
109. Klausner, *Jesus of Nazareth*, 31.
110. Lauterbach ("Jesus in Talmud," 541) insists that the fact that Akiba (fl. 110–135) spoke to the mother of the child precludes the possibility of that child having been Jesus.
111. Smith, *Jesus the Magician*, 47; contrast Goldstein, *Jesus*, 60; Klausner, *Jesus of Nazareth*, 20.
112. A third-century Babylonian.
113. A Babylonian town, a center of rabbinic studies.
114. Smith, *Jesus the Magician*, 47.
115. Klausner (*Jesus of Nazareth*, 23) thinks Miriam Měgaddělā', mentioned only by the Amoraim, was the wife of Pappos.
116. Goldstein, *Jesus*, 57–58, 60.
117. See Herford, *Christianity*, 38.
118. Lauterbach, "Jesus in the Talmud," n. 230, p. 542.
119. "Jesus: In Talmud and Midrash," *EncJud*, Vol. 10, cols. 16–17.
120. Lauterbach, "Jesus in the Talmud," 549.
121. Klausner, *Jesus of Nazareth*, 48.
122. S. Krauss, *Das Leben Jesus nach jüdischen Quelilen* (Berlin: Calvary, 1902) 246–47. This work includes a detailed study of most of the versions, and remains the basic scholarly work in the field. Chronological examination of the various fragments and versions reveals the development of the narrative. The complete medieval story has versions which are so different from each other in attitude and in detail that it is impossible that one author could have written it (J. Dan, "Toledot Yeshu," *Encyclopedia Judaica* vol. 15, col. 1208).
123. Bammel, "Christian Origins," 319, 325. He thinks these may be developments of earlier traditions which were less objectionable.
124. Solomon Schechter, "Some Rabbinic Parallels to the NT," paper read before the Hebrew class at University College, London, Oct. 19, 1898, in *Judaism and Christianity. Selected Accounts 1892–1962* (ed. Jacob B. Agus; NY: Arno, 1973) 415.
125. But it is not polemic per se; it relies on humor to convey its arguments. See Daniel J. Lasker, *Jewish Philosophical Polemics against Christianity in the Middle Ages* (NY: Ktav, 1977) 5, 21.
126. Bammel, "Christian Origins," n. 1, p. 325; see Klausner (*Jesus of Nazareth*, 51).

127. Goldstein, *Jesus,* 148–54.
128. Different texts give different dates.
129. The *Toledoth* legends regard Jesus as ben Pandera, but not ben Stada, even though they attribute to Jesus (as the Talmud does to ben Stada) the introduction of "spells from Egypt in a cut in his flesh"). The names of the husband and the villain vary in the different versions. If the husband is Joseph, the villain is Yohanan, and in those which name Yohanan as the husband, Joseph is the villain.
130. Some versions give his name as Pappos ben Yehudah.
131. Yohanan therefore could not prove who was the guilty party.
132. See tractate *Kallah* 51a.
133. Variant: Jerusalem.
134. Ps 2:7; he quoted also Ps 2:1–2 and Hos 2:4 ("Upon her children also I will have no pity, because they are children of harlotry").
135. Except the Yemenite version, in which Jesus is the son of a whore and therefore already liable to the death penalty (Krauss, *Leben,* 118; see Bammel, "Christian Origins," 320).
136. Dan, "Toledoth," col. 1209.
137. The husband is also said to have told R. Shimeon ben Shetah, who later reported it to others.
138. Relying here on the Sinaitic Syriac version of Matt 1:16.
139. Goldstein, *Jesus,* 156. Krauss ("Jesus in Jewish Legend," 170) thinks that "for polemical purposes it was necessary for the Jews to insist on the illegitimacy of Jesus as against the Davidic descent claimed by the Christian church."
140. Lauterbach, "Jesus in the Talmud," 475.
141. Freedman and M. O'Connor, "Bastard," 93.
142. Klausner (*Jesus of Nazareth,* 31, 36) thinks that the legend of Jesus' illegitimacy preserved by Celsus and the Talmud originated solely from the conviction of the Christians that Jesus was born without a human father. Cf. *Mary in the NT,* 262: it is likely that such anti-Christian polemics "presuppose the Christian claim of a virginal conception to which they oppose a more natural explanation . . . to attempt to find behind the Panthera story the 'true' circumstances of Jesus' birth is fanciful." The authors argue that it is possible to read all details as tendentious distortions of known Christian traditions rather than as reflections of independent sources. (See above, n. 139, on the views of Goldstein and Krauss.) I would agree, if I did not find the story of an illegitimate pregnancy also in the NT Infancy Narratives.
143. Cf. Herford, *Christianity,* 357–60.
144. Dalman, *Jesus Christ,* 11.
145. In some texts her conception is an erring, and she is condemned and repents. See G. C. Stead, "The Valentinian Myth of Sophia," *JTS* 20 (1969) 75–104; G. W. MacRae, "The Jewish Background of the Gnostic Sophia Myth," *NovT* 12 (1970) 86–101; Englesman, *Feminine Dimension,* chapters 5 and 6: Nils A. Dahl, "The Arrogant Archon and the Lewd Sophia," *The Rediscovery of Gnosticism* (ed. B. Layton; Leiden: Brill, 1981), 2.689–712; P. Perkins, "Gnostic Christologies and the New Testament," *CBQ* 43 (1981) 590–606.
146. An erroneous belief, according to the author. The mother and child are cast out of the city into a desert place (cf. Revelation 12). The motif of conception without intercourse is present in 7:31; cf. v 20 (MacRae trans-

lation, *OT Pseudepigrapha*, 1.717). On this document see W. Foerster, *Gnosis* (Oxford: Clarendon, 1974), 2.15; MacRae, "The Apocalypse of Adam," *Nag Hammadi Library*, 256.

147. Because the Spirit's union with the Father is to be understood symbolically, not literally, the Spirit remains a virgin. See E. Pagels, *The Gnostic Gospels* (NY: Random House, 1979) 53. She remarks that the author is making a radical suggestion "about the doctrine that later developed as the virgin birth." The authors of *Mary in the NT* speak of the virgin mother in some Gnostic texts as "no longer a human person but a symbol for a heavenly power" (p. 270).

148. E.g., in Egyptian stories of the god Amon and Queen Ahmose (see Boslooper, *Virgin Birth*, 163).

149. E.g., the form of a serpent in Suetonius, *Lives of the Twelve Caesars, Divus Augustus* 94:4; Plutarch, *Life of Alexander* 2:4; 1; cf. Zeus and Leda in Apollodorus, *Bibliotheca* 3:126.

150. E.g., Plutarch, *Table Talk* 8:1, 2–3; *Life of Numa* 4:3–4.

151. See C. H. Gordon, "Paternity at Two Levels," *JBL* 96 (1977) 101; "The Double Paternity of Jesus," *BAR* 4 (1978) 26–27, for the opinion that Egyptian, Mycenaean and NT stories confront us with "reflexes of the same principle: great personages in various segments of the biblical world could have two fathers, one human and one divine. However, one's position in society, notably kingship, was transmitted not through one's father in Heaven, but through the human husband of one's mother."

152. See Boslooper, *Virgin Birth*, 178. See, for example, Plutarch, *Life of Alexander* 2–3; Quintus Curtius, *History of Alexander* 1.

153. See the late second century Pseudo-Justin treatise, *On the Resurrection* (*Mary in the NT*, 273).

154. However, tales such as those told by Hesiod (*Theogony* 116) of the earth engendering heaven without the aid of a male element, or by Euripides (*Ion* 454; cf. Aeschylus, *Eumenides* 736–38) of Athena, without a mother, springing from the head of Zeus, would also lead some to think in terms of non-sexual conception.

155. If it was preserved and developed by some Jewish Christians as well, the evidence for this has been lost. See below.

156. J. N. D. Kelly (*Early Christian Doctrines* [2nd ed.; NY: Harper and Row, 1960] 145) remarks that the Apologists were preoccupied with the Logos, and evince surprisingly little interest in the gospel figure of Jesus.

157. Von Campenhausen, *Virgin Birth*, 22. See *Pistis Sophia* 8 (*NT Apocrypha* 1.403).

158. Machen, *Virgin Birth*, 12.

159. On growing ascetic and encratitic tendencies in the churches, preparing the way for new, independent Marian emphases, see *Mary in the NT*, 258. On early patristic misogynism, see R. Ruether, "Misogynism and Virginal Feminism in the Fathers of the Church," *Religion and Sexism* (ed. R. Ruether; NY: Simon and Schuster, 1974) 150–83.

160. Von Campenhausen, *Virgin Birth*, 70.

161. H. von Campenhausen, *The Virgin Birth in the Theology of the Early Church;* J. G. Machen, *The Virgin Birth of Christ;* see especially chapter 1: "The Virgin Birth in the Second Century"; A. Hoben, *The Virgin Birth* (PhD dissertation, University of Chicago, 1903) especially chapters 2 and 3; T. Boslooper, *Virgin Birth;* R. E. Brown, *The Virginal Conception and the Bodily Resurrection of Jesus,* especially pp. 47–52, "The Evidence from Early History." All of

these scholars hold that the belief in the virginal conception is found in both NT Infancy Narratives. See also *Mary in the NT*, 241–82.

162. Brown, *Virginal Conception*, 47; see 50, 52. Some hold that after the middle of the second century, the opinion prevailed that before, in, and after the birth of Jesus, Mary remained a virgin (A. Meyer and W. Bauer, "The Relatives of Jesus," *NT Apocrypha* 1.424).

163. Fitzmyer, "Virginal Conception," n. 44, p. 554.

164. The same scheme—according to the flesh, according to the Spirit; son of David, son of God—appears in *Eph.* 18:2; *Trall.* 9; *Smyrn.* 1:1–2; these texts stand in the line of tradition which leads back to Rom 1:3 and Phil 2:5–11 (J. N. D. Kelly, *Early Christian Creeds* [3rd ed; London: Longmans, 1972] 69–70).

165. C. Trevett ("Approaching Matthew from the Second Century: the Under-Used Ignatian Correspondence," *JSNT* 20 [1984] 62) concludes that Ignatius's knowledge and use of the Gospel of Matthew as we have it is much less certain than writers on that Gospel have sometimes led us to believe. His work also seems to reflect the influence of the Johannine prologue.

166. Von Campenhausen (*Virgin Birth* 19) holds that Ignatius lays great theological stress on the virginal conception, and "already regards it as an indispensable doctrine that has been handed down, and to which he refers in formal, almost confessional, language."

167. Ibid., 30. He nevertheless argues that in the framework of Ignatius's theology it is of highest significance that the primary miracle of the incarnation "is documented at this particular point by an obvious physical miracle," the virginal conception.

168. On this text, which may contain later interpolations, see *Mary in the NT*, 254. The *Testament of Joseph* 19:8 (second century?) mentions a lamb born of a virgin.

169. Kelly, *Creeds*, 146–48.

170. Kelly, *Doctrines*, 144–48. See *Acts of Paul* 1:14; 3:5, 12–14; *Shepherd of Hermas*, *Sim.* 9:1; 5:2–6.

171. See above, chapter 2, on the LXX translator's understanding of Isa 7:14, and on Matthew's understanding of that passage.

172. Brown (*Virginal Conception*, 32; *Birth*, 518) insists there can be no doubt that those who formulated these creedal affirmations believed in the bodily virginity of Mary.

173. His harmonization of conception Christology and preexistence Christology is clear in *Apol.* 1:21, 33. The coming of the Spirit and Power upon Mary is the coming of the Word.

174. Von Campenhausen, *Virgin Birth*, 31. He remarks that Justin hardly knows what theological line to take about it as a historical event.

175. He finds the same meaning in Isa 53:8 ("Who shall declare his generation?"); Gen 49:10 ("the blood of grapes"; this means for Justin that Christ derives blood not from the seed of man but from the power of God); Ps 110:3, and other texts.

176. Von Campenhausen, *Virgin Birth*, 33, 20.

177. See E. F. Bishop, "Some Reflections on Justin Martyr and the Nativity Narratives," *EvangQ* 39 (1967) 30–39.

178. Who may or may not be Rabbi Tarphon, a contemporary of Justin (see A. J. B. Higgins, "Jewish Messianic Belief in Justin Martyr's 'Dialogue with Trypho,'" *NOVT* 9 [1967] 298; J. Nilson, "To whom is Justin's 'Dialogue With Trypho' Addressed?" *TS* 38 [1977] 541). Acceptance of the identification

would not necessarily involve accepting all the statements attributed to Trypho as reliable expressions of contemporary Jewish beliefs. In fact, in his role as apologist Justin puts statements of Christian belief in Trypho's mouth which he could not have held.

179. Machen, *Virgin Birth*, 9–10.

180. "Those of your race."

181. Epiphanius and Jerome, who lived in the latter part of the fourth century and beginning of the fifth, say those Jewish Christians who accepted the virginal conception are called Nazarenes; those who denied it are called Ebionites. See Machen, *Virgin Birth*, n. 76, p. 22. See also S. Pines, *The Jewish Christians of the Early Centuries of Christianity according to a New Source* (Proceedings of the Israel Academy of Sciences and Humanities, II, no. 13; Jerusalem: Central Press, 1966). In the period before Origen, Irenaeus and (following him) Hippolytus mention only Ebionites who do not believe in the virginal conception. But their failure to mention the other division of Jewish Christians does not prove it did not exist in their time (Machen, *Virgin Birth*, 22. See A. F. J. Klijn and G. J. Reinik, *Patristic Evidence for Jewish-Christian Sects* [Leiden: Brill, 1973]).

182. Cf. 17:19: "And the Lord [would] not have said 'My [Father who is in] heaven' unless [he] had had another father, but he would have said simply '[My Father].' " This gospel is generally Valentinian in character, probably written in Syria in the second half of the third century c.e. (W. W. Isenberg, in *Nag Hammadi Library*, 131). The context here is confusing: Mary is spoken of as "the virgin whom no power defiled," but the belief that she conceived by the Holy Spirit is regarded as an error (55:23). See also 71:17–23: "Adam came into being from two virgins, from the Spirit and from the virgin earth. Christ, therefore, was born from a virgin to rectify the fall which occurred in the beginning." This is an interesting example of a document in which Mary is called a virgin, but the conception considered somehow both a natural and a heavenly event. It is not clear whether there is argument against the belief in a virginal conception, or symbolic interpretation of it, or ignorance of it (see *Mary in the NT*, 245, 269–70).

183. See P. Vielhauer, "Jewish Christian Gospels," *NT Apocrypha*, 1.118, 139.

184. The four evangelists are regarded as having an authority like that of the law and the prophets, and Marcion is condemned for mutilating Luke's Gospel by "removing all that is written respecting the generation of the Lord" (1.18.2).

185. See Von Campenhausen, *Virgin Birth*, 37.

186. In his adoption of the view of the Fourth Gospel, Irenaeus converts the virginal conception into "an advent or an incarnation in a more rigid and uniform sense than previously prevailed" (Hoben, *Virgin Birth*, 41).

187. Cf. Tertullian, *On the Flesh of Christ* 17. Sexual desire and the authority of death are linked in *Apocalypse of Adam* 2:8–10 (MacRae translation).

188. As Von Campenhausen remarks, the striking precision of this thought gives a false suggestion of logical necessity to which it has no claim (*Virgin Birth*, 47).

189. See Hoben, *Virgin Birth*, 43–44, 47.

190. See above, n. 79.

191. *Against Praxeas* 26.

192. See O. Cullmann, "Infancy Gospels," *NT Apocrypha*, 1. 366–68. They illustrate the heightened concern in the second century for Mary's honor and purity.

193. Cullmann, "Infancy Narratives," 372.
194. Num 5:11–31.
195. Von Campenhausen, *Virgin Birth*, 41.
196. See above, n. 202, p. 20; 180. Specialists now date the original of *2 Enoch*, which was probably in Greek, to the decades prior to 70 C.E. It exists in long and short recensions, both of which have been reworked by later scribes, and both of which contain the story of Melchizedek's conception. See J. H. Charlesworth, "The SNTS Pseudepigrapha Seminar," *NTS* 25 (1979) 316–18.
197. The author is blending the Matthean and Lucan accounts, and uses this motif to move from the Lucan to the Matthean, but I see no necessary reason for introducing it.
198. F. Scheidweiler ("The Questions of Bartholomew," *NT Apocrypha,* 1. 488, 508) assigns its original form to the third century.
199. In addition, two motifs are found also in *1 Enoch* 106 (on the birth of Noah): (1) the husband fears that the conception is from the angels (*Protevangelium of James* 14:1 ("I fear lest that which is in her may have sprung from the angels . . ."; *1 Enoch* 106:4–6; cf. 1QapGen 2:1); (2) a great light appears at the birth (*Protevangelium of James* 19:2; *1 Enoch* 106:2–3).
200. I agree with these scholars who think it was written by a Hellenized Jew: Scholem, Greenfield, Pines, Charles, Forbes, Hengel, Delcor, Perrot, Collins, Nickelsburg, Stone, Amusin, Andersen. Those who argue for a Christian origin include Daniélou, Vaillant, Rubinstein, Hay, Milik. For a summary of views, see A. M. Denis, *Introduction aux Pseudépigraphes d'Ancien Testament* (Leiden: Brill, 1970) 29; J. J. Collins, *Between Athens and Jerusalem* (NY: Crossroad, 1983) 229–30, 243.
201. The OT passages which mention Melchizedek (Genesis 14 and Ps 110) may be a source for the mythical motifs associated with him here in *2 Enoch,* as well as in the Epistle to the Hebrews and 11Q Melchizedek. See D. Flusser, "Melchizedek and the Son of Man," *Christian News from Israel* 17 (1966) 27; J. C. Greenfield, "Prolegomena" to *3 Enoch* (ed. H. Odeberg; NY: Ktav, 1973) xx; G. W. E. Nickelsburg and M. E. Stone, *Faith and Piety in Early Judaism* (Philadelphia: Fortress, 1983) 192.
202. See *NT Apocrypha,* 2.740.
203. J. Flemming, H. Duensing, in *NT Apocrypha,* 2. 643; A. K. Hembold, "Gnostic Elements in the 'Ascension of Isaiah,'" *NTS* 18 (1972); M. A. Knibb, "Martyrdom and Ascension of Isaiah," *OT Pseudepigrapha,* 2.150. Cf. *Acts of Peter* 23–24 (ca. 180–190).
204. J. H. Charlesworth, *The Odes of Solomon* (Oxford: Clarendon, 1973) vii. Von Campenhausen finds the gnostic imprint of the Odes indisputable (*Virgin Birth,* n. 2, p. 55).
205. Unless Charlesworth is right in his suggestion (p. 84) that the reference to "manifestation" in the last verse may be an example of the poet's love of double entendre; 'it is possible he means that she bore manifestly and according to the manifestation by Gabriel" (cf. Luke 1:26). Also, the last line could be translated, "And she acquired according to the Great Power" (cf. Luke 1:35). J. Lagrand ("How Was the Virgin Mary 'Like a Man'?" *NovT* 22 [1980] 99) thinks Ode 19:10a may be a poetic reflection of Matt 1:18b or may follow a trajectory from the idea he finds expressed in Matthew's Gospel, the attribution of a spiritual "male principle" to Mary.
206. See Charlesworth, *Odes,* 44; milk and word are linked conceptually in the first century (see 1 Cor 3:1–2). In Ode 35:5 the milk is "the dew of the

Lord." In the second century *Gospel of Truth* I, 3, 24:10, "the Father reveals his breast; but his breast is the Holy Spirit."

207. Lagrand, "How Was," 104. The translation preferred by Lagrand (p. 99) is: "She brought forth, as a man, by will." He thinks the *Gospel of Philip* 107 [103.23–26] ("Some said: Mary conceived of the Holy Spirit. They are in error. What they are saying they do not know. When did a woman ever conceive of a woman?") was possibly formulated originally as a very early Christian reaction against the error of assuming Mary had sexual intercourse with the Deity (p. 105), an error that may be present in Ode 19.

208. See Von Campenhausen, *Virgin Birth*, 22.

209. Machen, *Virgin Birth*, 274–75. Brown (*Birth*, 534) calls illegitimacy "the uncomplimentary explanation adopted by opponents."

210. Reactions to the possibility of rape often include conscious and unconscious denial, the proposal of other interpretations of the event, and anger and blame directed at the victim.

211. Hanke, *The Validity of the Virgin Birth* (Grand Rapids: Zondervan, 1963) 107.

212. Brown, *Birth*, 530.

Epilogue

1. R. P. McBrien, *Catholicism* (Minneapolis: Winston, 1981) 516, 517. A theologoumenon stands between a theological interpretation that is normative for faith and a historically verifiable affirmation. The Fathers of the church simply presupposed the virginal conception was historical, something which McBrien says NT scholarship does not claim can be disproved exegetically. McBrien does not consider the possibility of Jesus' illegitimate conception. Cf. Fitzmyer, "Virginal Conception," 542–50, 572–75.

2. McBrien, *Catholicism*, 518.

3. Brown, *Birth*, n. 29, p. 529; *Virginal Conception*, 33–38; "Liberals, Ultraconservatives," 319, 323: in his judgment, the Church teaches infallibly that Mary conceived as a virgin, without a male parent. Cf. M. O'Carroll, *Theotokos* (Wilmington: Glazier, 1982) 359–60, and the discussion by J. P. Kenney, "Was Mary in Fact a Virgin?" *Australasian Catholic Record* 56 (1979) 282–300.

4. V. Taylor, *Historical Evidence*, 132.

5. Daly, *Gyn/ecology*, 84, 111, 130. The Lucan annunciation scene, she claims, is about the rape of the mind/spirit/will of a terrified young girl, who, like all rape victims in male myth, submits joyously to degradation. Daly calls this "refined religious rapism," which makes physical rape unnecessary (p. 185; *Pure Lust*, 74).

6. Daly, *Gyn/ecology*, 85, 47.

7. Engelsman, *Feminine Dimension*, 152, 95–98, 129; Johnson, "Marian Tradition," 129.

8. On this term, see Ruether, *Sexism and God-Talk*, 46.

9. Daly, *Beyond God the Father*, 85.

10. In his discussion of the doctrinal value and significance of the "fact" of virginal conception, Box comments that even for the church to interpret the supernatural origin of Christ in a metaphorical or symbolical way would be disastrous, and endanger the doctrine of the Incarnation. "Sooner or later, the results would inevitably work themselves out in a 'reduced' Christology, and a 'reduced' Christianity" (*Virgin Birth*, 195). For our times, however, less may be more. Taylor asks "whether this so-called 'reduced Christianity' is not the true faith, as distinguished from a 'full Christianity' which in reality is florid and overgrown" (*Historical Evidence*, 130).

11. "The escape from sex and birth is ultimately an escape from death for which women as Eve and mother are made responsible" (Ruether, *Sexism and God-Talk*, 144). Cf. J. B. Phillips, *Eve: the History of an Idea* (NY: Harper and Row, 1984) 144: "The Church Fathers accepted, and then refined and promoted, the common view that the female body is a mysterious vessel which, if penetrated, becomes a symbol not only of sexuality and birth but also of corruption, sin, and death. Virginity preserves that body in its sealed state as a powerful symbol of Christianity's offer to humanity of the possibility of a return to a state of innocence or paradise—a sexless birth that cannot end in death." For Gordon, on the other hand, Mary "embodies our desire to be fully human yet to transcend death" ("Coming to Terms," 14).

12. Ruether, *Sexism and God-Talk*, 153–54, 152, 149.

13. Margaret Farley, "Feminist Consciousness and the Interpretation of Scripture," *Feminist Interpretation of the Bible*, 51. Compare my approach also with that taken by Mary Jo Weaver, *New Catholic Women* (San Francisco: Harper & Row, 1985) 201–11.

14. Brooten, "Feminist Perspectives," 57.

15. See Schüssler Fiorenza, *Memory*, 140, 142, on the Sophia God of Jesus.